Hyperbolic Realism

Hyperbolic Realism

A Wild Reading of Pynchon's and Bolaño's Late Maximalist Fiction

Samir Sellami

BLOOMSBURY ACADEMIC
NEW YORK • LONDON • OXFORD • NEW DELHI • SYDNEY

BLOOMSBURY ACADEMIC
Bloomsbury Publishing Inc, 1359 Broadway, New York, NY 10018, USA
Bloomsbury Publishing Plc, 50 Bedford Square, London, WC1B 3DP, UK
Bloomsbury Publishing Ireland, 29 Earlsfort Terrace, Dublin 2, D02 AY28, Ireland

BLOOMSBURY, BLOOMSBURY ACADEMIC and the Diana logo are trademarks of
Bloomsbury Publishing Plc

First published in the United States of America 2024
This paperback edition published in 2025

Copyright © Samir Sellami, 2024

2666 by Roberto Bolaño. Copyright © 2004, The Heirs of Roberto Bolaño,
used by permission of The Wylie Agency (UK) Limited.

For legal purposes the Acknowledgments on pp. x–xi constitute
an extension of this copyright page.

Cover design: Eleanor Rose
Cover image © Getty Images

Excerpts from AGAINST THE DAY by Thomas Pynchon, copyright © 2006
by Thomas Pynchon. Used by permission of Penguin Press, an imprint of Penguin
Publishing Group, a division of Penguin Random House LLC. All rights reserved.

Excerpts from Against The Day by Thomas Pynchon. Copyright © Thomas Pynchon.
Reproduced by permission of the author c/o Rogers, Coleridge & White Ltd., 20 Powis
Mews, London W11 1JN. All rights reserved.

Excerpts from 2666 by Roberto Bolaño, translated by Natasha Wimmer. Copyright ©
2004 by The Heirs of Roberto Bolaño. Translation copyright © 2008 by Natasha Wimmer.
Reprinted by permission of Farrar, Straus and Giroux. All Rights Reserved.

All rights reserved. No part of this publication may be: i) reproduced or transmitted in any
form, electronic or mechanical, including photocopying, recording or by means of any
information storage or retrieval system without prior permission in writing from the publishers;
or ii) used or reproduced in any way for the training, development or operation of artificial
intelligence (AI) technologies, including generative AI technologies. The rights holders expressly
reserve this publication from the text and data mining exception as per Article 4(3) of the
Digital Single Market Directive (EU) 2019/790.

Bloomsbury Publishing Inc does not have any control over, or responsibility for, any
third-party websites referred to or in this book. All internet addresses given in this
book were correct at the time of going to press. The author and publisher regret
any inconvenience caused if addresses have changed or sites have ceased
to exist, but can accept no responsibility for any such changes.

Library of Congress Cataloging-in-Publication Data
Names: Sellami, Samir, 1987- author.
Title: Hyperbolic realism : a wild reading of Pynchon's and Bolaño's late
maximalist fiction / Samir Sellami.
Description: New York : Bloomsbury Academic, 2024. | Includes bibliographical references and index. |
Summary: "A philosophically grounded exploration of the hyperbolic realism of Pynchon and Bolaño within
the broader context of modern literature and post-war maximalist writing"– Provided by publisher.
Identifiers: LCCN 2023030368 (print) | LCCN 2023030369 (ebook) | ISBN 9781501360497 (hardback) |
ISBN 9781501374555 (paperback) | ISBN 9781501360503 (epub) |
ISBN 9781501360510 (pdf) | ISBN 9781501360527
Subjects: LCSH: Realism in literature. | Hyperbole in literature. | Maximalism (Literature) | Bolaño,
Roberto, 1953–2003–Criticism and interpretation. | Pynchon, Thomas–Criticism and interpretation.
Classification: LCC PN56.R3 S44 2024 (print) | LCC PN56.R3 (ebook) |
DDC 809/.912–dc23/eng/20230927
LC record available at https://lccn.loc.gov/2023030368
LC ebook record available at https://lccn.loc.gov/2023030369

ISBN:	HB:	978-1-5013-6049-7
	PB:	978-1-5013-7455-5
	ePDF:	978-1-5013-6051-0
	eBook:	978-1-5013-6050-3

Typeset by Integra Software Services Pvt. Ltd.

For product safety related questions contact productsafety@bloomsbury.com.

To find out more about our authors and books visit www.bloomsbury.com
and sign up for our newsletters.

For Johanna—and all the other good enough mothers of all things.

CONTENTS

Acknowledgments x

β) Introduction: Why Long Novels? 1

Part I

1 Realism on an Expanded Canvas 9
   Why Study the Real? 9
   New Realism and the Return of Speculative Philosophy 12
   Ontology's Unlikely Friend: Postwar Phenomenology beyond Personal Experience 14
   Marc Richir's Quantum Phenomenology 17
   And Yet Another Return of the Real 19
   The Many Lives of Realism 22
   Concepts of Reality, Possibilities of the Novel 27

2 Notes on Hyperbole 31
   The Risky Truth of Hyperbole 31
   The Rare Occurrence of Hyperbole in Literary Criticism 33
   Hyperbole as *Figura* 35
   Phenomenology's Hyperbole 38
   Hyperphenomena, Hyperobjects 41

Part II

3 Abundant Discourses 47
   The Maximalist Novel: Lovers & Haters 47
   Amalfitano's Case for the Long and Difficult Novel 51
   Cruft vs. Craft 55
   2666 and ATD in the Context of Modern Maximalism 57

4 Anthropophagic Intertextuality 63
Abundant Intertextuality 63
Pynchon's Reparative Genre-Poaching 65
Bolaño's Intertextual Name-Dropping 69
Metabolic Intertextuality, Anthropophagic Form 79

5 The Visible and the Invisible 85
It's Always Night, or We Wouldn't Need Light 85
Flickering Lights in Otherwise Perfect Darkness 87
The Visible and the Invisible in Richir and Merleau-Ponty 90
Santa Teresa as *Centro Intermitente* of *2666* 93
Perfect Darkness and Capitalist Sorcery in *ATD* 100

6 Flat Fictionality 107
Métaphores Filées 107
A Facilitator of Passages 111
The Secret Trade of Metaphor 114
Flat Fictionality 118
The Dismal Metonymies of the Dead 126

7 *Sed Tamen Effabor* 131
Practical Disbelief 131
Extravagant Doubt and the Suspension of Mimesis 134
Lucretius Reacts to the Myth of the Ineffable 136
Sin Embargo: Ontological Simulacrum and
Hyperbolic Stubbornness 138
Pynchon's Hyperbolic Carnival 139
The Penultimate Self-Portrait of Edwin Johns 141
The Melancholy of Totality 145

8 Ekphrasis beyond Imagination 149
Ekphrasis between Rupture and Longue Durée 149
Photography as Modern Alchemy 152
Bolaño's Negative Epiphanies 155
Dehiscence and Phantasia at the Margins of Perception 158

Andrea Tancredi's Impossible Avant-Garde Art 165
Hyperbolic Realism's *Phantasia* 168

Part III

9 Slow Adventures 175
    The Adventure Novel after the End of Adventures 175
    Bolaño's Poetic Fracasology 177
    Pynchon's Slow Adventures 180

10 The Labor of Figuration 187
    Hyperbolically Realist 187
    Against Ineffability 195

ψ) Epilogue: A Fifth Concept of Reality 203

References 211
Index 226

ACKNOWLEDGMENTS

Anything that could ever possibly matter in a person's life comes from the metabolization of friendship. You don't have to write an entire book to discover such an obvious truth, but here, at the margins of one, is probably not the worst place to briefly remember it. In our culture, books are supposed to be the arduous outcome of a solitary heroic effort; and if it is probably true that the process of writing itself is impossible without the luxury of loneliness, the product will never forget what it owes to the privilege and miracle of the shared adventures of a generous past.

Once, Clarice Lispector suddenly felt as if she were the mother of all beings. I don't know of a better way to name our relation to the world, our often-irresponsible responsibility for each other and the infinite joy of all those moments when celebration and care coincide. Above all, then, I must thank the evolving innermost circle of my good enough co-mothers of all things: Fred, Johanna, Amelie, Fernanda, Mathias, Jonathan, Micha, Matteo, Wanda, Rike, Nele. I also thank Tobias, hyperbolic editor-in-arms, and Sanaz who opened new horizons still waiting to be explored.

There are so many more who deserve my gratitude, and I should (and probably could) mention you all by your name. But the space is limited and this is not an obituary or a monument, so I hope that you won't be offended if I thank you anonymously, but with no less fervor. Working myself yet another time through my manuscript, I encountered your presence at every turn, in a singular thought, a surprising question, a specific sentence or reference, or in a simple gesture I once received as your unconditional gift.

Some people have shaped my academic and intellectual adventures a bit more than others or have supported me in crucial moments, as rather unconscious or, at least, perfectly discreet mentors. I thank, among many others, Philipp Ekardt, Gert Mattenklott, Oliver Lubrich, Anne Eusterschulte, Tanja Nusser, Ernst Osterkamp, Ingrid Hotz-Davies, Martin Bauer, Héctor Hoyos, Gabriel Giorgi, Marc Redfield, Lothar Müller, Silvia Fehrmann, Jens Bisky, Teresa Koloma Beck, and my incredible supervisors Fernando Resende and Jonathan Pollock.

Special thanks go out to LECKEN, which is gradually transforming itself from a party collective into a full-fledged support system, cultivating the sex appeal of the inorganic still better than anyone else.

I thank my fellows from *Interzones*, the whole staff at the Ibero-American Institute in Berlin where so many parts of this book were written, my lovely former colleagues at the Hamburg Institute for Social Research for creating an intellectual home across our home office isolation, and my friend André, *hyperbolique lecteur mon semblable mon frère*, who helped me, tirelessly, with an earlier version of *Hyperbolic Realism*.

Finally, I thank my wonderful editors Amy Martin, Agalya Mayandi, Katherine de Chant, and everybody at Bloomsbury Academic who had a part in the making of this book.

Nothing of this could exist without the ongoing love and support of my family. I thank my brother, Faruk, for sharing with me the room that was our own and for planting the seeds of my earliest curiosity in my little head. I thank my grandparents in Germany for being there for us through all these years and for being so proud and so modest at the same time. I thank my grandma in Ksour for her quirky charm and the many times we mocked the language barrier with our secret ways of communicating. And I thank my whole family in Tunisia who, at an early age, introduced me to the craftsmanship of unsparing hospitality.

At last, I thank my parents for their often unspoken trust in my decisions and for stirring up in us the thirst for discussion and disagreement; my father for his admiring generosity and for letting me learn my own lessons; my mother for an involuntary yet brilliant incapacity to turn herself over to her class antagonists and, much more importantly, the priceless legacy of her untamable tongue.

Berlin / Fortaleza, September 2023.

β) Introduction: Why Long Novels?

> *Hell yes, need advice bad.*
> *Any man who writes a trilogy needs advice*
> *(and a good physician).*
>
> JOHN DOS PASSOS

Why do we still read long novels? What I mean are novels that are both really long and real, not brick-sized page turners that purport to bring news from distant lands, telling marketable standardized stories in standardized prose and dim-witted dialogue, books whose only remarkability is their unremarkable style, written by authors whose claim to fame is nothing but fame itself. No, the type of novel I am referring to is that really long novel—"long" as in difficult, complex, exuberant, encyclopedic—that strikes many as coming closer to an adequate representation of the real than the most dedicated realist narrative. As we speak, that novel is still being read, and not only within academia, where it arguably enjoys particular popularity. As a literary genre, it may well be past its prime, but its days are not yet numbered. Against the odds, the long and difficult novel has managed to survive, as a ritual object for a loyal circle of readers whose devoted attention operates both within and against the all-encompassing digital condition of fragmented realities and fleeting perception. It is not easy to find the time and patience required to come to terms with these novels, and yet they are still read and re-read by more than just a happy few.

About a century ago, an exceptionally gifted Irishman by the name of James Joyce was the first to bring the genre to rare perfection only to bring it, ultimately, all the closer to its own demise. Whereas in *Ulysses*, excess and abundance are still somehow contained in the confines of a "work," in *Finnegans Wake,* the "book" has disappeared to make room for a heretic confusion of inexhaustible expression and universal unreadability. One more century prior to that, years before the births of Joyce's two opposite twins, a novelist from, say, Russia could count on the coming of a cold, long winter as the perfect excuse for his prospective readers to plunge into his novels' ranges and depths. Today, in the first quarter of the twenty-first century, however, a writer with maximalist ambitions can no longer hope for such assistance from the natural course of events. Not only are our winters becoming drastically shorter and warmer, we can also spend them—in the precious time between professional and private obligations, seasonal depression and, if one has the means, temporary escapes to warmer climes—almost entirely in front of our screens.

A series of questions arise: What more than nostalgia for the analog could lie behind this digital era's sustained interest in maximalist literature? How can books like *Infinite Jest*, or Bolaño's *Savage Detectives*, for that matter, still serve as a major point of reference for whole generations (at least parts of them)? How does the long and difficult novel survive and maintain the interest of a reader who has been raised in a post-literate age of ever-declining attention spans (McLuhan 1962; Powe 1987)? How can the maximalist novel hold ground against the rise and ambition of the TV series as the dominant cultural format responsible for sprawling narratives? And how, in the first place, do both formats, the maximalist novel and the maximalist TV show, justify their commitment to long stories if postmodernism has so successfully proclaimed the death of master narratives? Moreover, is the human-scaled default setting of literature capable of coping with the most pressing phenomena of our time, the elusive and massively distributed realities of cybernetic inflation, financial capitalism, and climate change? And how can literature keep up with the defining mode of contemporary writing dominated by seemingly authorless codes and algorithms?

Over the years, many names have been invented for prose works that violate ordinary expectations of length, coherence, scale, range, and complexity. It seems plausible to place these texts in one line with the great epic poems from Homer to Camões, with the sprawling travelogues and grotesque adventure tales of Rabelais, Cervantes, or Melville, with the encyclopedic achievements of Burton, d'Alembert, and Diderot, and with all other works that manifest a desire for a *Gesamtwerk* or even a *Gesamtkunstwerk*. But does it really matter if we call these works "maximalist novels" (Ercolino 2014), "mega novels" (Karl 2001), "systems novels" (LeClair 1989), "encyclopedic novels" (Mendelson 1976), "modern epics" (Moretti [1994] 1996), "cartographies of the absolute" (Toscano & Kinkle 2015), "geopolitical novels" (Irr 2014), "alephs" (Hoyos 2015), "*discursos de la abundancia*" (Ortega 1992), "*novelas supremas*" (Padilla 2004), "novelas without witnesses" (Corral 2001), or "*novelas totales*" (Vargas Llosa 1991: 9–58)? And what could be the merit of less celebratory or outright dismissive reactions to maximalist writing, reactions that criticize some of the most lauded maximalist novels as "too hard to read" (Franzen 2002), as illustrations of the "dull new global novel" (Parks 2010) or as agents of a preposterous literary movement denounced as "hysterical realism" (Wood 2000)?

There is, of course, more than a grain of truth in the assertation that the maximalist novel is notoriously hard to read. Simply because of its sheer length, instead of being read through from page one to three hundred, it asks to be studied, consulted (Cortázar 1967: 137), interrupted, resumed, admired, despised—or abandoned. In this book here, however, realism does not present itself as the opposite of opacity. Instead, my two guiding concepts, *hyperbole* and *realism,* shall lead ways into and cut swaths through the thicket of two relatively recent cases of the maximalist novel, Roberto Bolaño's *2666* and Thomas Pynchon's *Against the Day (ATD)*.[1]

On first view, realism and hyperbole seem to be antagonists, the former concerned with creating an adequate reproduction, a corresponding image of the world as (we think) we know it, the other on a constant mission to challenge, distort, mock, and violate our regular and ordinary, normal and normative expectations. Seen that way, the novel would be perceived as the result of a formal compromise, which would open the door for well-rehearsed dialectical solutions, in which realism and hyperbole would be gradually mediated into sublation (and potentially into oblivion). The critical strategy I want to perform in this book, however, refrains from dialectical ready-made solutions. Adhering to the conviction that contradictions exist only in logic, but not in reality and certainly not in literature, I see the realistic and the hyperbolic as *two distant yet interrelated modalities* invested in one and the same aesthetic project, sometimes conflicting, sometimes converging, sometimes not interacting at all. Consequently, as my "wild readings" (Stengers [2002] 2011; Lévi-Strauss 1962) of Pynchon's and Bolaño's late maximalist novels unfold, there are at least two crucial points that I hope to make clear: The world has always had and will always have its fair (and often unfair) share of hyperbole; any act of formalized exaggeration entails oblique and twisted comments on the reality that grounds and conditions their excess.

Let's have a quick look at the structure of the present book. In two separate chapters, Part One will introduce "realism" not as a genre, but as an ongoing open problem in aesthetics and the history of art, as well as hyperbole as rhetorical device and aesthetic figure. Part Two handles most of the hermeneutic work, close-reading crucial aspects, procedures, and poetic strategies of *ATD* and *2666* under the lens of what I came to call *hyperbolic realism.* Chapter 3 reacts to the first and foremost problem any study of maximalism must deal with: the problem of the too-much, of excess, abundance, and over-abundance, of how to make sense of the mega-novel's

---

[1]Since I will refer extensively to both novels throughout this whole book, all quotes will be indicated with the short title (*ATD* & *2666*) and page number directly behind the quoted passage.

questionable whims to constantly invite the "sand-grained manyness of things" (DeLillo 1997: 60) to the party. The rest of the chapters in Part Two close-read (or should I say: wild-read?) salient aspects of hyperbolic realism such as the digestive incorporation of intertextuality (Chapter 4); the flickering distribution of light and darkness and the interplay of the visible and invisibility (Chapter 5); the metonymic, horizontal interlacing of hyperbolic metaphors (Chapter 6); the non-dialectical labor of doubt and uncertainty, or the explosive use of ekphrasis (Chapter 7) in the service of imagination's hyperbolizing energies (Chapter 8).

Part Three, then, weaves together some of the scattered results from the previous chapters to celebrate the adventurous and often mannered labor of figuration that is perhaps the most salient compositional (though not always syntactic) aspect of hyperbolic realism. For this part, the last two chapters of my book contest the myth of ineffability, which modern literature has significantly (but not exclusively) inherited from romanticism. My aim, however, is clearly not to endorse the boastful triumphalism of some of our most distasteful contemporaries (such as a former US-American president) against the virtues and values of diversity, doubt, and uncertainty— metafictional, metalinguistic, and metapragmatic virtues that happier forces within modernity and postmodernism have entrusted us with.

If my strategy of "wild reading" has a distinctly philosophical dimension, my aim is not to write an epistemology of the novel (Gess & Janßen 2014; Rancière 1992). Instead, I will concentrate myself on literature's innate power to amplify, accommodate, and acuminate phenomenological and ontological motifs within its highly fictionalized and formalized folds. Hyperbole's role in this strategy is not only to help bring these motives to the surface; it also acts as a "facilitator of passages" (*ATD*: 433) which fuels the trade between two hitherto irreconcilable departments of experience.

Over the entire course of the book, while studying the aesthetic features of *2666* and *ATD*, I will keep at least half an eye on those novels' underlying concept(s) of reality, which can only gradually and reflexively be carved out of the texts as they unfold in front of our eyes and in the grip of our hands in simultaneously linear *and* nonlinear ways. The concrete phenomenality of those epiphanic moments, when the real in its contemporary *gestalt* seems to appear on the surface of the text—their rhythm of appearance, disappearance, and re-appearance—will turn out to be an integral part of hyperbolic realism's core conception of reality as a whole. In a short, concluding epilogue, I discuss how Pynchon's and Bolaño's novels are taking part in spelling out a new concept of reality, not only through reproduction (i.e., representation in the classical sense), but through co-production and co-creation. At the same time, I want to show that this new concept of reality is not so entirely new, rather, it has been anticipated or prefigured by postwar phenomenologists such as Maurice Merleau-Ponty, Marc Richir, or Emmanuel Levinas, and newly promoted by intellectuals who pioneered the emerging field of Anthropocene theory such as Quentin Meillassoux, Dipesh Chakrabarty, Claire Colebrook, Karen Barad, and many more.

The expropriation of aesthetic material from the literary text toward an elucidation of structures and styles of the world, of environment and the planet, of sensation and perception, of body and earth is of course not possible without the critic's ongoing investment and integration of risk and exaggeration into his own critical discourse. In this book, the inevitably hyperbolic investment of the critic (= me)—always more and less than illustration or conceptualization, always more and less than methodology or interest—is conceived as a synonym to theory. As theory never blindly trusts the self-healing powers of truth and evidence, it does not seek to repress or eradicate the penchant of hyperbole to distort, impress, and persuade. Critically applied, hyperbole does not aim beyond truth, it rather settles beneath and besides it, and should not be used in absolutist term, as a tool of triumphalism. (Critical) hyperbole has an irreducibly intrusive dimension; however, its seizure on our attention relies on consensus. If the trope is overacting, its force should not become violence; it should feel like bondage, not capture. As a counterpart to self-evident truth, hyperbole is often not concerned with making fully substantiated claims, but if it does (and it does so at times), it makes simultaneous room for doubts and uncertainty, failure, illusion, melancholy, and even despair. The hyperbolic mode is allergic to both the absolute *and* nothingness; it does not seek to attain or embody "the Alpha and Omega, the first and the last, beginning and end" (Revelation 1:8, 21:6, 22:13) of existence. It aims toward the very-large and almost-nothing, the second(ary) and pen-ultimate, the superfluous and vanishing, the smallest audible and near-deafening units of perception. It stands in for the way-too-much, the way-too-little or the by-far-not-enough, it aims too high or falls too short, it is either too late or too early. "Hyperbole," writes hyperbole's leading hyperbolist, Christopher Johnson, "is the *beta* and *psi* of the apophatic experience" (Johnson 446). Not the *alpha* and *omega*, just the *beta* and *psi*.

Any act of institutionally untamed reading runs the risk of landing on the side of arbitrariness or, perhaps worse, apoliticality. Wild readings entail irredeemable hyperbolic dimensions, leaps into the unknown, and minor moments of madness. Following a strong undercurrent of literary modernism, from Stéphane Mallarmé to Mahmoud Darwish, they act like an unsolicited throw of the dice. So even where, in this book, glimpses into the infrastructure of the real—as it could present itself at the beginning of our current century—are probed, chance and hazard are not abolished. Each gazing into the face of the world—or its abyss, as Bolaño would have it—comes with the costs of partial blindness.

The stance I seek to cultivate in this book aims to be more (and less) than a "hermeneutics of suspicion" (Ricœur [1965] 1970) following the imaginary footsteps of Bolaño's bookish characters, savage hermeneutic detectives embroiled in ongoing acts of reading and overreading, in short: hyperbolic reading. Instead of universally applied suspicion (which is meant to be a critical tool, but all too often ends up being an agent of indifference and loss of curiosity), *Hyperbolic Realism* seeks to promote a wild way of reading, a *savage* hermeneutics of *corrupted pilgrim's guides,* to adopt Pynchon's adorable formula, an exploration of twisted, apocryphal maps that will lead us on sinuous paths to some well-lit and prominent places, to other places almost entirely unknown and to yet others "not strictly on the map at all" (*ATD*).

My hyperbolic, exaggerated and exaggerating hermeneutics resonate with César Aira's poetic dictum of the *fuga hacia adelante*, which refers to a constant, improvisational flight of the writer from the text—staged within the text. My intention, however, is not to promote a flight from, but a "plunge into reality" (O'Connor [1957] 1970: 78), "not a disentanglement from [it], but a progressive *knotting into*" (Pynchon 1973: 3). Clearly operating on the side of materialism's critical legacy (quite like Hoyos 2019), but in a decidedly less pessimistic key than some of its dominant proponents, my hermeneutics' adventurous mood might sometimes appear to come dangerously close to the carefree ingenuousness of Pynchon's aeronauts, the "Chums of Chance". But what hopefully excuses me and, to a certain extent, them, is the fact that their naïveté is not ideological, but experimental. As a mode of experimentation, the aim of "wild reading" is not to abolish critical thinking, but to merge it with a materialist and phenomenological curiosity that can guide us through *hyperbolic realism*'s "wild and free creation" (Stengers [2002] 2011) of aesthetic concepts. To follow a sometimes-unreliable, but all in all trustworthy guide, should not lure us to where catharsis and redemption are confidently waiting for us. It will rather bring us, I hope, to more of those half-hidden places so typically cherished by Bolaño and Pynchon; places both ordinary and eerie, "where salvation does not yet exist" (*ATD*: 566).

PART ONE

1

Realism on an Expanded Canvas

*At last, at last, there was no symbol,
there was the "thing,"
the orgiastic thing.*

CLARICE LISPECTOR

Why Study the Real?

For Spivak, at least, the answer is clear: "Because we must" (Spivak 2012: 1, 2, and 12). Admittedly, her essay concerns the slightly different question of its title: *Why study the past?* But the grounding tensions between understanding and action, analysis and existence, study and life are more or less the same no matter if we look at past, present, or future. Allowing these tensions to shape our critical practice promises to "protect […] us from the horror and randomness of planetarity" (2012: 1), to provide us with a protective skin of ambiguity, contingency, and becoming that helps us gaining "language and poise in the face of catastrophes, suffering, chaos and crisis" (Böhme 2009, my transl.). But once we shift to the field of action, the benefit of ambiguity becomes dubious. "The field of work, the field of life," writes Spivak, "is best described by a double bind, contradictory instructions coming at once. You acknowledge that this description must be immediately converted into a single bind—strictly speaking an 'erroneous' description—so that a choice can be made. You cannot not decide if you are actually in the field of social justice" (Spivak 2012: 11).

Critically addressing Deleuze and Guattari's concept of nomadic counter-historiography, Spivak objects that while quintessentially postmodern figures such as the nomad, the rhizome, or schizoanalysis are helpful tools to wrestle away the past from "the sedentary point of view [that acts] in the name of a unitary State apparatus" (Deleuze and Guattari [1980]

1987: 23), they are a lot less useful at the level of decision and agency: "The schizo's 'and then ... and then'," Spivak concludes, "stands as a reminder of the double bind, but it's not agentially useful" (Spivak 2012: 11).

Of course, theory must never be reduced to support concrete action through practical advice, nor should it advocate a new positivism that privileges perception over reflection. But if it wants to be "agentially useful" (2012: 11), it must account to some extent for both sides of the situation: for the double bind of the *image* as well as for the single bind of the *decision*. What Spivak advocates is thus a tight alliance between historiography (in a broad and plural sense) and activism (from an equally pluralistic perspective). The challenge to make informed and justified claims in favor of *specific* grounding errors, which inevitably underlie our meaningful practices, has a fundamentally ethical dimension:

> You can't just say for the practice of freedom that Kant shows us that the production of the discourse of freedom is always programmed by the lack of access to pure reason, so we say "ok, we wash our hands, just let's make mistakes." [...] Because just *any* grounding error is not O.K. You have to choose between structures of violence, structures of *violating* the double bind of life and work and thinking, and so on, you have to choose, and that's the democratic choice. (2012: 11).

Two of Spivak's names for such specific violations of complexity are "affirmative deconstruction" (2012: 11) and "broad reading" (2012: 3). From their vantage point, we begin to view the past—and this should be true even more for the present—not as a "manifest image" (Sellars 1963: 5), but as a "relief map," emphasizing "contemporaneous diachronies" (Spivak 2012: 3), but fully aware of the inevitability of our not completely reversible grounding errors.

To bring back irreversibility to the core of cultural theory marks a decisive rupture with the postmodern age, which was in a way based on the idea of a general reversibility of cultural and symbolic relations in a time after the end of history. It also marks the advent of something new, and the by now widely established name for this new cultural epoch is of course: the Anthropocene. But the Anthropocene is not only the name for a new cultural epoch, it also signals an emerging geological era, which is why Dipesh Chakrabarty, in his Anthropocene lecture at the Berliner *Haus der Kulturen der Welt* in 2013, claimed that the spectacular comeback of nature calls for the study of our history and culture "on an expanded canvas" (Chakrabarty 2009)—not only in their global and geopolitical contexts, but in their complex environments on a planetary scale and with a renewed attention to the natural sciences.

At the example of Giovanni Arrighi, a leading Marxist scholar of global history, Chakrabarty points to a recent change in the analytic mood—from a predominantly Euro-American reflection on capital's internal globalization

(Arrighi [1994] 2010) to a focus on planetary "lineages" (Arrighi 2007) in the wake of the Cold War, which is "more concerned with the question of ecological limits to capitalism" (Chakrabarty 2009: 200):

> [The] critique that sees humanity as an effect of power is valuable for all the hermeneutics of suspicion that it has taught postcolonial scholarship. It is an effective critical tool in dealing with national and global formations of domination. But I do not find it adequate in dealing with the crisis of global warming. [...] We may not experience ourselves as a geological agent, but we appear to have become one at the level of the species. And without that knowledge that defies historical understanding there is no making sense of the current crisis that affects us all. Climate change, refracted through global capital, will no doubt accentuate the logic of inequality that runs through the rule of capital; some people will no doubt gain temporarily at the expense of others. But the whole crisis cannot be reduced to a story of capitalism. Unlike in the crises of capitalism, there are no lifeboats here for the rich and the privileged. (2009: 221).

Chakrabarty's call to redraw the outlines of the field of social and cultural critique is of course not the only programmatic statement that demands a radical conversion of the humanities (see e.g. Latour 2004). But his four theses about historical research in times of anthropogenic climate change serve as an acutely condensed aide-mémoire for any future Anthropocenic theory to come. In a nutshell, Chakrabarty's four theses state: (1) that we must overcome the binary between natural and human history, (2) that the concept of modernity must be fundamentally revised, (3) that the history of globalization must enter into a dialogue with the history and evolution of the human species, and (4) that to consider capitalism from the perspectives of the species and the planet probes the limit of capital itself.

According to Chakrabarty's four theses, Anthropocenic theory must think the limits (and the possible afterlives) of capitalism, but should not forget that any contemporary critique of capitalism cannot be articulated from within the logic and history of capital only. The intellectual outcome of our "new cultural geology" (McGurl 2011) differs greatly in purpose, style, and quality (Garcia 2018), but there is a minimal set of shared concerns to all Anthropocenic critical thinking, which can be defined, roughly, by the following questions: How can we think an outside not only to the (transcendental) subject, but also to the status quo of capitalism, human superiority, and the hegemony of Western modernity? How can we think nature on its own terms without reducing the political, the social, and the cultural domain to biologically determined products? How can we think the real in complex, broad, and pluralistic ways while at the same time accounting for the Anthropocenic problem of planetary decision-making under extreme time-pressure? What kinds of *new realism* can we invent without regressing to a *new doxa* that merges the neo-positivist angst in the face of cultural complexity with an accelerationist celebration of techno-euphoric and post-democratic "solutions"?

New Realism and the Return of Speculative Philosophy

On April 27, 2007, the neo-Marxist philosopher Alberto Toscano invites four philosophers—Ray Brassier, Iain Hamilton Grant, Graham Harman, and Quentin Meillassoux—to London for a workshop with the title *Speculative Realism* (Mackay 2007: 307–449). Although it would later be rejected by all four participants, the label has survived even as its date of origin slowly fades into oblivion. But also outside of that meeting of the minds in London, 2007 marks a moment in which a renewed interest in both ontology and speculative philosophy comes to the fore.

The most influential participant of Toscano's workshop on what would continue as a perpetual search for new realisms is Quentin Meillassoux. In the following paragraphs, I will not engage in a comprehensive discussion of Meillassoux's fascinating and intricate chain of arguments in *After Finitude*, a book hailed by no one else than Alain Badiou as a small philosophical revolution. A few things must be said, however, since hardly any discussion of Anthropocenic theory, new realism, and the renewed interested in speculation can afford to bypass Meillassoux's argument.

At its beginning lies a daring concept that allows Meillassoux, hyperbolically, to comprehend the totality of philosophy since Kant under a common denominator. This concept he calls *correlationism,* and it describes the widely shared understanding that everything which exists for us, exists in relation to a knowing, perceiving, or otherwise intentionally invested (human) subject. According to Meillassoux, what practically all philosophical projects since Kant have in common is either that they start from the constitutive unknowability of Kant's noumenon or Ding-an-sich, or that they completely deny the epistemological relevance of anything outside the subject and its transcendental structures. For correlationists, knowledge is only possible in relation to a knowing subject, and everything that appears, appears in relation to a more or less intentionally directed faculty of that subject.

It is not against this or that theory, this or that philosopher, that Meillassoux's argument is directed, but against the entire field of critical philosophy, harking back to its fundamental grounding error, correlationism, that is. Meillassoux attacks the whole paradigm of philosophy that Harman calls *philosophies of access*—a philosophy based on the idea that reality is somehow *over there*, that it can only be accessed through the various filters of a subject *over here*, and that it has neither value nor structure apart from that relation.

Instead of our access to reality, Meillassoux and others prefer to speak of our contact with a real that, to some extent at least, can be assessed on its own terms. "Intentionality," writes the French philosopher Jocelyn Benoist, "is absolutely not a condition for accessing the real, as if access to it were ever necessary; it presupposes instead a previous contact with it" (Benoist 2011: 89, my transl.). Contact as a mode of relation is completely different from the mode of access; in fact, it is not really a relation at all, but an embodiment, an environmentally oriented entanglement of the subject with material, organic, and immunological processes. This ecological dimension of contact is clearly expressed by the German phenomenologist Lambert Wiesing: "The metaphor of access to the world is an unecological hubris. Humans don't have access to the world, but live in the world as a part of the world—until the day they must go" (Wiesing 2009: 69, my transl.).

To redefine our primordial relation to the world in terms of contact is the main material(ist) purport of *After Finitude*. On its speculative side, we follow Meillassoux to an assessment of the real in its most general form, not as a particular and concrete piece or section of reality. "Speculative Philosophy," says Whitehead, a central figure of reference for the recent ontological turn, "is the endeavour to frame a coherent, logical, necessary system of general ideas in terms of which every element of our experience can be interpreted" (Whitehead 1929: 3). It is the real in its most general form, the real as absolute, which is at stake in Meillassoux's project, and the *arche-fossil* is his by now well-known term for a mode of the real that is essentially knowable without being reduced to its existence for a human subject. The *arche-fossil* names any kind of evidence from a world before the emergence of the human such as a "zircon, the oldest rock in the world" (Wark 2017: 286). It refers to an event hidden in deep time, which took place long before the advent of our species-being (the arche-function), an event that has nevertheless been preserved and can be described, at least, in mathematical terms (the fossil-function).

Meillassoux's second anchor is *ancestrality*. It names the temporal register in which the *arche-fossil* exists. Correlationism, no matter if in its strong or weak form (Meillassoux [2006] 2008: 30), cannot make sense of an ancestral proposition, as for example the claim that zircon is 4.4. billion years old, not only for us, but regardless of whether we exist or not.

As the metaphysical spearhead of Anthropocenic thought, Meillassoux's work combines speculative philosophy's risky strategy of radical and consequent dehistoricization with the pristine fantasy of a pre-human wilderness (2008: 21–2) and the looming post-apocalyptic situation in which our planet, after the comparatively brief episode of human existence, will have become a toxic wasteland (2008: 112). Ancestrality, extinction, and imminent catastrophe are in fact cornerstones of the Anthropocene's geological reconceptualization of time. Relying on the warnings of postmodern Marxism (Jameson 1981: 9), one may take this as evidence of a dangerous ignorance of power dynamics and historical conditions of asymmetry on the part of the thinkers of the Anthropocene. With the same right, one could point to those thinkers' commitment to conceptualize history and the world on an expanded canvas. It calls for an expansion of a focus on *bios,* which has been an important critical tool but remains ultimately too narrow, in order to open up social and cultural critique toward natural history and geological time. Following Meillassoux, the task is to devise an archaeology of ancestrality; in the wake of Claire Colebrook, we have to engage with an "ethics of extinction" (Colebrook 2014: 40).

All too often, the great number of critics of Meillassoux and the whole paradigm of new realism and Anthropocenic metaphysics play an easy game by merely calling out the alleged political conservativism of those new metaphysical concerns (Galloway 2013). In my opinion, we should stop asking if contemporary metaphysics does in fact address social and political issues (which they indeed often do) and start to explore if the metaphysical turn has the potential to add fresh insights to our social and political predicament. For it has always been the task of metaphysics to provide a general frame in which more specific problems and concerns can be discussed under different conditions. More than anything else, to criticize metaphysics for not being outspokenly liberal or emancipatory enough amounts to a confession that one is actually quite at ease with the given conditions even where one acts as those conditions' strongest critic.

Ontology's Unlikely Friend: Postwar Phenomenology beyond Personal Experience

It is hard not to admire Meillassoux's argument for its razor-sharp efficiency. Yet, we could also accuse him of a flaw that some of the not so ambitious newer contributions associated with the ontological exhibit. Inspired by an early and disregarded contribution from the French context (Rosset 1977), we could describe this unsatisfying feature as the sadness and solitude of the real. For in those accounts, the only thing that is undeniably real seems to be that which stubbornly resists all kinds of symbolic appropriation, all that which remains speechless, insignificant—with one word: idiotic (see also Speranza 2005). To base an entire philosophical endeavor on the singularity and unavailability of the real, one risks to stare at it the way some people stare at goats—seeing something that doesn't reveal anything else than its self-contained, mute, and inoffensive presence.

Despite the constant claim on novelty, new realism does of course take cues from history and the tradition, referring back to writers like H. P. Lovecraft (Harman 2012), cultural theorists like Mark Fisher (Hoffmann 2017), classical philosophers like Friedrich Wilhelm Joseph Schelling (Grant 2006), canonized modernist philosophers like Martin Heidegger (Harman 2002), and some who were once famous, but are today neglected like Alfred North Whitehead (Shaviro 2009; Stengers [2002] 2011). In this book, I will probe the unlikely alliance between new realism and a certain strand of postwar phenomenology represented by Maurice Merleau-Ponty, Emmanuel Levinas, and—the unjustly unknown—Marc Richir.

In 1959, Maurice Merleau-Ponty started working on a new project that his sudden death in 1961 would turn into his unfinished legacy. Published posthumously by Claude Lefort as *Le Visible et L'Invisible* in 1964, the book consists of four chapters edited by Merleau-Ponty himself and an appendix of about 150 pages, the so-called *notes de travail*. Among those notes, a few ideas for working titles can be found, revealing a deep interest in nature and the real that seem quite odd for a phenomenologist: *Being and Meaning, Genealogy of the True, The Origin of Truth, The Visible and Nature*. From the very first note onwards, it becomes clear that Merleau-Ponty envisions his project as a break with his own philosophical tradition: "Necessity of a return to ontology—The ontological questioning and its ramifications/ the subject-object question/the question of inter-subjectivity/the question of Nature" (Merleau-Ponty [1964] 1968: 165).

Against the assumption of phenomenology as a philosophy of the subject or its reduction to nothing more but a thick description of experience, Merleau-Ponty promises to use ontology as "the elaboration of the notions that have to replace that of transcendental subjectivity, those of subject, object, meaning" (1968: 167), trying to make sense of the fact that before perception and logical thinking lies a pre-reflexive and pre-linguistic contact with the real and an embodiment in nature. Sensual experience, language, and the inter-subjective relation to the other are still seen as *openings* toward a world, but "the objective transcendence is not posterior to the position of the other: the world is already there, in its objective transcendence" (1968: 172). The distinction between a life-world already imbued with sense and meaning and a pre-logical world *tout court*, a world "in its objective transcendence," offers a promising way out of the correlationist dogma; contrary to the charges brought forth by Meillassoux and many new realists who view phenomenology as that dogma's most crippling sermonizer.

Now, philosophy's reconsidered task is not only to work through the distinction of these two worlds but to give an account of the various ways of transition and passage between them. This is why most of Merleau-Ponty's working titles and subtitles all contain an element of evolution and passage: history, genealogy, origin etc. "In showing the divergence between physics and the being of Physis, between biology and the being of life, what is at issue is to effect the passage from being in itself, the objective being, to the being of the *Lebenswelt*" (1968: 166–7). Not unlike Levinas, but much less hermetically, Merleau-Ponty claims that the real is not that ready-to-hand material we find in front of us and try to get access to; it is that which simultaneously contains and excludes us as it passes through our bodies without ever conceding to be fully controlled. In the life-world of phenomenal experience, the real thus only manifests itself in "the form of traces" (1968: 101), involving us in experiences "both irrecusable and enigmatic" (1968: 130), which are not produced by a subject, but lie "dormant in our ontological landscape" (1968: 101).

This could not remain without serious consequences for the concept of the phenomenon itself. In *The Intertwining—The Chiasm*, the famous last completed chapter, which sounds like the subtitle of a David Lynch series, Merleau-Ponty introduces a new understanding of the phenomenon as "wild Being" [*être sauvage*] (1968: 165). No longer the pure presence of immediately given sensory data (Husserl) nor the ontic material that needs to be reconnected to the fundamental ontology of *Dasein* (Heidegger), Merleau-Ponty's wild beings are appearances that flicker, like erratic animations of *chiaroscuro* shapes, between the visible and the invisible, the phenomenal and the ontological: "My flesh and that of the world therefore involve clear zones, clearings, about which pivot their opaque zones" (1968: 148).

A phenomenon in that sense is neither fully given to us nor entirely absent, it is the result of a dynamic intertwining [*entrelacement*] between body (both *chair* and *corps*) and world, between nature and its virtual products, which are interdependent of, yet not entirely reducible to each other. As a result, philosophy must move beyond the Euclidean imagination, that "network of straight lines" (1968: 210), into a space defined by Merleau-Ponty as topological, a space "cut out in a total voluminosity which surrounds me, in which I am, which is behind me as well as before me" (1968: 213–14). While remaining a distinct practice, philosophy shares the central demand with literature that it mustn't believe that it can "soar over [*survoler*] its objects" (1968: 27). Instead, like literature but with distinct methods, it must "plunge into reality" (O'Connor [1957] 1970: 78). Only then can literature make sense of its imbrication with a nature from which it emerges and in which it remains grounded, no matter how far it might travel into the weightless world of aesthetic ramifications.

In the last paragraph ever written by Merleau-Ponty, not so different from the tone of Levinas in the final section of *Otherwise than Being*,[1] he

---

[1] "Here the human is brought out by transcendence, or the hyperbole, that is, the disinterestedness of essence, a hyperbole in which it breaks up and *falls upward*, into the human. Our philosophical discourse does not pass from one term to the other only by searching the 'subjective' horizons of what shows itself, but embraces conjunctions of elements in which concepts subtended as presence or a subject break up" (Levinas [1974] 1991: 184).

redefines philosophy's task as the production and preservation of "an almost carnal existence of the idea" as a "sublimation of the flesh" (Merleau-Ponty [1964] 1968: 155). Language has an important part to play in this, but its role is much more complicated than most theories of communication would have us believe (1968: 162). It does not come as a surprise, then, that, in trying to embrace the full philosophical extent of language, Merleau-Ponty's last words turn to hyperbole:

> In a sense the whole of philosophy, as Husserl says, consists in restoring a power to signify, a birth of meaning, or a wild meaning, an expression of experience by experience, which in particular clarifies the special domain of language. And in a sense, as Valery said, language is everything, since it is the voice of no one, since it is the very voice of the things, the waves, and the forests. And what we have to understand is that there is no dialectical reversal from one of these views to the other; we do not have to reassemble them into a synthesis: they are two aspects of the reversibility which is the ultimate truth. (1968: 155).

Marc Richir's Quantum Phenomenology

The Belgian phenomenologist Marc Richir takes up on Merleau-Ponty's reorientations and radicalizes them. For most of the few but extremely devoted experts of his vast and fascinating work, discussing Richir in the context of new realism might seem completely senseless. Instead of a hyperbolic speculation beyond the limits of phenomenology (Levinas) or its refoundation on ontological grounds (Merleau-Ponty), Richir's philosophy has been read as a "phenomenological relaunch of the transcendental question" (Forestier 2015: 2, my transl.), as a radicalization of phenomenology's in-built "strong correlationism" (Sparrow 2014: 86–113). Returning rigorously to the phenomenon as *rien-que-phénomène* [nothing-but-phenomenon] (Richir 1998), there seems to be no room in Richir's approach for an ontological return or the expansion of phenomenology beyond phenomenalization.

And yet, Richir will be the most important philosophical informant of this book—not only because he disposes of a fascinating and subtle conception of hyperbole (see Chapter 2), but also because he adds nuance and contour to the exploration of "the birth of [...] wild meaning" (Merleau-Ponty [1964] 1968: 201) left by Merleau-Ponty's last words as an open task for any future phenomenology.

Richir's first move strips off any idea of full and immediate givenness[2] from the concept of the phenomenon: "all that is given must be thought of as the product of a genesis" (Forestier 2015: 5). If in Merleau-Ponty's words, the phenomenon still appears as a *Gestalt*, a compositional figure produced by a *clearing* of visibility and its invisible surroundings (Merleau-Ponty [1964] 1968: 148), Richir pushes the centrifugal forces at the heart of phenomenalization even further to the extreme. The phenomenon as *rien-que-phénomène*, then, represents being in its wildest form—untamed, internally fractured, contingent, and entropic. Beyond the common protocols of perception and imagination, phenomenality erupts "in discontinuous manners" (Richir 2000: 312, my transl.), flickering as "Protean, fleeting, fluctuating and intermittent flashes [*clignotement*]" (2000: 148) through otherwise perfect darkness. Tracing the *adventure of meaning in the making*—Richir's version of the "naissance du [...] sens sauvage" (Merleau-Ponty 1964: 201)—, phenomenality occurs in a quasi-autonomous realm of its own with no guaranteed continuity to other spheres of our being and no need to be translated into gestalt-like figures, recognizable images or symbolic meaning. The plurality, contingency, and entropy of experience cannot be domesticated nor fully synthesized by logical or semantic operations.

Richir's second blow against classical phenomenology consists in relegating Husserl's method of eidetic reduction (the discovery of essence through variation) to anarchist grounds. Against Husserl's unnecessary obsession to reinvent philosophy as a strict or rigorous science (Husserl [1911] 1956), the eidetic in Richir's understanding does not need to overcome its phenomenal origins to become solid, although it is then only graspable according to an intermittent blinking [*clignotement*] of being (Richir 2000: 480). Instead of a rigorous essence of things, what we should look for is again a "wild proto-eidetic" (Forestier 2015: 5) that allows for a heterogeneous and incomplete, yet structured account of the genesis of ideas and anything else that comes out as a sedimentation of the incessant labor of phenomenalization.

Setting out from Merleau-Ponty's redefinition of the phenomenon as *wild being*, Richir's phenomenology bifurcates into two complementary directions: a genetic one and an architectonic one, as he puts it. The genetic line asks questions like: What are the concrete and contingent, but structured processes initiated and inaugurated by the labor of phenomenalization? How is the transposition from one register (like affectivity) to another (like semantics) possible and how does it take place? On the other hand, the

---

[2]The charge of the so-called "myth of givenness" (Sellars [1956] 1997) is one of the greatest challenges for phenomenology as a whole. Derrida ([1967] 1997) and Meillassoux ([2006] 2008) are only the most prominent among a wide cast of critical voices. Richir's refoundation of phenomenology does not render this critique fully obsolete, but it makes it significantly harder to maintain.

architectonic line asks: How do those transpositions [*schématismes*] make sense in a larger architecture of distinct, yet related processes of sense-making? And what kind of infrastructure is needed for the adventurous unfolding of meaning-in-progress (Richir 1991)?

The architectonic side of Richir's thinking seems to become more and more important in his later works. Reading through Husserl's lesser-known writing on image and imagination, Richir revives an interest for the phenomenological sphere prior to imagination in a narrower sense, a sphere already described by Husserl, albeit somewhat hesitatingly, as *phantasia*. *Phantasia* refers to a level of phenomenality on which what appears is far from becoming a fixed or fully coherent image and certainly in no danger to become a carrier of symbolic or mythological content and meaning (Richir 2004). In Richir's efforts to grasp the ungraspable character of *phantasia*, the *phantastic* phenomena increasingly become the privileged model for the phenomenon as a whole: "*phantasia* appears and disappears in a flash (*blitzhaft*), intermittently and discontinuously, it is protean (*proteusartig*) and certainly not fully present (*nicht gegenwärtig*)" (Richir 2003: 26, my transl.).

Over the course of this book, I will often return to Richir's difficult and fascinating philosophy. For now, it suffices to say that what differentiates Richir's speculative phenomenology from some of the speculative pathways opened by Anthropocenic thought is his interest in the microscopic, the infinitesimal, the very-small, the almost-invisible undercurrents of human experience, society, and nature. While much of speculative Anthropocenic thinking puts a lot of emphasis on the macro-scale of reality (ancestrality, extinction, apocalypse, imminence, the Great Outdoors, etc.), Richir's "quantum phenomenology" (Maurice 2013: 910, my transl.) zooms in on the particle plane of experience. Since hyperbole is not only interested in the larger-than-life, but also in levels of attention beneath the human scale, phenomenology as it has been radicalized by Levinas, Merleau-Ponty, and Richir provides an overlooked and underestimated framework for the inhumanist challenges to the humanist preconceptions targeted by Anthropocenic thinking. In that sense, it serves as an unexpected ally for a new conception of the real aspired by contemporary scientists, artists and intellectuals alike who all try to study and invent history, the present and the future on an expanded canvas.

And Yet Another Return of the Real

Not only the humanities and philosophy have turned their attention back to realism and the real, something similar occurred within the ranks of literary criticism. It is tempting to read that return as a conservative reaction to the long dominance of modernist and postmodernist paradigms, which seemed to push literature and the arts further and further away from their supposedly original mimetic mission. In Chapter 3, we will indeed see that some of the most distinguished voices calling for a return to the real, to realism or even mimesis cannot or do not even want to deny the traditional tinge of their preferences. Not at least because it is all too easy to silence these voices from the snobbish heights of the postmodern connoisseur, in this book I promise to look at ways of returning to realism and the real that have been suggested by two writers who have been canonized by many as quintessential and outstanding postmodernists.

But let us first look at some of the ways in which the *return of the real* has been proposed. Hal Foster's eponymous and highly influential book of art criticism sees the 1990s as a certain closing point of high postmodernism, but also considers its afterlife in ideas, styles, and modes of production (Foster 1996). Marc McGurl's groundbreaking literary history of postwar fiction in North America from the perspective of creative writing programs questions the unchallenged dominance of postmodernism and places postmodernist writing (roughly defined as *technomodernism*) on one and the same spectrum with other movements such as innovative genre fiction, high-cultural pluralism and lower-middle-class modernism (McGurl 2009).

For early postwar Latin America, a similar role to that of postmodernism in the United States is assumed by the literature of the boom from the 1950s and 1960s, a heterogeneous cultural phenomenon that would soon find itself to be trapped in the misleading category of *magical realism*. As a consequence, for a growing readership both global and domestic, realism became one important element in a whole set of expectations directed toward the Latin American novel. At the same time, everything that was not to some extent *magical,* and this is perhaps even true for the influential genre of the fictional dictatorship memoir, would be moved to the second rank. Not only was Latin American realist or socially invested writing, which was too hard to fit into the magical box, excluded from this US-led marketing strategy; the same fate befell the branch of experimental, cerebral, and conceptual writing, which has been a strong and lively tradition in Latin American letters, at least since Borges.

In 1996, during a period of Latin American literature wrongly labeled as unproductive, Alberto Fuguet and Sergio Gómez from Chile published an anthology of texts by younger Latin American writers who all set themselves apart from the founding fathers of magical realism. They called their anthology *McOndo*, a brilliant pun not only on the most popular village in literary history, but also on a world where Macs, McDonald's, and *condominios* have replace colonial gallantry, myths, and natural wonders.

In our McOndo, just like in Macondo, anything can happen. In our version, of course, when people fly it's because they're on a plane or they're very high. Latin America, and somehow Hispanic America (Spain and the whole Latino USA) seems to us as magically realist (surrealistic, crazy, contradictory, hallucinating) as the imaginary country where people levitate or predict the future and humans live forever. Here the dictators die and the *desaparecidos* do not return. The climate changes, the rivers overflow the banks, the earth trembles and Don Francisco colonizes our unconscious. (Fuguet and Gómez 1996: 15, my transl.).

The horror of colonialism and military dictatorships was not eradicated in Latin America; it was translated into the subtler violence of neoliberal privatization, "cultural imperialism" (Dorfman and Mattelart [1971] 1975) or evangelical churches, which is why Fuguet in another brilliant move has coined the term "magical neoliberalism" (Fuguet 2001) as a name for his generation's historical moment. It is a moment in which "the great creative mystery of cultural métissage" (Uslar Pietri 1986: 137, my transl.) has finally had its day as the cultural dominant of that ultimately ideological construction called Latin America (Mignolo 2005: 95–162). Instead of using the sentimental and slightly racist metaphor of *métissage*, which casts a precious veil on a history of genocide, rape, and dispossession, we should view the world of McOndo as a "bastard culture" (Fuguet and Gómez 1996: 17), a world of MTV Latinoamérica, Comandante Marcos, foreign debt, NAFTA, and Mercosur (1996: 16), a world where kitsch-indigenous mythologies have been replaced by digital nomadism: "Aquí, no hay realismo mágico, hay realismo virtual" (1996: 13).

McOndo is not the name for a unified school or movement. It communicates the frustration and irreverence of several generations of Latin American writers who have tried to make literary sense of their world without seeking refuge the theme park of magical realism. Regardless of Bolaño's aesthetic singularity, we must see him as an integral part of those and similar articulations of the post-Boom and post-dictatorial generations, which have opened up new aesthetic territory during the last few decades in Latin America.[3] Although deeply invested in experimental, playful, and oblique modes of representation, the words realism, reality, and the real are no strangers to these poetic discourses. But if there is one thing they all share, it is the conviction that if a realism for the twenty-first century is possible in Latin America, it will certainly not be magical.

---

[3] Another famous example is the Mexican CRACK movement (Castañeda et al. 2004).

The Many Lives of Realism

If we consider the general vagueness and ambiguity of aesthetic concepts into account, realism is still a special case. In his brilliant essay "On Realism in Art," Roman Jakobson famously maps out four or five distinct and partly incompatible definitions of realism. While type A classifies a specific work as realistic "if it is displayed by its author as a display of verisimilitude, as true to life" (Jakobson [1922] 1987: 20), type B relies on the reader's judgment concerning verisimilitude of said work. Type C refers to the well-known use of realism as a historiographic signifier for a specific epoch, school, or movement, most prominently in the context of mid-nineteenth-century visual arts and the novel. Type D, finally, has a technical dimension pointing at the accumulation of seemingly superfluous detail, atmospheric empathy that mediates between the social fabric and the character's innermost feelings, thick description and narrative detour—rhetoric devices, in short, contributing to what Roland Barthes has famously called the *effet de réel* (Barthes [1984] 1989).

With the rise of modernism, a fifth type comes to the fore in which the concept of realism threatens to implode. As the aesthetic dimension in modern art and literature is converted from an external system of regulation into a reflexive feature of the text itself (Iser 1966), Type E realism points to *"the requirement of consistent motivation and realization of poetic devices"* (Jakobson [1922] 1987: 27). According to such a definition, almost any kind of aesthetic decision can serve as an agent of realism as long as it is sufficiently motivated from within the text itself: "Thus, the Czech novelist Čapek-Chod in his tale, 'The Westernmost Slav', slyly calls the first chapter, in which 'romantic' fantasy is motivated by typhoid delirium, a 'realistic chapter'" (1987: 27).

As early as 1922, Jakobson's concise essay masterfully demonstrates that not only do we encounter different types and variants of realism in the history of art, there are completely different, even contradictory conceptions of it, both historically and systematically. But as we are in the messy realm of culture and not in Husserl's fairy world of *rigorous science,* discussing realism again and again may be worth the trouble no matter how shaky the grounds on which such a discussion stands. In his seminal book on *Realism and Literature*, Federico Bertoni leaves no doubt that this is the path any contemporary study of realism should follow. Having assembled an illustrious group of writers and thinkers (Friedrich Engels, George Eliot, Roman Jakobson, Erich Auerbach, Ian Watt, Georg Lúkacs, etc.) and their diverging opinions on the right understanding of realism, Bertoni concludes:

> We could go on forever, but perhaps we should stop here and limit ourselves to a temporary, minimal statement: not only, as Thomas Pavel reminds us, are there "realisms of different kinds," which result from the

different approaches with which each writer represents the world; there are also different *conceptions* of realism, which are historically, culturally and ideologically conditioned. Their partial and often vigorously idiosyncratic visions have been accumulated over the years, layer upon layer, without any chance to merge into a univocal or at least fairly homogeneous system. (Bertoni 2007: 226–7, my transl.).

This leaves us with three basic options. The first option consists of completely dropping the notion of realism either by deconstructing its inconsistent or even ideological internal structure or by stressing the rather obvious fact that even the most impressive *effet de réel* is the result of a laborious effort of figuration. The second option is to follow Fredric Jameson's famous advice to "always historicize" (Jameson 1981: 9), to follow the emergence and development of realism throughout the nineteenth century, to understand how it taps into the long history of mimesis (Auerbach [1946] 2003) or to discuss its complicated afterlife in modernist and postmodernist writing (Jameson 2013). The third option, finally, promises a philosophical solution to the problem. Here, we can ask if and how literature relates to an underlying *concept* of reality and the real, if and how this concept is developed or merely reproduced in a particular text and what this tells us about the relation between literature, philosophy, and the social sphere.

While it is this third approach that this book will mostly subscribe to, it is needless to say that depending on what one is trying to do the other two are equally legitimate concerns. More importantly perhaps, the most innovative contributions move elegantly back and forth among these three options instead of dogmatically sticking to one of them. Sometimes, however, there is a remaining risk that the analysis becomes as elusive as the category it is interested in, like in the moment when Bertoni defines his book "not as a general theory nor as a systematic history of realism and even less a manual or encyclopedia" (Bertoni 2007: VII). Yet it is a risk worth taking, especially if one is invested in contemporary writing for which the concept of reality is still in the making, still contested and controversial.

Contemporary critical discussions of realism in literature and the arts are of course more than aware of the many risks and vagaries that come with its object of study. For that reason, many critics start by claiming that the realism they are interested in belongs to some kind of second order; a realism promising no direct representation of the real, but questioning its own expressive decisions with the same movement that it tries to bring home some sense of the world out there. This world, our world, is of course characterized by the urgency of environmental concerns, radical transformations of our everyday lives through digitalization and social media, searing inequality both within and among the countries, the geopolitical reordering of power relations after the Cold War, the rise and return of nationalism and right-wing extremism all over the world, to name just of its most salient features. New realism in art and literature faces the dual challenge that it can no longer confine itself to the outlines of a specific society or nation, but must come to terms with the global entanglements of even the smallest detail as it faces a world run by the anti-literary algorithmic logic of Facebook and finance and the legal acrobatics of edgy lawyers and international organizations that are basically inventing at will the realities they need for their projects.

Realism 2.0 is acutely aware of the fundamental conflict between type A and type B realism, a conflict between residual reality and emerging reality as the backgrounds against which the degree of verisimilitude of any text is judged. At the same time, it reckons with the possibility that type C realism, no matter how close it might feel itself to its contemporary moment, may not be sufficient to deal with the madness of the real the way it presents itself to us at the turn of the century. This is what motivates a gifted critic like Mark Fisher to group a whole generation of widely different cultural products under the same pejorative category of *Capitalist Realism* (Fisher 2009), accusing them of providing support for a generalized capitalist aesthetics even where their formal structures deviate from its protocols. In Fisher's view, realism *is* capitalism, as its aesthetic and cognitive proxy; only an avant-garde or punk attitude has a limited potential to disrupt the contiguities between realistic aesthetics and capitalist realities. Against this gloomy perspective, a highly experimental and self-conscious writer like Ricardo Piglia reminds us that in a way both realism *and* the avant-gardes have been canonized by a literary market that has the capacity of turning every formal decision into a marketable cultural unit:

> Today, avant-gardism is one of the spontaneous ideologies of every writer. (The other is realism.) If being avant-garde means being "modern," we writers all want to be part of the avant-garde. Modernity is the great myth of contemporary literature. At the same time, the avant-garde has presently, at least in Argentina, come to form a genre. By now, there exists a fixed method, so full of conventions and rules that an avant-garde novel could be written with the same ease [*la misma facilidad*] as a police novel for example. (Piglia 2000a: 86–7, my transl.).

At the end of the twentieth century, realism, the avant-garde, and genre fiction have all become conventional, none of them more noble than the other, all of them limited templates that any future aesthetic invention has to traverse and transgress. In a typical Latin American move, however, Piglia finds a way out of the dilemma by claiming that it is the reader, not the author, who must adopt the avant-garde attitude: "Finally, we must say that the problem is not so much whether a certain work belongs to the avant-garde or not; the fundamental question for any writer today must be if the public and the critics reveal themselves as belonging to the avant-gardes" (2000a: 87).

If we read Fisher and Piglia together, the message becomes compelling: writing at the end of the twentieth century comes late in a dual sense—both after realism *and* after the avant-gardes. It seems that everything contemporary writing must hope for is the reader.[4] If she adopts an avant-garde state of mind, the post-avant-garde text offers her a lot to discover and uncover despite the rumor that literature seems doomed to forever repeat itself. Redefined as rigorous contextualism, realism at the turn of the century can serve as both an expansion and a reduction of what usually counts as real. David Foster Wallace, for instance, can casually claim that metafiction is merely realism of a higher order—*real* realism, so to speak: "Metafiction, for its time, was nothing more than a poignant hybrid of its theoretical foe, realism: if realism called it like it saw it, metafiction simply called it as it saw itself seeing itself see it" (Wallace 1993: 161).

If metafiction *as* realism represents an expansion of the real by presenting itself to itself as mediated self-reflection, a new realism as ascetic reduction is also an option. In what is probably the most sophisticated take on the problem in Latin America, Luz Horne explores the deflationist side of new realist sentiments. In line of what I have called the philosophical solution, Horne starts from the observation of a "new cultural configuration" (Horne 2011: 12, my transl.)—characterized by the rise of documentary cinema, the new popularity of autobiography, the presumed presence of the real and the body in contemporary art and the triumph of reality TV—and analyzes how the literary text relates and reacts to such a new conception of the real prompted by cultural transformations.

The principal dynamic captured by Horne's compelling semiotic method is the waning of the symbolic dominance and a corresponding rise of the indexical function in literary texts from celebrated Latin American authors such as Abreu, Aira, Chejfec, Eltit, Noll, and Ruffato. The texts of Horne's corpus all play in some way or another with repetition, absurdity and the limits of language to reveal "something of the order of the real" (2011: 14). By pointing toward the elevation of seemingly trivial statements such as *this is real* (reality TV) or *I am here* (social media) to the most indicative of reality effects, these texts demonstrate that the real reduced to itself is an extremely boring and idiotic (non-)event (Rinck 2015; Speranza 2005; Rosset 1977).

---

[4]Benjamin Loy's readings of Bolaño must count as the practical realization of this insight; in infinitely generous and knowledgeable readings, Loy portrays Bolaño above all as an avant-garde reader who turned his findings into simultaneously post-avant-gardist and neo-realistic poetic masterpieces (Loy 2019).

The aesthetic result is an often-criticized flatness of characters, an absence or irregularity of plot, a melodramatic theatricality and triviality of dramatic conflicts and in some cases the allegation of bad writing.[5] What emerges from such a deflationary attitude is a way of writing that Horne describes as "merciless realism" (Horne 2011: 32), a realism in which the real is exposed as pure flesh, as brute and wild being, as *rien-que-phénomène*. The concept of the literary character is dissolved or marginalized; language excludes personality by turning around itself; and all this despite the ubiquity of sensual stimulations and seemingly infinite possibilities to consume.[6]

Any serious discussion of nineteenth-century realism must conclude that there has never been such a thing as realism 1.0, if only because no ambitious nineteenth century novelist has ever really believed in the naive conception that a rigid representation of reality is possible or desirable. Looking back on Horne's corpus and other writers and theorists such as Fisher, Piglia, and Wallace, it becomes clear, on the one hand, that they must not necessarily be seen as completely separate from the long arc of realist aesthetics. Yet, as Horne's work shows much more in detail than I can reproduce here, we can also register a clear rupture with the descriptive, mimetic, and symbolic confidence of nineteenth-century realism, even where Flaubert & Co. may have ironically deconstructed that confidence. Either way, realism remains a challenging problem. On the one hand, it points to an aesthetic intention that seems obsolete today, no matter how far we bend its definition; on the other hand, it names an explicit if sometimes-vague commitment to create some kind of meaningful connection between a "new cultural configuration" (Horne 2011: 12) and new modes of writing engaged in an exploration of the actual version of a specific "order of the real" (2011: 14). In that sense, ambitious realist writing always aims to more than mirroring its time. More than trying to show what is evident and obvious, it wants to show what is possible.

---

[5] Among writers of indexical realism, the mise en scène of bad writing is a popular technique which serves both as a reality effect and a creative act of irreverence against the establishment's demands of well-written, rule-consistent prose. See, e.g., the beginning of João Gilberto Noll's *Berkeley em Bellagio* (2002), where the narrator presumably loses his ability to speak his mother tongue and becomes exiled in his own language—a crisis of identity that produces the poetic text that we are about to read. The provocative peak of bad writing in recent Latin American literature is arguably Mario Levrero's kind of maximalist novel *La novela luminosa* (Levrero 2005).

[6] In that context, Horne writes about the final scene of César Aira's *La prueba* (1992), which is set in a supermarket, the simple, but plausible image of a reality that seems infinitely diverse, but nevertheless caught in a bad infinity, the never-ending repetition of the same, where experience and material reality are perpetually flattened into commodified products. The novel demonstrates "that subject as consumer – the subject in the supermarket – is nothing but pure flesh. This opens up a space between life and death, between the subjective and the objective, between language and the non-linguistic where single words ('with neither nor feet') refer ostensibly (mercilessly) to torsos and extremities, in short: to mutilated bodies" (Horne 2011: 166, my transl.).

Concepts of Reality, Possibilities of the Novel

A philosophical approach to realism in the novel looks at the conception or conceptions of reality in the way they emerge from the novelistic universe. Going through a few positions that reveal a new interest in ontological questions in Anthropocenic theory, phenomenology, literary studies and the arts, we have seen that the many lives and meanings of the term make it seem futile to work with realism as a well-defined concept with a purpose. Rather than a clearly defined concept, it is a concern, an object of desire, which speaks to issues as different as the critique of corporate neoliberalism, the representation of climate change or the elaboration of a neo-materialist aesthetics. Most of the time in the main part of this book, I won't speak about Type C realism (the Bourgeois and/or nationalist realism of the nineteenth century), but often implicitly and sometimes explicitly about the writer's or text's realistic intentions (Type A), the reader's realistic discoveries (Type B) and the various moments where realistic intentions and effects appear only indirectly and as the result of an investment of speculative interpretation (Type E).

The six chapters of the main part of this book can be read as case studies that bring to the forth specific relations between hyperbolic writing modes and the conception of reality as they unfold temporally and intermittently throughout these spacious and fascinating novels. Here, realism always appears as a realism of possibility, the literary invention of a world not determined but shaped and enhanced by its underlying reality, a reality, in turn, of which the text is itself an integral part, scanning the world's contours as it is passing through.

Such a modal conception of literature and its relation to the real is inspired by a groundbreaking essay of the German philosopher Hans Blumenberg, a text that has not gained the attention it deserves, not even in Germany where Blumenberg has been rediscovered in the last years (Bajohr & Geulen 2022; Goldstein 2020; Zill 2020; Rüter 2018). Blumenberg's essay starts with a hyperbolic assumption, which sets the speculative tone for everything that follows: "The history of Western literary theory can be summed up as continuous debate on the classical dictum that poets are liars" (Blumenberg [1964] 2015: 29). Plato's infamous disapproval of the poets' claim to (a higher) truth puts the very possibility of poetic realism at risk, makes it appear as delusional oxymoron. But Blumenberg directs our attention to another implication of that sentence. If the poets are capable of lying, it must also be in their power to say the truth, at least in principle. According to Blumenberg, the claim that poets are liars and not or not only madmen—an available option within the conceptual range referring to the *poeta vates*—establishes two types of relations between poetry and the real, which will from now on accompany and even dominate Western writing and the writing about that writing (poetology, literary history, literary criticism, literary theory, etc.).

The first type views reality as something which is already given and to which the poet can thus choose to relate in a mimetic or non-mimetic way. The second type of relation points to the fact that literature itself produces a new piece of reality, which supplements, contests or surprises reality as we think we know it (2015: 30). In a way, to repeat Blumenberg's clearly hyperbolic initial statement, the whole Western tradition can be read in light of this dual relation between literature and the real: on the one hand, as a reproduction of reality; on the other hand, as its creation.

Hyperbolically covering the ground of the entire Western tradition, Blumenberg sets out to reconstruct four principal concepts of reality and sketches the ways in which literature has elaborated on them. His analysis focuses on the novel as the "most comprehensively 'realistic'" [*das welthafteste und welthaltigste*] (2015: 42) literary genre. The first concept comprehends the Platonic understanding of reality as "instantaneous evidence" (2015: 31), inaccessible for primitive perception but immediately accessible for the philosophical eye, which has purified itself through a constant commerce with the department of ideas. The second concept is that of a "guaranteed reality" (2015: 31), according to which the individual's relation to the world is mediated and controlled by a third instance, an absolute witness such as god or the church. The third concept emerges with the triumph of modern science and epistemology, considering reality as the "actualization of [a coherent] context" (2015: 32). Coherence, consistency, and intersubjectivity are the pillars of a paradigm that produced transcendental subjects, positivism and the free market and cut through the Medieval triangle to knot its threads into complex fabrics of mutual interconnectedness. The fourth concept, finally, which is supposed to be ours as well, is that of modernity proper. Here, reality appears as the "experience of resistance [...], *as that which cannot be mastered by the self*" (2015: 34). Real for the modern mind is what resists appropriation, what withdraws from sight and touch, what remains stubbornly intact when all the routes of access are clogged. It is an absolutely negative object, like Kant's *Ding an sich*, an ontological gold standard that no clear-minded soul would even try to study or understand.

Comparable to Foucault's epistemic regimes, Blumenberg's concepts of reality form the background against which every single novel can be read. However, if each of the concepts can be roughly identified with a specific historical epoch—Antiquity, the Middle Ages, Early Modernity, Industrial Modernity—we must not see them as isolated and deterministic lawmakers. On the contrary, various aspects of each concept can and usually do overlap or clash in one and the same text. Take the high modernist novel as an example. Its basic structure is defined by a more and more autonomous, extremely dense internal coherence of its social and symbolic content, its formal patterns and poetic strategies (C3). At its heart sits an impenetrable bloc of reality (C4)—time, art, consciousness—, sheltering an enigmatic truth whose concrete shape may or may not flash up in rare and non-repeatable epiphanic moments (C1). As far as the premodern concept of reality as guaranteed truth (C2) goes, there seems to be no room for it in the modernist novel—unless we suggest that the elaborate mise-en-scène of the artists as negative priest serves as the god-like authority that tightens the twisted bond between the text and its readers.

Speaking about contemporary literature, as this book will do most of the time, we are faced with the difficulty that the novel's underlying concept of reality oscillates between an emerging and a dominant pole. Keeping in mind the two modes of how literature relates to the real, we must conclude that on the one hand the novel refers to a dominant concept of reality as already given; on the other, the literary text helps to produce that same concept as an emergent and not yet fully established framework.[7] As provocatively speculative as Blumenberg's discussion of the four concepts of reality and their relation to the novel may be, I will use them heuristically as a silent companion of my readings of Pynchon's and Bolaño's hyperbolic realism. As our near-contemporaries, those authors' late maximalist novels do not merely reflect what is or was already there; they produce or co-produce the fundamentals of our relation to the real.

Against a philosophical approach that discusses the novel under primarily epistemological aspects, my work is thus more interested in its ontological and phenomenological dimensions. Phenomenology is such an important informant for my approach because it frees the real from its idiotic solitude and sharpens our senses for the messy ways in which it is brought to our attention—through excess and abundance (Chapter 3), intertextuality (Chapter 4), the interplay of light and shadow (Chapter 5), metonymically composed metaphors (Chapter 6), doubt and uncertainty (Chapter 7), images and artworks (Chapter 8). Against a widely accepted accusation, however, phenomenology does not have to give up its ontological rootedness but can hold on to the real (the body, nature, the environment) as a grounding factor of its phenomenological explorations.

It should go by itself that ontology, in my understanding, does not refer to a unified and eternal being, but is invested in the principal structure of how the real must be conceptualized in our time and the various ways of worldmaking that emerge from this underlying conception. If the novel is indeed a world—or worlds, the following chapters try to introduce to the reader two fascinating ways of how such particular worlds make sense of ours. One of today's world's salient features, the world both in its appearance and its being, is its perpetual excess, its unfathomable abundance, its orgiastic exaggeratedness, in short: its hyperbolic character. It is thus to hyperbole that we will now turn our attention.

---

[7]My uses of the terms *dominant* and *emerging* are evidently inspired by Raymond Williams (1977), 121–7.

2

Notes on Hyperbole

> *Bigger and better.*
> *Good greater greatest totally great.*
> *Hyperbolic and hyperbolicker.*
> DAVID FOSTER WALLACE

The Risky Truth of Hyperbole

If it is true that all poets are liars, but do—"somehow, anyhow" (Lowry [1947] 1971: 44)—speak the truth (or are even in a privileged position to do so), then it is hardly surprising that hyperbole bears a deep affinity with poetry. In a decisive moment of the history of the hyperbole, the Roman orator and theorist Quintilian places the intricate relationship between truth and illusion at the heart of a concept which operates at the same time as an "Amplification and Attenuation" (VIII 6.68) of perception, experience, and reality. In his influential *Institutio Oratoria,* Quintilian saves hyperbole for the very end, the *summo loco,* of the chapter on tropes in book VIII, which begins with "the commonest and far the most beautiful of Tropes" (6.5): metaphor.

To make hyperbole appear at the eccentric margins of the chapter on tropes is, of course, an intrinsically hyperbolic move that resonates with hyperbole's peculiar ontology. Not only is it both an amplification and attenuation of speech and discourse; it can be seen at the same time as the most essential and the most auxiliary element of figurative language. On the one hand, then, hyperbole only appears in conjunction with other and more prominent figures of speech such as comparison, synecdoche, or metaphor. On the other hand, it marks the essence of figurative speech whose ultimate mission is to create a distorted, synthetic picture of the world more real than the world itself: "It is enough to say that *hyperbole* lies, though without any intention to deceive" (6.74).

As a (logical) subtype of amplification, hyperbole tends toward accumulation. This paves the way to one of hyperbole's central contributions to the history of art—the outdoing of individual predecessors and historical models (Curtius [1948] 2013: 162–5). Using the example of a Pindar poem, Quintilian demonstrates how hyperbole often inaugurates a rhetorical breakthrough at the end of a long chain of failing acts of designation—a procedure central to Bolaño's (and to a lesser extent Pynchon's) aesthetic behavior, as we will see in Chapter 6.

As it is notoriously difficult to decide on the question of rhetorical adequacy [*decorum*] within hyperbolic speech, the question whether a specific use of hyperbole represents an "appropriate exaggeration of the truth" (6.68) cannot be answered from the far, but only by way of close, attentive and contextualized readings of concrete passages and scenes. Either way, hyperbolic conduct always remains a risky endeavor. On the one hand, it inevitably involves the courageous transgression of trained conventions and hackneyed phrasing; on the other hand, a "certain sense of proportion" of hyperbolic speech "is necessary" for "there is no surer route to affectation [*cacozelia*]" than over exaggerated exaggeration (6.73).

Just like the poet trying to step out of Plato's shadow, but cannot escape his eidetic claws,

> hyperbole is a liar, but does not lie to deceive. We must therefore consider how far it is appropriate to exaggerate a thing which is not believed [...].
>
> It is in ordinary use, too, among the uneducated and with country people, no doubt because everybody has a natural desire to exaggerate or minimize things, and no one is satisfied with the truth. It is pardoned, however, because we do not vouch for what we say. Hyperbole only has positive value when the thing about which we have to speak transcends the ordinary limits of nature. We are then allowed to amplify, because the real size of the thing cannot be expressed, and it is better to go too far than not to go far enough. (6.74–6).

Let us use this little phrase as a signpost for our exploration of the deeper intentions of Pynchon's and Bolaño's late maximalist novels: *It is better to go too far than not to go far enough*. In a historical moment and on an endangered planet, where literally everything "about which we have to speak transcends the ordinary limits of nature," hyperbole seems to be a privileged source for such an effort of expression. In contrast to the self-reflexivity of irony, the privileged figure of postmodernism, hyperbole's self-reflexivity is not defensive. Its gambling strategy is not to perpetually withdraw and escape from what it has just stated. Quite the contrary, while constantly being aware of its possible and even likely failure, it prefers to fall back into ridiculousness [*pervenit haec res frequentissime ad risum*, 6.74] instead of failing "the real size of the thing" it is being summoned to grasp.

Inspired by Spivak's words in *Why Study the Past?*, we could ask: Why exaggerate? For Quintilian, the answer is clear: Because we must.

The Rare Occurrence of Hyperbole in Literary Criticism

Regardless of its prominence in rhetoric, poetics and philosophy from Quintilian to Góngora, hyperbole has fallen out of the scope of most literary criticism after the Baroque era. In a rare occasion where hyperbole appears as the core concern of a critical contribution, Jonathan Arac takes its very unfamiliarity within the critical discourse as a happy occasion for gaining new and fresh insights into the literary text, which in this particular example is George Eliot's novel *The Mill on the Floss*.

> My figure of hyperbole bears the same name as a geometrical figure defining a shape generated from dual foci but from no center, suggesting the complexity and instability I wish to emphasize. Furthermore, I find useful the arbitrary excess of such a geometrical metaphor for the "form" of a literary work; as a term it is so alien, falls so far short of our usual critical metaphors, that its tentativity and purely exploratory value remains always in view. Such an analogy is much less likely to mislead us into false consequences than the organic, architectural, or textile metaphors that are more common. The barrenness may be fruitful as fresh provocation. (Arac 1979: 673).

By setting the crucial word *form* in quotation marks, Arac points toward hyperbole's role as a more than subjective force that gives form to and stabilizes aesthetic structures but also transcends and pushes them toward what Bataille has famously called the *informe* (Bataille [1929] 1985: 31). Beyond its energetic aspect, hyperbole as a figure for literary criticism embodies an analytic promise without an obligation to harmonize its findings within an organic system with a single and clearly defined center. Against the two dominant trends of using hyperbole pejoratively as a synonym for bad exaggeration (as in: *don't believe the hype*) or warning against its use (as in: *let's not exaggerate*), Arac revives the forgotten rhetorical figure to demonstrate how Eliot's transitional novel dramatizes the "clash between the hope of a fitting language and the recognition that language is never at one with reality, any more than the world is at one with itself" (Arac 1979: 690).

Critical efforts often deploy hyperbole to emphasize and prioritize processual features over sedimented forms or more easily definable structures. The "wayward, hyperbolic energy" in Eliot's novel, which "ensures that all the literary types that help to structure the book are different in their return" (1979: 689), is one example of this; another one is Leo Spitzer's discussion of Proust's sinuous syntax, where he distinguishes bad hyperbole, the pretentious inflation of relatively simple basic structures, from hyperbolic exuberance as a stylistic strategy that embodies the most profound aesthetic commitments and "vision" of the author (Spitzer [1928] 1961: 375).

But even in the rare occasions where hyperbole is used in a positive mood or mode, critics feel urged to defend themselves. Just like Arac needs to make a case for the analytic purport of a non-organic concept, Spitzer must protect hyperbole from the charge of being hypertrophic by legitimating its inevitable use as an essential element of the artist's inner vision and character. In a short essay called "Hyperboles," Gérard Genette claims that what we see at work in the more daring efforts of comparative literary criticism is "the hyperbolic power of language, which, to or from as far as possible, *projects* (or brings back) something we might as well call thinking" (Genette 1966: 252, my transl.). But after all, his plea for the importance and autonomy of such a *raison hyperbolique* remains a timid and inconsequential poke in the well-fed belly of formalism's *bon sens*.

Even those critics with a thing for hyperbole, then, seem to be excessively wary of Quintilian's warning that too much is simply too much, that more often than not hyperbole walks on the wrong side of the thin line that separates wit from madness. This modern predicament of hyperbole can be seen as a long-term result of its loss of currency and quasi-extinction as a figure of thought with the Enlightenment. Toward the end of the seventeenth century, as Christopher Johnson masterfully demonstrates in what is without a doubt the bible of hyperbolic criticism, hyperbole's reign comes to an end as a consequence of the rise of Cartesian clear and distinct reasoning. In Dominique Bouhours's *La Manière de bien penser dans les ouvrages d'esprit* from 1688, Johnson discovers a watershed moment at the end of the seventeenth century when hyperbole's line of supply is cut through by a fresh demand for harmony and tasteful balance (Johnson 2010: 478). From now on, hyperbole can only hope to survive in the niches of this emerging culture (or cult) of reason as a "decorous" element predicated on the audience's familiarity with a particular hyperbolic trope or image, a familiarity which "acts like its passport" [*sert comme de passeport à l'hyperbole*] (2010: 480).

But as the eighteenth century came along, a more expensive travel ticket had to be found for hyperbole's restricted mobility. It was the triumph of irony, that quintessentially modern figure, which acted at the same time as a voucher for hyperbole's precarious survival and as a symptom of its slow, but steady decline. It was a triumph with consequences; not only "symptomatic for an important historical shift in hyperbole's reception" (2010: 481), but one that inaugurated a cultural dominance that found its apex in high postmodernism, defined by some as "the age of irony" (Giroux 2002; Purdy 1998).[1]

It is beyond the scope of this book to provide a full account of Johnson's precious and elaborate defense of hyperbole as the central figure for Baroque thinking and writing and its influence beyond the seventeenth century. But despite the different historical context and the much larger corpus that he analyzes, there are many things to be retained from Johnson's broad comparatist frame for hyper-close readings with a speculative touch, readings that reach, in good hyperbolic fashion, far beyond the limits of its chosen epoch. As hyperbole demands, Johnson's methodological approach is not merely formalist nor is he adhering to an orthodox version of discourse analysis aiming to fully externalize its historical content. If the specific kind of *realism* evoked in this book has to do with writing that creates speculative pathways between the phenomenal and the noumenal realm, between being and appearance, *hyperbole* serves as its concrete tool and figure, a versatile figure that moves along and across the margins of history, experience, form, and epistemology. With Anselm Haverkamp's radicalization of Hans Blumenberg's "theory of non-conceptuality" (Blumenberg [1979] 1996), we might say that Johnson's and my intentions converge in the sense that we're both not so much interested in the Heideggerian project of *Seinsgeschichte*, but rather in what Haverkamp calls *Gesagtseinsgeschichte*, the history of what has been said—figuratively, metaphorically, hyperbolically (Haverkamp 2002, 2004).

Hyperbole as *Figura*

It is one of the basic convictions of this book that hyperbole is most useful when it is not reduced to its descriptive role as a trope or figure of speech. Emancipated from its decorous functions, so to speak, hyperbole acts as a versatile agent moving in and out of discourses, affective constellations and

---

[1]Purdy's essay resonates with my intentions in this book insofar as it shows that irony has a strong, almost-inevitable tendency toward ethical detachment and self-immunization, but that "rescuing irony from itself" and "enriching" it from within is not impossible. From a hyperbolist point of view, however, Purdy's slightly elitist and moralizing remedy for the wrong kind of irony ("an intelligent and resourceful irony") marks an important, yet insufficient step. Against the rallying cry for *new sincerities*, hyperbole tries to rescue irony from itself by pushing it further into two opposite directions, calling for stronger commitments to the world and riskier forms of detachment all at the same time.

ethical attitudes, and performs a shift from figure to *figura,* from its manifest appearance to a much less obvious, latent potential of the text that draws together poetic, perceptual, and conceptual dimensions. The notion of *figura* is of course reminiscent of Erich Auerbach's famous study (Auerbach 1939), but its role in this book is even better explained with the help of one of the most important texts of the Latin American tradition. In *Rayuela,* Julio Cortázar creates a fine and complex network of aesthetic ideas with the help of a motley crew of characters. After commenting on a brief passage from Bataille (fittingly), the fictional writer Morelli jots down a few notes that we can adopt as a heuristic definition for the fundamental analytical ethos of this book:

> To accustom one's self to use the expression *figure* instead of *image,* to avoid confusions. Yes, everything coincides. But it is not a question of a return to the Middle Ages or anything like it. The mistake of postulating an absolute historical time: There are different times *even though* they may be parallel. In this sense, one of the times of the so-called Middle Ages can coincide with one of the times of the Modern Ages. And that time is what has been perceived and inhabited by painters and writers who refuse to seek support in what surrounds them, to be "modern" in the sense that their contemporaries understand them, which does not mean that they choose to be anachronistic; they are simply on the margin of the superficial time of their period, and from that other time where everything conforms to the condition of *figure,* where everything has value as a sign and not as a theme of description, they attempt a work which may seem alien or antagonistic to the time and history surrounding them, and which nonetheless includes it, explains it, and in the last analysis orients it towards a transcendence within whose limits man is waiting. (Cortázar [1963] 1966: 479–80).[2]

Operating "on the margin of the superficial time of [its] period," hyperbole as figura marks its always oblique presence as a "*totius*

---

[2]"Acostumbrarse a emplear la expresión *figura* en vez de *imagen,* para evitar confusiones. Sí, todo coincide. Pero no se trata de una vuelta a la Edad Media ni cosa parecida. Error de postular un tiempo histórico absoluto: Hay tiempos diferentes *aunque* paralelos. En ese sentido, uno de los tiempos de la llamada Edad Media puede coincidir con uno de los tiempos de la llamada Edad Moderna. Y ese tiempo es el percibido y habitado por pintores y escritores que rehúsan apoyarse en la circunstancia, ser 'modernos' en el sentido en que lo entienden los contemporáneos, lo que no significa que opten por ser anacrónicos; sencillamente están al margen del tiempo superficial de su época, y desde ese otro tiempo donde todo accede a la condición de figura, donde todo vale como signo y no como tema de descripción, intentan una obra que puede parecer ajena o antagónica a su tiempo y a su historia circundantes, y que sin embargo los incluye, los explica, y en último término los orienta hacia una trascendencia en cuyo término está esperando el hombre" (Cortázar [1963] 2003: 659).

voluntatis fictio, as a figment of a continuous intention, manifesting itself more often implicitly than explicitly and, *apparens magis quam confessa* without laying bare its intention" (Haverkamp 2002: 82, my transl.). It wouldn't lead us very far to build our readings on those moments in Pynchon's and Bolaño's novels where hyperbole appears as a clearly recognizable trope. Instead, its role as a latent or, rather, intermittent figure will require from us to ground our readings in a larger theoretical framework, which in my book will be composed of fragments from postwar phenomenology, Anthropocenic thought, traces of a critique of postmodern reason and the implicit aesthetic reflection of my authors and some fellow hyperbolists.

This is not to say that hyperbole in *2666* and *Against the Day (ATD)* does not have its spotlight moments, which is one of the reasons why I do not, like Haverkamp would, speak of *latency*, but of *intermittence* as hyperbole's preferred mode of appearance. To name just a few examples, the hyperbolic potential breaks through the text's surface:

> as apparently colloquial superlatives in inconspicuous scenes of daily life ["The metro at that hour was the saddest thing in the world" (*2666*: 804), "all of a sudden the most beautiful actress in Hollywood appeared in the middle of this big, repulsive restaurant" (*2666*: 315)].

> as excessive quantities and numbers ["surrounded or partially surrounded by forty-one million square miles of salt water" (*2666*: 22)];

> as a hint to hyperbolic geometrical structures and weird spatial realities ["the bright, flowerlike heart of the hyper-hyperboloid" (*ATD*: 1085)];

> or as instants of paradox and mystical speech ["like a trick photograph that isn't a trick, floating, floating pensively in the skies of Paris, weary, sending messages from the coldest, iciest realm of passion" (*2666*: 182)]; *thinking without thinking, thinking with shaky images* (Bolaño 2004a: 463; *2666*: 370), "the blindness[3] at the heart of a diamond" (*ATD*: 109).

In Pynchon's and Bolaño's maximalist novel, the hyperbolic is to be found both on the surface, as "the blindness at the heart of a diamond," and in the niches, the undercurrents and underworlds from where the rich and complex textures of these astonishing books is constantly nourished. Just like in Merleau-Ponty's unfinished project of a phenomenological

---

[3]For the relationship between blindness and hyperbole see Klein (1973).

ontology, the world is neither just what we see nor all that is left unseen, neither pure presence nor an enigmatic absence that, like Heidegger's true being, has to be spectacularly uncovered. It is the flickering and erratic unfolding of both the visible *and* the invisible, both surface *and* underworld—"an organization in depth, a relief." (Merleau-Ponty [1964] 1968: 205).

Phenomenology's Hyperbole

Despite its loss of prominence in modern times, hyperbole has remained a secret concern for philosophy throughout the centuries, and the Belgian phenomenologist Marc Richir is perhaps its most self-conscious thinker. Although the question whether Richir makes coherent use of the term is controversial among specialists, Richir's philosophical project is of invaluable use for my purposes as he demonstrates that hyperbole can find a home in philosophical thinking beyond the Baroque.

Richir's interest in hyperbole starts with the claim that since no act of thinking has a logically justified beginning, each thought is born as a risky leap into the unknown: "every true act of philosophizing starts with a hyperbole, a 'moment of madness'" (Richir 2015: 69, my transl.). One of Richir's favorite examples for such an inaugurating moment of madness that both conditions and exceeds the framework of a system of thoughts is Fichte's famous first act of the spirit [*erste Tathandlung des Geistes*] that postulates a self that is identical with itself (Ich = Ich, I = I). For Richir, the equals sign is where hyperbole hides itself embodying the madness of identification of Fichte's *geist* with itself:

> We know that hyperbole is first of all a rhetorical figure of exaggeration; but I'd prefer to say that it is more fundamentally a moment of *hubris*. The point is that hyperbole implies a risk that is in fact fantastic and fictional [*fantasmatique*], that if I push it too far, I will become mad (2015: 69).

Fully in line with what we have said above, Richir's approach transcends the view of hyperbole as merely rhetorical and defines it as attitude and *ethos*, as an affective, aesthetic, and ethical state with a strong inclination toward violating the laws of proportion and propriety. Despite the task to recover and reintegrate retrospectively what is projected by the hyperbolic impulse, what it unleashes can and should not be completely tamed and locked into a system of tightly inferential reassurances. For Richir, as for Bolaño, Pynchon, and a few more hyperbolists casted into this book, at the heart of each thought, each act of writing and, eventually, life itself lies a hyperbolic moment, an abyss, a "fundamental void":

It is very difficult to constantly live hyperbolically, because at some point you lose track of what you're talking about. This is why it represents a moment of madness in the sense that if one stays there, one really becomes mad, as Artaud has beautifully described it. So there is a fundamental void at the bottom of thinking, which makes it impossible for me to recover what has been thrown forward by hyperbole [*reprendre ce qui a été jeté par l'hyperbole*], and therefore to temporalize it with language and thought. (2015: 69).

Hyperbole dwells in each beginning; but it comes with the irreducible danger that if you dwell in it for too long, you may lose track of your thoughts and—eventually perhaps—of yourself. It is a risk and a danger that must not be excluded from the philosophical project if philosophy does not want to lose its meaning or even its right to exist. The fundamental void left behind by the hyperbolic moment of madness at the heart of "every true act of philosophizing" must be vanquished over and over again, and its unsettling potential should not be disarmed too hastily.

Against the distorted view of hard-boiled anti-rationalists, Descartes was acutely aware of hyperbole's explosive potential. Its unsettling force reliably surfaces whenever Descartes prepares himself to cast off the certainties of experience and sensation in order to venture into the unknown. The vessel of this memorable venturing into modernity is, of course, what Descartes has famously called *le doute hyperbolique*. What awaits us at the bottom of this hyperbolic doubt, is Descartes's no less famous philosophical fiction of the *deus malignus*, that malicious force with the potential to turn all our certainties into a potential source of deceit and illusion.

In Richir's hyperbolic re-reading of the rationalist tradition, from Descartes via Kant and Fichte to Husserl, the *deus malignus* acts as a constant reminder that wherever systems of knowledge with claims to sovereignty are produced, doubt and uncertainty are never far away and in fact irreducible (Richir 2014: 13–47). Irreducible—since for modern philosophy proper any dogmatic "warrantor of truth" (Richir 2015: 154) must be forever out of reach. From now on, neither Descartes's God nor Kant's transcendental ego that accompanies all our mental states nor Fichte's tautological, terroristic self nor Husserl's immediacy of experience can hope to fill in the gaps left open by hyperbolic doubt and the threat of a general irrealization. To adopt a Nietzschean perspective, we could say that, with the advent of a post-classical concept of nature, it is becoming increasingly impossible to distinguish between the *deus malignus* and a well-meaning God who, after all, could be a malicious invention of the *deus malignus* himself. Descartes's ego reveals itself as a fideistic fiction impossible to sustain without a hyperbolic leap outside of the rationalist system; and Fichte's self-assuring self gets lost on its way toward itself somewhere in the space left open by the equality sign, which may guarantee mathematical identity, but cannot guarantee an existential agreement of the self with itself.

In light of this paradigmatic shift, Richir radicalizes the methodological moment of madness—contained in Descartes's hyperbolic doubt, in Kant's awakening from his dogmatic slumber or in Fichte's unaccountable *Tathandlung*—toward a full-fledged philosophical method, where hyperbolic doubt becomes a constant companion of the philosophical adventure, which no cognitive act can ever abolish once and for all.

Hyperbolic epoché is Richir's name for a method based on a new understanding of what a phenomenon essentially is (Chapter 1). In their wildly flickering mode of existence that entails both givenness and illusion, both the symbolic shapes and their primitive energies (which are itself grounded in nothingness), phenomena are complex and dynamic quasi-entities which are impossible to disentangle in a way that the rational elements can be clearly and once and for all separated from the "bad," contaminated aspects. From the "fundamental void" at the heart of the phenomenon radiates an "originary multiplicity" that liberates the pulsating phenomenon from its reductionist role as a guarantor of immediate experience:

> This requires a "meaning" or "sense", the phenomenological "sense", which is the sense of what is "trembling", "vibrating" or "circulating" in that which seems to give nothing but itself, and the sense of *letting* it happen or vanish, despite and beyond the rigidity of philosophical language. And it is at this point, we might say, that an architectural problem emerges concerning God and the Evil Genius—only God can *ensure* and *guarantee* the symbolic institution. (Richir 2015: 153–4).

Beware of "the stupidest structuralism" (Richir 2015: 161) where everything is reduced to (the structural aspects of) language or text, radical phenomenology provides a space for the proto-symbolic vibration of the phenomenon as it is letting "happen or vanish" what lies beyond or rather beneath language, that most important of all symbolic institution. But unlike the deplorable grain of the vast majority of postmodern phenomenologists, Richir does not fall back to a vitalist celebration of the plenitude of givenness or, even worse, the religious surrender to pure and immaculate experience, which tends to treat language, philosophy, and politics as annoying and inconvenient sins. Instead, as I have indicated above, what Richir defines as pure phenomenon is the flickering force of those "full wild being[s]" (Richir [1982] 1993: 66) that are constantly passing through, informing and unforming our ritualized habits, well-founded institutions, and codified symbolic systems. Thinking, experience, and our very being neither take place in a mystical realm completely outside of language nor are they solely the product of our transcendental constructions; they occur where the *phénomène-du-monde* and the *phénomène-du-langage* clash and converge in always syncopated, reliably erratic, and never fully predictable ways.

Hyperphenomena, Hyperobjects

A theory of hyperbole doesn't care much about Hegel's absolute or Sartre's abstract nothingness. It is much more interested in the not-nothing (Rosa [1956] 2015: 19) or almost-nothing, in what is more and less than nothing, more and less than everything (Moten 2018: 1). Wherever the shudder in the presence of abstract infinity is replaced by "the vertigo of hyperbole" (Baudelaire [1855] 1976: 559, my transl.), one must not be terrified by the "infinite immensity of spaces" (Pascal [1670] 2008: 26).

The most diligent philosophical exploration of hyperbole is that of the German phenomenologist Bernhard Waldenfels. In his book *Hyperphenomena. Modes of Hyperbolic Experience,* Waldenfels starts from the simple definition that hyperbole is produced wherever there is "something that appears as *more* and *different* than what it actually is" (Waldenfels 2012: 9, my transl.) Waldenfels' hyperbole, similar to but less radical than Richir's, is the force that interrupts the self-containment of a specific order without the intention to destroy or abolish that order: "The hyperbolic we have in mind represents a mode of moving-beyond. It is a well-known motif that appears under various names at the margins of large and small orders, but also in the midst of them" (2012: 9–10). Apart from the by-now familiar tendency of excess and transgression, two things can be gained here for our purposes: first, that hyperbole is often hiding out under various names, and second, that, despite its eccentricity, it does not only appear at the edges of time, religious experience, norms and the law, art, hospitality and trust, but sometimes at the heart of these fields of experience.

With an eye on the hyperbolic in Pynchon's and Bolaño's late maximalist novels, we must say: not only sometimes, but above all in "the midst of them." For it is often from the most inconspicuous and trivial setting that the hyperbolic carves its way into the heart of Bolaño's and Pynchon's literary cosmos. For example, both Pynchon and Bolaño avoid a graphic description of war, dating their plots to times of pre–, inter–, or invisible war: the First World War in *ATD*, the bloody drug wars between the cartels in *2666*. Violence, although omnipresent in both novels, is rarely narrated as an immediate, deadly attack on a vulnerable body, but sneaks in obliquely from the perspective of sad results, blurred traces, and troubled reports. And only occasionally are mental and moral incapacities relegated to the clinic (*2666*: 88–92, *ATD*: 626); more often do they spread through the police, the military, capitalist corporations, the media, the university, and other deceitful institutions.

In *2666*, the abyss or void (*abismo*) is Bolaño's favorite milieu for the hyperbolic. Despite his predilection for peripheries and remote locales (the desert at the Northern edge of Latin America, a mental asylum in the Swiss Alps, the *casa de los escritores desaparecidos*), the clearly designated or suggested abysses in his fiction reliably crack open in the middle of the world as the following examples demonstrate: "as if they were bypassing the abyss of daily life, the abyss of people, the abyss of conversation" (2666: 663); "in the middle of a salt lake, she saw a tunnel" (2666: 558); "but both moved, twined their limbs, communed, as if they were on the edge of the abyss" (2666: 725).

In Pynchon's *ATD*, characters and readers alike frequently encounter what they know from genre fiction (especially science fiction) as gates or portals, hidden thresholds, real and/or imaginary ones, drug-like substances that operate as "facilitator[s] of passage between the worlds" (*ATD*: 433), connecting realms that are usually held separate "by only the thinnest of membranes (*ATD*: 130)."[4] But the countless portals, voids, and underworlds in Pynchon's and Bolaño's late maximalist novels do not merely invite and provoke hyperbolic experience; they often challenge and threaten the possibility of experience as such. Several times in *2666*, something like an "unfathomable void" (2666: 720) emerges, a "terrible, immense abyss into which, upon falling, all is forgotten" (2666: 432); and if experience at that extreme edge of the world is still possible, it is only possible as "*experiencia abismal*" (Bolaño 2004a: 397–8).

In Waldenfels's account, where humans and their institutions reliably remain the ultimate point of reference, this last consequence is not spelled out. The hyperbolic in Pynchon's and Bolaño's novels is not only that of experience, but often that of the world and reality itself. The hyperbolic exudes its traumatic presence in the realm of the human, but is only graspable as a flickering *clignotement* (Richir), where real, illusionary, and fictitious elements intermingle, reaching out to something not only at the limits of experience but, to say it with Levinas, to something otherwise-than-experience (Levinas [1974] 1991). Waldenfels's hyperbole does not go far enough to get to this dimension of non-experientiality as he seems to be calculating in advance for a homoestatic compromise between the

---

[4] In *Gravity's Rainbow*, Pynchon's use of the membrane seems a bit different and perhaps slightly more radical. While *ATD* stresses the technical role of membranes as mediators between two different ontological orders, *Gravity's Rainbow* explores the membrane as a vibrant interface, an almost living skin, which becomes the site of action and the preferred milieu of the narrative voice.—"Now that he [= Dog Vanya] has moved into 'equivalent' phase, the first of the transmarginal phases, a membrane, hardly noticeable, stretches between Dog Vanya and the outside. Inside and outside remain just as they were, but the *interface*—the cortex of Dog Vanya's brain—is changing, in any number of ways, and that is the really peculiar thing about these transmarginal events" (Pynchon 1973: 78–9).

hyperbolic force traversing a particular order and the stability of that very order. Hyperbole can thus not unfold its full and "unemployed negativity" (see Chapter 5); its unsettling centrifugality is tamed too precociously. To account for a non-experiential realm that is nevertheless part and parcel of the real, we have to take a step beyond the homely precincts of human-centered phenomenology.

As we have seen in Chapter 1, it is both from phenomenology and from the renewed interest in ontological questions in Anthropocenic theory that such steps can be dared. Although his work comes with its own troubled baggage, Timothy Morton is perhaps the most outspoken theorist within the latter group who engages directly with the problem and concept of hyperbole. His concept of hyperobjects tries to conceptualize those monstrous and complexly entangled chunks of reality, "things that are massively distributed in space and time" (Morton 2013: 1), hyperbolic not in relation to the human, but in relation to other things and objects. A strong example for a hyperobject is global warming, which is now accepted as all too real although it is indefinitely hard, if not impossible to directly experience it. Despite the sustained reality of climate denialism, climate change undeniably exists, it can be measured and even to some extent visualized with the help of geophysical data, statistical models, probability theory, and advanced visualization procedures. Climate change is hyperreal or, as we could also say, hyperbolically real, even though and, to some extent, precisely because the full impact on both the life of humans and the life of the planet (organic and otherwise) is impossible to predict in any meaningful way of the word prediction.

Exceeding by far the capacities of our bodies and minds, hyperobjects cannot be contained by transcendental minds, they act as autonomous or at least "semi-autonomous materials" (Negarestani 2008) with higher impact and sovereignty than any human individual can ever hope to attain: "Hyperobjects haunt my social and psychic space with an always-already" (Morton 2013: 29). Hyperobjects call for a complete reorientation of our thinking, agencies, art practices, and political organizations. Hyperobjects ultimately bring to an end the fantasy of an outside of our world from which our thinking can take place, they end the possibility of transcendental leaps "outside" physical reality. Hyperobjects force us to acknowledge the absolute immanence of thinking, and yet at the same time the independent existence of the real, which means to give up the environmental fantasy of our embeddedness in nature or the "lifeworld" (2013: 2).

Rather than bringing us home to nature, the Anthropocene confronts us with the fact that we are expelled into environments of "ultimate toxicity" (Povinelli 2016: 165), which have been created but can no longer be controlled by us. This is the founding paradox of the Anthropocene—that we were so successful in the creation of hyperobjects that they now threaten to eliminate our whole species. In such a situation, the most devastating events "carry with them a trace of unreality" (Morton 2013: 28), which then weirdly becomes "the very sign of reality itself. Like a nightmare that brings news of some real psychic intensity, the shadow of the hyperobject announces the existence of the hyperobject" (2013: 32).

The difficult search for hyperbole's precise location (Waldenfels 2012: 10) is not only a technical intricacy, but a structural feature of hyperbole's peculiar ontology. The hyperbolic often invites strangely familiar, yet inherently excessive and uncontainable experiences. It appears within a specific order as a threatening and destabilizing force without necessarily destroying nor abolishing that order. It appears suddenly and surprisingly, as shock, or traumatism, or witty turn, but not only at the margins where we would somehow expect it, but often in the midst of the most common and institutionalized settings. It refers not only to experience, but can touch upon the very fabric of reality itself. It usually prefers to speak figuratively, but it rarely ventures into complete nonsense or indulges in anti-language. It often appears under different names or guises.

Waldenfels' trenchant definition is a good start but we can elaborate its two parts, by expanding them into what could be called the hyperbolic fourfold. In such an expanded framework, the hyperbolic would be defined as that which appears and is different from itself, excessively more, almost nothing or involved in a dynamic of self-contradiction. Alterity and paradoxality (1), excess and abundance (2), unemployed negativity (3), and pervasive fictionality (4) become the signatures of the hyperbolic, which flickers in erratic shapes and formations through and between the phenomenal and the ontological realm. Literature is a privileged site where this flickering can be observed and playfully (co-)produced in all its richness and complexity. High time, then, to turn our attention to the literature of Thomas Pynchon and Roberto Bolaño, to their late maximalist novels—to their *hyperbolic realism*.

PART TWO

3

Abundant Discourses

What abundance, what consolation.
CLARICE LISPECTOR

The Maximalist Novel: Lovers & Haters

In the beginning of a minimalist essay on maximalist novels, John Barth makes a long story short by playing with numbers. As we hear him counting the pages of each book on his impressive list of over-long novels without saying anything about their content or form, we could think that his playful approach is just another example of a postmodernist's anti-hermeneutic sentiment. But the decision to use minimalistic means to talk about maximalist outcomes underscores Barth's central argument, which claims that there is no hope for the eternal quarrel between maximalism and minimalism to be settled once and for all. It cannot and should not be settled even though "other things equal, less surely *is* more" and even though minimalist writing supposedly fits better into "our distracted century" (Barth [1967] 1995a: 74). Although the modern ecology of attention seems to encourage minimalist writing, nothing can replace the "metabolistic mode" (1995a: 78) championed by "the exhaustive but inexhaustible, exhilarating novel" (1995a: 88).

In a particularly funny moment of *It's a Long Story. Maximalism Reconsidered*, Barth claims that he "once declined to review Gaddis's formidable novel [*The Recognitions*, 956 pages] on the minimalist pretense that anything worth saying in literature can be said in 806 pages," which refers to the exact page count of his own longest novel, *The Sot-Weed Factor* ([1960] 1995c: 79). Measured against Barth's Sot-Weed test, Roberto Bolaño's *2666* (1119 p.) and Thomas Pynchon's *ATD* (1085 p.) must appear as far too long. And this although they are much shorter after all than novelistic monsters like Hugo's *Les Misérables* or Richardson's *Clarissa,* shorter than the epic and life-devouring endeavors of Rabelais, Proust, or Musil, less obsessively encyclopedic and easier to read than Joyce's *Ulysses* or Pynchon's own *Gravity's Rainbow* whose 730 and 763 pages still operate within the limits of the test.

By taking the Sot-Weed factor more seriously than its inventor probably did, we seem to have the choice between two different attitudes toward overabundant novels—either we judge them, more by their weight than their cover, as hopelessly overwritten, redundant, pretentious; or we praise them as genre-bending attempts from insubordinate writers who defy the values of conservative critics and the literary market.

Since the earliest beginnings of literary criticism, many have opted for the first alternative. In the rhetoric tradition, such discussions have turned around the central notion of *copia*. If the guidebooks recommend the use of all available tropes and figures to amplify, embellish, and variegate one's discourse, there are also recurrent warnings that too much *copia* can harm the poet's integrity. Within the more specific history of the modern mega-novel (Karl 2001), the reactions to *Moby-Dick* from Melville's contemporaries have set a skeptical tone that can still be heard today. While some of his critics complain about his "mad" use of language, others share with us their suffering from the "dull and dreary" effect of Ishmael's declamatory style, Ahab's ravings, and the stilted learnedness of the book's pseudo-encyclopedic chapters (Higgins & Parker 1995: 356, 412). As one critic bluntly concludes, the book "repels the reader instead of attracting him" (1995: 359).

Today, of course, the situation has changed. *Moby-Dick* is widely considered as one of the greatest books ever written although it took more than a century to establish this consensus (Buell 2014). Complex, sprawling, and difficult novels are at the core of literary canons both in the United States and Latin America, and a figure like James Joyce is celebrated for being the author of the two highlights of the maximalist genre: the ultimate multi-encyclopedic novel *Ulysses* ([1922] 1992) and the ultimate defiance of readability *Finnegans Wake* ([1939] 2000).

Nevertheless, voices hostile to the maximalist ambition in the tradition of Melville's critics persist. One of its loudest amplifiers is the British literary critic James Wood, famous for his attacks on *hysterical realism*, as he calls it. "The big contemporary novel," writes Wood, "is a perpetual motion-machine that appears to have been embarrassed into velocity. It seems to want to abolish stillness, as if ashamed of silence—as it were, a criminal running endless charity marathons" (Wood 2000). Written as a roast of Zadie Smith's *White Teeth,* some of the most respected postmodern writers are included in Wood's blacklist, namely, Rushdie, Pynchon, DeLillo, and David Foster Wallace. According to Wood, the strongest flaw of Smith and her peers is their failure to create credible characters. Instead of real "life," there is only inhuman "spectacle," the quality of the writing "undulates" and the language is denounced as "extremist." Like some of Melville's more moderate critics, he acknowledges the writers' talent, but laments that there is simply too much of everything: too many words, too many stories and plot lines, too many unbelievable inventions, too much entanglement: "what above all makes these stories unconvincing is precisely their very profusion, their relatedness. One cult is convincing, three cults are not" (2000).

But not only are these novels considered to be too long to be convincing, they are also deemed too difficult. This view has found an even more prominent spokesperson in Jonathan Franzen, a writer of long, but not too difficult novels. In a controversial essay for the *New Yorker*, Franzen (2002) rebels against the aesthetics of difficulty identified with the work of William Gaddis. As a starting point, Franzen defines two conflicting author-reader-models: the Contract model and the Status model. While the Contract model "entails a balancing of self-expression and communication" and demands from the author to respect the reader's wish for quick pleasure and continuous entertainment," the Status model "is the tool of socially privileged readers and writers" who despise the average reader's consumer values and declare to aspire to the sublime goals of poetic novelty, literary genius and artistic subversiveness. Adherence to the Status model produces a "literature of emergency" that intimidates and tortures the reader with its pretentious "encyclopedia of phonyness" (2002).

Toward the end of his essay, Franzen's argument becomes somewhat more ambitious. The problem of the Status model, he writes, is not only that it is arrogant and elitist, but that it is based on a series of fallacies, namely, the idea that the novel could or should "capture" reality in all its complexity; that voices and motifs should be composed like symphonic waves; that its major aesthetic value lies in the novelty of its form; and that a notoriously "Stupid Reader" must be provoked by difficult art that irritates his narrow-minded expectations. Close to Wood's opinions, it is the presumed inhumanity of difficult art, exemplified by though not limited to the maximalist novel, that poses a threat to the essence of fiction, that "most fundamental human art" (2002).

It would be an all too easy task to point out the major inconsistencies at the core of Wood's and Franzen's criticism.[1] What I am more interested in is to unveil the unquestioned aesthetic humanism implicit in their argument.

---

[1] The fundamental inconsistency at the core of Wood's and Franzen's arguments has to do with their conception of "life." Whereas both critics complain about the over-abundant, "hysterical" vitalism of difficult, maximalist novels, they build their counter-aesthetic model on the unquestioned value of life and a by no means self-evident claim that being human essentially means to tell each other *stories*. In that way, they share a common flaw of humanist thinking; instead of an exploration of humanity as a project, an exploration of what it could mean to be human, they take humanity as an accomplished given and allow dissent only about the ways in which it should be narrated. For a critical response to Franzen see Marcus (2005). For a critical analysis of Wood's tactics as a literary critic see Deresiewicz (2008).

For Wood, the unique criterion for accomplished literature seems to be the successful representation of character. To achieve that goal, a character must obtain "a life of its own." Chekhov is the outstanding model for such an "unhostaged writer" (Wood 2000) whereas the opposite model is represented by Flaubert whose characters are the "doomed" victims of their author's relentless mental construction (Wood 2014).

Like Wood, Franzen centers on Flaubert as the prime example of his Status model. He almost seems to be copying his colleague when he describes *The Recognitions* as "a huge landscape painting of modern New York, peopled with hundreds of *doomed* but energetic little figures, executed on wood panels by Brueghel or Bosch" (Franzen 2002, my emphasis). Franzen only differs from Wood in what is the core value of his aesthetic humanism: not character, but *story* shall be the major bond which creates "a sense of connectedness" between the writer and the reader. "Shorter, warmer books," as Franzen bluntly puts it, seem to be more capable of creating such an affective connection.

Wood and Franzen are talented writers, and their attacks against *hysterical realism* or *the literature of emergency* include provocative, eloquent, and entertaining moments. However, the weakness of their account has to do with a hidden but pervasive moralization of their argument. If we take a closer look at their own use of metaphors, it becomes clear that, in their view, the novels in question are not only aesthetic aberrations, but moral and dietetic sins. They suffer from "binging in any kind of illusion" (Wood 2000), and instead of serving a balanced "many-course meal," they are "more closely associated with the lower end of the digestive tract" (Franzen 2002). The endless stuff they are piling up is not only linguistic and fictional shit; it's shit with the wrong moral attitude. *Hysterical realism* is not only bad, but wrong; the *literature of emergency* not only flaky, but pretentious, phony, and fake.

Both critics' provocations intimate the long and difficult novel's precarious situation at the beginning of the twenty-first century. Although some younger specimens like *Infinite Jest, Underworld,* or *2666* have found a huge fan base among readers, critics, and academics alike, sometimes subjected to an almost cultish adoration, they have also faced the incomprehension and impatience of readers and professional critics.[2] There seems to be a stubborn suspicion that behind the Status writer's quest for complexity, entanglement, and urgency lies not much more than the dishonest intention of showing off. The Contract writer, in contrast, is not exposed to a similar general suspicion, as long as they come along with a good story (one, not many) and all too human characters with a life of their own. The example of Melville shows that modern writing invested in copious form has struggled with this

---

[2] For a cautious evaluation of DeLillo's *Underworld* see Tanner (1998). Tanner's critique, however, does not target DeLillo's experimentalism. On the contrary, the author sees in DeLillo's by far longest novel a relapse into more conventional narrative style.

general suspicion long before the postwar period. And the example of John Barth reveals that even committed writers (and avid readers) of maximalist works are painfully aware of the risks involved in the writing (and reading) of books that may be too long.

Amalfitano's Case for the Long and Difficult Novel

One of Bolaño's most fascinating characters, the Mexican philosopher Amalfitano, who lives as a single parent with his teenage daughter in the semi-fictional city of Santa Teresa at the border between Mexico and the United States, has a completely different opinion of the maximalist novel than his Anglophone opponents. In a conversation with the son of the dean of the Faculty of Arts and Letters where Amalfitano teaches, the young man, who thus far has given the image of a hedonist playboy, confesses his love for poetry to the distracted professor, especially the poetry of Georg Trakl. At the mention of Trakl, Amalfitano's mind starts to digress and jumps back to Barcelona, reminding him of an encounter with a young pharmacist who used to read books when the pharmacy was on night duty. Asked one night by a curious Amalfitano which kind of book he likes most:

> Without turning, the pharmacist answered that he liked books like *The Metamorphosis*, *Bartleby*, *A Simple Heart*, *A Christmas Carol*. And then he said that he was reading Capote's *Breakfast at Tiffany's*. Leaving aside the fact that *A Simple Heart* and *A Christmas Carol* were stories, not books, there was something revelatory about the taste of this bookish young pharmacist, who in another life might have been Trakl or who in this life might still be writing poems as desperate as those of his distant Austrian counterpart, and who clearly and inarguably preferred minor works to major ones. He chose *The Metamorphosis* over *The Trial*, he chose *Bartleby* over *Moby-Dick*, he chose *A Simple Heart* over *Bouvard and Pécuchet*, and *A Christmas Carol* over *A Tale of Two Cities* or *The Pickwick Papers* (2666: 227).[3]

---

[3]"El farmacéutico le contestó, sin volverse, que le gustaban los libros del tipo de *La metamorfosis*, *Bartleby*, *Un corazón simple*, *Un cuento de Navidad*. Y luego le dijo que estaba leyendo *Desayuno en Tiffanys*, de Capote. Dejando de lado que *Un corazón simple* y *Un cuento de Navidad* eran, como el nombre de este último indicaba, cuentos y no libros, resultaba revelador el gusto de este joven farmacéutico ilustrado, que tal vez en otra vida fue Trakl o que tal vez en ésta aún le estaba deparado escribir poemas tan desesperados como su lejano colega austriaco, que prefería claramente, sin discusión, la obra menor a la obra mayor. Escogía *La metamorfosis* en lugar de *El proceso*, escogía *Bartleby* en lugar de *Moby Dick*, escogía Un *corazón simple* en lugar de *Bouvard y Pécuchet*, y *Un cuento de Navidad* en lugar de *Historia de dos ciudades* o de *El Club Pickwick*" (Bolaño 2004a: 289).

Amalfitano's reaction to the young pharmacist's confession of his unease with the long and difficult novel is often cited as a crucial metafictional of Bolaño's own attempt to create great, imperfect, torrential works:

> What a sad paradox, thought Amalfitano. Now even bookish pharmacists are afraid to take on the great, imperfect, torrential works, books that blaze paths into the unknown. They choose the perfect exercises of the great masters. Or what amounts to the same thing: they want to watch the great masters spar, but they have no interest in real combat, when the great masters struggle against that something, that something that terrifies us all, that something that cows us and spurs us on, amid blood and mortal wounds and stench (227).[4]

Now, it goes without saying that no critical reading of literature should ever confound character speech with authorial intentions. However, especially when reading Bolaño, one can hardly stop oneself from correlating to some extent his character's views on art, literature and their relation to life with the author's aesthetic convictions. Bolaño loves to send his characters to the front where they express strong, opinionated, and often-hyperbolic statements, which could call into question the author's credibility if he voiced those statements somewhere else than in fiction.

Amalfitano's plea for maximalist adventures calls to mind his first appearance in part one where he meets the three literary critics on their search for the reclusive German writer Benno von Archimboldi. In a tirade against the Mexican state intellectuals, oscillating between reluctant doubt and hyperbolic accusation, he draws a devastating sketch of the literary establishment and intellectual in Mexico. His own speech serves as a counter-example to the accused quietism of the official intelligentsia, delivered in a broken style, wild and discontinuous, almost mad. It suggests Amalfitano's ambivalent position as a subversive yet marginal figure. After his enigmatic claim that to become a Mexican intellectual you must first renounce your own shadow, Amalfitano guides his audience to an imaginary proscenium where the sponsored part of the Mexican intellectuals (Sánchez Prado 2018) gathers to "translate or reinterpret or recreate" (2666: 162) the weird sounds heard from "something like a mine shaft or the gigantic opening of a mine" (2666: 121). A mine that could also be a cave. From its hidden

---

[4] "Qué triste paradoja, pensó Amalfitano. Ya ni los farmacéuticos ilustrados se atreven con las grandes obras, imperfectas, torrenciales, las que abren camino en lo desconocido. Escogen los ejercicios perfectos de los grandes maestros. O lo que es lo mismo: quieren ver a los gran des maestros en sesiones de esgrima de entrenamiento, pero no quieren saber nada de los combates de verdad, en donde los grandes maestros luchan contra aquello, ese aquello que nos atemoriza a todos, ese aquello que acoquina y encacha, y hay sangre y heridas mortales y fetidez" (Bolaño 2004a: 289–90).

center radiates unintelligible sound, "onomatopoeic noises, syllables of rage or of seduction" (121). Only the "spectators who are closest to the stage" can discern a certain shape even if it is not the real shape, but "only the shape of something" (121). The only function of the cultural ambassadors who represent the Mexican intellectual establishment is to "translate or reinterpret or recreate" those sounds, a secondary work which is "it goes without saying" of a rather "low standard" (121–2).

Faced with a phenomenal realm that eludes their methodological routines, the Mexican intellectuals lay down their symbolic arms. With their backs turned to the abyss, they have no interest in translating the wild cacophony coming out of it. They fail to account for the murmuring and whispering and moaning, to give shape to proto-symbolic fragments of reality not yet crystallized into fixed shapes or recognizable forms. "They employ rhetoric where they sense a hurricane, they try to be eloquent where they sense fury unleashed, they strive to maintain the discipline of meter where there's only a deafening and hopeless silence. They say cheep cheep, bowwow, meow meow, because they're incapable of imagining an animal of colossal proportions, or the absence of such an animal" (*2666*: 122). Similar to Amalfitano's complaint about the shy pharmacist are afraid of venturing beyond the realm of small and perfect *cuentos*, monstrosity is a key word in this scene. But differently from Plato's unmistakably echoed allegory, the task is not to emancipate the prisoners of the cave by guiding them from the world of shadows to the earth's surface where they become eligible to encounter the archetypes of ideal being. Instead, according to Amalfitano, a real intellectual must do justice to the phenomenality of the cave in its very un(re)presentability[5] and untranslatability by creating an expressive framework that integrates its monstrous, more-than-human and spectral elements.

The state intellectuals' inability to face the metaphorical abyss of reality is an eerie foreshadowing of the complicit role of culture in a system that incites violence against and the murdering of women while at the same time denying the structural and systemic conditions of such a deadly violence. Over the course of part IV, the part of the *feminicidios*, it becomes painfully clear that the whole cultural apparatus both in Mexico and abroad is programmed to drastically underestimate and misrepresent the

---

[5]It may sound awkward, but *unpresentable* is the better word than *unrepresentable*. While the latter term conjures a wrong image of impossible representation that reproduces the myth of ineffability (that I will set out to debunk in Chapter 10), the neologism is more precise, claiming that no act of representation can hope to make any phenomenon *fully* present. See Merleau-Ponty ([1964] 1968: 227–8): "A certain relation between the visible and the invisible, where the invisible is not only non-visible (what has been or will be seen and is not seen, or what is seen by an other than me, not by me), but where its absence counts in the world (it is 'behind' the visible, imminent or eminent visibility, it is *Urpräsentiert* precisely as *Nichturpräsentierbar*, as another dimension) where the lacuna that marks its place is one of the points of passage of the 'world.'"

phenomenon. In their adherence to the neo-classicist[6] ideals of symbolic enchantment, abstraction, and ahistorical beauty, the Mexican intellectuals miss at least two important expressive possibilities: the "cold," fact-based, observational approach of crime reporter Sergio González Rodríguez,[7] and the "hot," neo-surrealist, counter-factual, visionary style exemplified by Hans Reiter/Archimboldi who, according to his critics, tries to follow darkness "to the bottom, with his eyes [wide] open" (2666: 639). In part IV, Bolaño will tap into both expressive modes, the documentary *and* the neo-surrealist, bring them together and eventually transcend their respective limits by gradually integrating them into the larger socio-environmental context of Santa Teresa.

Amalfitano's rant provides a powerful counter-example to the stylized anti-realism of his adversaries. It is directed against miniaturization, against polished perfection, against aesthetic solutions designed to tame and mortify reality in all its irreducible monstrosity. It is hyperbolic in that it refuses to remain silent about whereof one cannot speak. It tries to gain poise on the slippery path between the ineffable and the obvious without pretending to exhaust the formless [*informe*], to say it with Bataille's famous concept ([1929] 1985: 31; also Bois and Krauss 1997).[8] Not only is it replete with eccentric images and metaphorical pretension; it is also full of concessions, precautions, and Amalfitano's tangible fear that, in the end, his words could make no sense at all. On the one hand then, Amalfitano's hyperbolism meets Agamben's appreciation of a style that does not conceal what might otherwise remain hidden in its own act of saying, a style that radiates into two directions at the same time pushing forth while regularly reflecting back on its blind spots and tacit assumptions (Agamben 2009: 8). On the other hand, Amalfitano demonstrates that hyperbolic expression often operates at the edge of intelligibility. After all, even hard-boiled hermeneuts like

---

[6] Their favorite writer is Paul Valéry.

[7] Like Santa Teresa, the fictional Sergio González Rodríguez has a very real model in the late Mexican journalist, reporter, and novelist Sergio González Rodríguez. His fascinating and terrifying account of the *feminicidios* in Ciudad Juárez, *Huesos en el desierto*, is widely considered to be the central source and inspiration for Bolaño's work on part IV of 2666 (Rodríguez 2002).

[8] Here's the entire quote just because it's so irresistible: "A dictionary begins when it no longer gives the meaning of words, but their tasks. Thus formless is not only an adjective having a given meaning, but a term that serves to bring things down in the world, generally requiring that each thing have its form. What it designates has no rights in any sense and gets itself squashed everywhere, like a spider or an earthworm. In fact, for academic men to be happy, the universe would have to take shape. All of philosophy has no other goal: it is a matter of giving a frock coat to what is, a mathematical frock coat. On the other hand, affirming that the universe resembles nothing and is only formless amounts to saying that the universe is something like a spider or spit."

Liz Norton, professionally at ease with hermetic and difficult language struggle to make sense of Amalfitano's abyssal rhetoric. After having patiently listened to everything he has to say, everything Norton returns is this simple reply: "I don't understand a word you've said" (*2666*: 123).

Cruft vs. Craft

A recent contribution to the field of maximalist studies registers a comparable polarization at the heart of maximalist writing. The "agony and ecstacy" felt upon reading "Big Books" (Letzler 2017: 1) can be judged as "punishment" (Franzen 2002), or as invitation to an adventure that rewards our substantial investment of time and attention with infinite jest. For many admirers of the maximalist novel, its encyclopedic "style of connectedness" (Moore 1987) serves as a pretext to embark on a fanatic quest devoted to deciphering every single reference to historical reality, to the history of art and literature as well as the entire machine of intra—and intertextual relations and metafictional allusions. The *PynchonWiki*[9] is an obvious symptom for the "hermeneutic fury" (Hörisch 1998) of a digital community committed to reverse tracking Pynchon's excessively researched, notoriously dense and hyper-allusive texts.

In *The Cruft of Fiction*, David Letzler offers a clever alternative to the simplistic opposition of stubborn rejection and blind endorsement. He starts from the claim that most information in the maximalist novel is simply "pointless" (Letzler 2017: 3):

> Instead of feeling thralldom, then, to every nonstandard usage, gratuitous datum, fleeting impression, broad parody, wandering subplot, and enigmatic symbol that a mega-novel contains, we ought to investigate how our minds manage an overwhelming amount of text with ambiguous function, how they work through material that is often pointless and boring, and how they adjudicate the intelligent use of stupid text (2017: 29).

Letzler seems to argue in the wake of demands for an emancipated reader whose primary task is not to slavishly obey the text's apparent order, but to react to the presented material with an independent mind (or body). In the case of the maximalist novel, this means above all *not* to read everything. The diligent critic who is desperately trying to understand everything, who believes that his first civic duty is to reconstruct the meaning and context of each and every single detail, is a pathetic figure. Putting his finger in

---

[9]https://pynchonwiki.com.

the wound, Julio Cortázar made fun of those among his critics who were actually reading his quite maximalist novel *Rayuela* twice just because he offered them two different ways to read it (Cortázar 1967: 138).

To conceptualize those massive amounts of pointless information, Letzler adopts the term *cruft* from the jargon of computer programming. Defined by the dictionary as "[e]xcess; superfluous junk; used esp. of redundant or superseded code; poorly built, possibly over-complex" (Letzler 2012), *cruft* refers to those components of a computer program that could easily be eliminated for reasons of efficiency and elegance. As experience (and theory) demonstrates, some *cruft* will always inevitably remain, at least in those systems not entirely reducible to mathematical axioms. And yet we are left with the question: why does the maximalist novel purposefully accumulate so much *cruft*, which, according to its critics, makes it so unnecessarily bulky and destroys its narrative economy? Why does it punish the reader with so much excess, so much abundance, so much stuff that no one needs? Why does it place an additional burden to a literary market already troubled to find good and reliable readers?

There are several answers to these questions. One important thing that *cruft* does is precisely to defy the traditional literary value of *craft*. The definition of literature as craft has a long and complex history, certainly not independent from revolutionary developments in science, technology, the modern organization of labor and the increasing importance of the dictionary. The paradigmatic moment of craft in the history of modern writing is probably Flaubert's remark that literature has less to do with the outpouring of genius and more with the hard and sweaty search for the right word [*mot juste*]. Directed against inspiration, Flaubert's Protestant vision has reorganized the whole literary field, exerting a sustainable influence on writers across the whole confessional spectrum, from Catholics like T. S. Eliot to neo-mystics like Henry James. James's adherence to craft is of course related to his famous dictum *show don't tell,* which prefers technique to improvisation, sophistication to spontaneity, efficiency to affluence. Since narrative economy is one of the central pillars for any aesthetics of craft, the maximalist novel must naturally come under suspicion for its sprawling exuberance.

As Mark McGurl (2009) has shown in *The Program Era,* his seminal study of US-American postwar literature, the triumph of literature as craft has been assured by its institutionalization through the creative writing programs that were set up in the whole country after the model of the Iowa Writers Workshop. It is thus almost impossible to overhear the echoes of the "Iowa doctrine" in Franzen's and Wood's critiques, which are based on the premise that the maximalist novel is merely showing off instead of showing that which should not be told. Besides this rather moralizing argument, there is a quite practical reason why craft is more apt to guide the institutionalized debate about what constitutes literature and how it should be written and read. Short texts are not only easier to imitate (for aspiring writers), they are also more convenient to teach (to aspiring professional readers). In the context of the higher education, Pynchon's *Crying of Lot 49* has acquired "college textbook" (2009: 191) status, occupying a far more important position than his way more important *Gravity's Rainbow*. If the influence of creative writing programs is not the same in the Latin American context, teachers of Bolaño's literature may for pragmatic reasons at least still pick his shorter fiction (*Distant Star, By Night in Chile*) before burdening their students with *2666* or *The Savage Detectives*. This having said, Pynchon's and Bolaño's shorter texts do of course not easily sit next to the "perfect exercises of the great masters" (*2666*: 227). On the contrary, their sprawling, multilayered, and inconclusive complexity is crammed into the tightest space, creating role models of a quite remarkable and understudied literary species: the maximalist miniature.

2666 and *ATD* in the Context of Modern Maximalism

Already at first glance, Pynchon's and Bolaño's late maximalist novels, *ATD* and *2666*, seem to occupy a quite peculiar position in the field of crufty fiction. Both novels constantly play with the allure of the too-much (Haberkorn 2021)—both through their sheer length, their intention to provide a sense of the "sand-grain manyness of things that can't be counted" (DeLillo 1997: 60), and through their constant gesturing toward a reality that even the most detailed and loaded discourse can neither contain nor exhaust. Judging the books by their looks and the previous works of their authors, we may prepare ourselves for a dizzying and "hysterical" reading experience (Wood 2000) with constant changes of direction, perspective, and focus. But unlike the celebrated earlier maximalist masterpieces, *The Savage Detectives* and *Gravity's Rainbow*, the narrative pace of these later texts is strikingly slow. Especially in the case of *ATD*, the elaborate journeys at the crossroads into the twentieth century unfold with an "ominous slowness" (*ATD*: 146). Pynchon's protagonists make regular use of airships, regional trains, and steamboats, but their favorite means of transportation are their feet. Their wanderings are frequently referred to as *pilgrimages,* and a description that imposes itself as metafictional self-description of the novel speaks of it as a "corrupted pilgrim's guide" (Severs & Leise 2011). The *Inconvenience* of that illustrious boy group, the Chums of Chance, serves as an epitome of what was then the technological avant-garde, but the leisureliness on board has nothing to do with the rush of hysteria familiar from works like *Manhattan Transfer*, which simultaneously denounce and celebrate the unsettling rhythms of modern life. The Chums of Chance's few encounters with rivaling airships proceed in respectful, comradely, and undramatic manners, a rather strange uneventfulness if we take the *Pequod*'s dramatic encounters with other ships or the adventurous life onboard of Jack London's *Ghost* as a model.

In Bolaño's *2666*, suddenness is an important mode of aesthetic appearance,[10] but sudden events are still rare and embedded within long passages where nothing substantial happens. To some extent, Bolaño's protagonists seem to experience the novel's Baudelairian motto as they stumble into unpredictable situations often accompanied by unexpected outbursts of violence, briefly dwelling in an "oasis of horror" in the midst of an otherwise vacuous "desert of boredom" (2666: ix). But Bolaño's excessive repetition of the same always leaves room for sometimes almost imperceptible variations. In part IV, excessive repetition will confront the reader with a moral challenge. As the narrator endlessly uses the same clinical phrases to refer to the state of the corpses and the circumstances of the crime, the reader might have difficulties to dedicate the same amount of attention and compassion to each and every new case. Caused by the relentless inflation of sexist, deadly violence and its forensic reproduction in part four of *2666*, an increasingly exhausted reader might start "soaring over" (Merleau-Ponty [1964] 1968: 27) the individual cases and miss some of the particularly horrendous details in what is already a desert of horror. In the next chapter, I will insist on an extraordinarily shocking case and look at the narrator's touching attempt to do justice to it. Until then, however, we record what might be a shared experience of most readers of *2666* and especially part IV. Through tiny variations and an epic commitment to provide a complete or near-to-complete list of these crimes, Bolaño restitutes at least a fraction of their singularity to the faceless victims of such hyperbolic, feminicidal violence. But the tedious repetition of the same and the failure to give full tribute to the dead leaves us behind with a bitter, melancholic aftertaste (see also Chapter 7), a sense of agential powerlessness in the face of rampant crime and injustice that disguises itself as metaphysical, unspeakable evil.

ATD and *2666* are outstanding examples of abundant literary discourses whose broken totality is very hard to comprehend in a single reading, but the remarkable slowness of their unfolding distinguishes them from what Letzler, in yet another pathologizing turn, has described as literature modeled on a generation suffering collectively from ADHD (Letzler 2017: 236). Their slowness distinguishes them from a hyperactive classic like *Infinite Jest*, which translates Joyce's grotesque encyclopedianism into the early

---

[10] For a classical account of suddenness as a mode of aesthetic appearance see Bohrer ([1981] 1994).

digital age of television (Fitzpatrick 2006). We should thus keep in mind that the *Ulysses* line is often not very helpful for *hyperbolic realism* insofar the latter's aesthetic signature is less dependent on a frantic reinvention of new styles and idioms. And an even less useful model for our novels is, of course, Joyce's relentless and almost hostile experimentalism in *Finnegans Wake*.

Unlike *Mason & Dixon, 2666* and *ATD* are not written in a highly stylized, manufactured idiom, in which the character's more-or-less historical accents are comically reproduced and inflected, and this despite the fact that Pynchon, at least, makes such excessive use of historical genres in bringing to life the twentieth century's prehistory. On the other hand, our two novels are much noisier than such a fascinating and by all means maximalist novel like DeLillo's *Underworld*, which nevertheless clings to rather conventional or even conservative montage of consistent narrative arcs. In contrast to DeLillo's panoramic take on Cold War America, then, the borders of Pynchon's and Bolaño's places and periods are significantly fuzzier.

Let us continue for a little while with this game of contrasting different maximalisms. José Lezama Lima's *Paradiso* ([1966] 2011), to add an example from Latin America, is hyperbolic to the core, more explicitly so than 2666 and *ATD* together, but it is based on the underlying design of a hyper-intellectual *Bildungsroman*, breathlessly but chronologically panting after Lezama's asthmatic *alter ego* José Cemí and his two friends and part-time rivals Foción and Fronesis.[11]

As a whole, *ATD* and 2666 come closer to the seemingly less daunting *roman-fleuve* even if they are not novelistic cycles, but clearly designed as single books—despite the fact that Bolaño, apparently for financial reasons, played with the idea to publish the five parts as five autonomous novels. From the flow of events, Bolaño and Pynchon single out characters to spend some limited time with their destinies, to bring some plot lines and motives to the fore while others recede into the text's background or even into oblivion. Some are led to a kind of conclusion, which often insists on its temporariness; some are abandoned or sharply interrupted.

In that sense, hyperbolic realism provides the sense of a structure that is less "composed" and articulated than for instance the structure(s) of Proust's *Recherche,* even if, in Proust's case, it is often late, too late, when the characters or even the reader become aware of a decisive pattern. Another important thing that sets them apart from the life-defying narrative performance which is the *Recherche,* are the stakes in their struggle against time: for reasons I will explore in Chapter 5, among others, nothing in *hyperbolic realism* is so definitely lost at their beginning so that it would have to be heroically and definitely regained at their end.

---

[11]Could there be a better name for a precocious alpha male aspiring to become an intellectual tyrant? (Phronesis is, of course, the Greeks' term for intelligence and wisdom.)

Their dominant mode of juxtaposing motifs, metaphors and themes is, as I will show later, clearly metonymic and contiguous. Essayistic passages are less visibly emphasized and more organically integrated into the narrative flow or, as we have seen with Amalfitano, voiced in character speech.

Unlike *Rayuela,* to make another comparison, *ATD* and *2666* are not introduced with a metafictional warning that invites its readers to experiment with different modes of reading. It is certainly possible and rewarding to jump around, flip pages, compare and re-read scenes and passages, but nowhere is it explicitly recommended to do so. Bolaño's infamous part IV is certainly the section most suitable to interrupt the internalized linear reading mode, and I know through personal conversations that this is the part where readers are most likely to give up. Instead of blaming those readers for their lack of discipline, however, we should acknowledge the novel's power to repel a previously sympathetic reader to the extent that they might give up on a reading project in which they have already invested so much.[12]

In sharp contrast to Pynchon's and Bolaño's earlier maximalist masterpieces *Gravity's Rainbow* and *The Savage Detectives,* their later *ATD* and *2666* respectively cannot even remotely be described as symphonic orchestrations of voices. While *The Savage Detectives,* especially in its middle part, juxtaposes a high amount of partly conflicting and irreconcilable *testimonios* from mostly minor characters who have some kind of relation to the disappeared protagonists Ulises Lima and Arturo Belano, the narrative voice of *2666* appears as a somewhat anonymous force neither directly involved in the diegetic universe nor completely auctorial. The earlier novel also represents, *en passant,* a little encyclopedia of (not always mimetically correct) Latin American idioms whereas *2666* seems to settle in an almost context-free idiom that some have taken to be the equivalent of the neoliberal and late capitalist conditions that shape its social fabric. In *Gravity's Rainbow,* perspectives shift and switch within a sentence if the ontology of perspective is not altogether abolished in that book. In *ATD,* we are rarely in doubt about perspective and characters are almost always recognizable even where their actions seem eccentric and implausible.

In Pynchon's and Bolaño's later novels, then, language itself seems to be less in crisis or at stake. Objects and shapes do not constantly dissolve into perceptual fragments, noise, sound, and confusion. We are therefore inclined to read these novels as essentially late phenomena where some of the most radical formal gestures, thematic peculiarities and philosophical concerns of earlier maximalist novels, at least from *Moby-Dick* to *Infinite Jest,* are somehow taken for granted, resumed, revamped, and recycled without the

---

[12]Perhaps this is not the most negligible of many reasons behind Bolaño's decision to tackle its deep scandal so late in the book.

need to demonstrate the same experimental fury and stylistic aggressiveness than some of their celebrated predecessors. Metafictional self-referentiality is still a common feature but it is far less explicitly marked: not as a preface (*Rayuela*), not in footnotes (*Infinite Jest*), not in long essayistic passages (*Man Without Qualities, Paradiso*). The same is true of those novels' use of cruft, which is so efficiently hidden within a larger textual environment that they sometimes appear as very long but essentially well-crafted conventional novels.

Situated at the end of a long trajectory of modern, North and Latin American maximalism, *ATD* and *2666* convey a sense of constitutive lateness and appear to be long and difficult books after the end of the book (Derrida [1967] 1997: 86), after the end of modernism, postmodernism, and even maximalism. In that sense, they invite their readers to read with the same emancipated investment they have developed through earlier reading experiences of seemingly more radical instances of the genre. Readers already familiar with maximalist writing are prepared to encounter in these books the same amount of cruft, metafictional play and defiance of narrative (and narrativist) self-confidence than in more openly experimentalist and "difficult" examples of the genre. Trained in a tradition of maximalist reading or encouraged by experts, critics, or fans to adopt a typical maximalist's investigative curiosity, some readers might invest an amount of attention and readiness high enough to break through what often appears as those texts' conventional surface, the conventional surface of naïvely mimetic realism.

The ethos they hereby adopt is closely related to Cortázar's playful celebration of the active, emancipated reader ready to make multiple use of a single text, an ethos which calls for commitment but also promises the discovery of hidden and almost infinite jest.[13] Cortázar's aesthetics of reception is, of course, hyperbolic to the core, not only because it is folded into the poetic text itself, where it creates that hermeneutic vertigo typical for hyperbole (Baudelaire [1855] 1976: 559), but because it perpetually instigates the reader to venture beyond the text to come back to it later with an awareness energized and refined by its hyperbolic leave from the text. But there is also a realistic side to this attitude as it brings itself on par with the basic concept of reality and existence in our time, not as a distant bystander nor as a fully immersed agent of intuition, but as a body and subject that is complexly entangled into the very structure it tries to make sense of. Aesthetic theory, as much as phenomenological and ontological patterns and preferences, is neither to be found completely outside the literary text nor comfortably embedded in its symbiotic, distanceless immanence, but

---

[13]Remember: The hyperbolic mode keeps its safe distance from both the metaphysics of the absolute and infinity.

continually emerges, disappears and re-emerges from its poetic condition and context in the exact same moment these conditions and contexts are born. But before we get to a point where we can justifiably project our literary findings on more-than-literary fields of concern, we must first find them. In other words, we must read—as active, participatory readers relying on strong contextual and environmental fundaments. In the next chapter of this book on *hyperbolic realism*, it is not only me who is reading, it is me reading our authors reading (and, perhaps sooner rather than later, it is they who read us). In fact, not only in the next chapter, but in all the ones that remain.

4

Anthropophagic Intertextuality

I ate him.
OSWALD DE ANDRADE

Abundant Intertextuality

Pynchon and Bolaño do read an awful lot, so much that their use of intertextuality becomes a direct function of their use of cruft. Today, after the lasting impact of post-structuralist contributions on the topic, intertextuality is reliably associated with dialogism, the plurality of meaning or the death of the author. The French structuralist Michel Riffaterre, however, saw intertextuality as a force that limits the context and reduces the range of interpretative options, which leads to an increase of hermeneutic objectivity. "Intertextuality is a linguistic network connecting the existing text with other preexisting or future, potential texts. It guides reading" (Riffaterre 1994: 786). In contrast, the dynamic that opens a text toward an unmanageable abundance—the abundance of literary history, writing, or reality as a whole—is associated with the term hypertextuality, a category often applied to texts that seem to mimic the rhizomic nature of digital networks, by now-familiar but still quite new and controversial in 1994 when Riffaterre wrote his essay: "Here lies, I think, the first principle differentiating intertextuality from hypertextuality: the latter collects every available datum, but this exhaustive inclusion exposes the reader to a wealth of irrelevant material. Intertextuality, by contrast, excludes irrelevant data" (1994: 786).

Maybe not surprisingly for an orthodox structuralist, Riffaterre's approach ultimately pleads in favor of the controllable displacement of intertextuality and against the frenzy (or should we say: hysteria?) of hypertextual over-connectedness. Acknowledging hypertextuality as a source of (subjective) creativity, Riffaterre holds that the intertextual mode enriches the text in a more objective manner since it "provides clues that are not historical and subjective in nature, but grammatical or lexical, and objective" (1994: 785). Hypertextuality, in contrast, leads to a dangerous inflation of information or data, to the (cognitive and ethical) disorientation of the reader and the loss of reliable criteria for measuring relevance. Intertextuality does not provoke a similar failure; it "provides clues."

If this privileging of intertextuality over hypertextuality is already in itself questionable, it becomes even more problematic as it denies a reality in which the excess of data and information is gradually becoming our natural habitat. Accordingly, Letzler's defense of *cruft* points in the opposite direction and claims that abundant hypertextuality or intertextuality is an occasion for readers to train their forces of judgment that conservative critics consider in danger. Encouraged to creatively filter out and reorganize the masses of text in front of them, the readers' main activity has to shift from being a specialist of decoding meaning to becoming a choreographer of their own attention.

In *Palimpsests,* Gérard Genette's impressively systematic analysis of paratextual dynamics, we read: "The less massive and explicit the hypertextuality of a given work, the more does its analysis depend on constitutive judgment: that is, on the reader's interpretive decision" (Genette [1982] 1997: 9). This couldn't be less true for crufty fiction. There, hypertextuality is always massive and often explicit, and yet it is precisely this explicit massiveness of references that activates the reader since she is asked to decide which traces to follow, which dots to connect and how to deal with all the rest that remains neglected or falls into oblivion.

Already in his otherwise-useful definition of hypertextuality at the beginning of the book, Genette's underestimation of massiveness becomes visible: "By hypertextuality I mean any relationship uniting a text B (which I shall call the *hypertext*) to an earlier text A (I shall, of course, call it the *hypotext*), upon which it is grafted in a manner that is not that of commentary" (1997: 9). This is a crucial point: hypertextuality's tendency toward deterritorialization, which Riffaterre sees skeptically while Genette remains rather neutral, is nourished by the fact that it establishes a relation which is "not that of commentary," that crucial activity of classical hermeneutics. Therefore, hypertextuality provides options for attacking the literary illusion of textual self-containment. If this option becomes available for us by way of Genette's theory (or perhaps we should better say: methodology), his conception of hypertextuality still implies a limitation that tries to explain everything that happens in a relation from one text to another even if that relation is somewhat more complicated than more conservative takes on intertextuality admit. As I will try to show in the following, such a textualist approach, however commonsensical it may appear, will not suffice to fully grasp the intertextual or hypertextual dynamics at play in *ATD* and *2666*.

Pynchon's Reparative Genre-Poaching

For more than half a century, the steadily growing number of readers of Pynchon's novels have learned that one of the major difficulties and major pleasures of reading this author lies in the task of tracing back and hunting down the uncountable intertextual allusions and references. As Simon Malpas and Andrew Taylor have shown, already in Pynchon's first novel V. intertextuality is not only "a background to the plot, but it rather *is* the novel itself, its milieu, medium, style, and the source of its search for the central, titular enigmatic figure, V. herself" (Malpas & Taylor 2013: 88). A little above, they had already made a similar claim, namely, that "allusion and intertextuality are not sub-textual structures that the narrative seeks to hide, but are rather explicitly presented on the surface of the text" (2013: 88).

More than forty years later and especially in *ATD*, intertextuality is still not a substructure but the very milieu out of which this longest Pynchon novel emerges. At the same time, the intertextual presence on the text's surface seems a lot less aggressive than in Pynchon's early, arch postmodern texts such as *V.* or *Crying of Lot 49*. As early as *Gravity's Rainbow*, as Brian McHale (2011) argues, Pynchon shifts the core of his intertextual milieus from singular texts or authors to whole literary genres or modes of writing.[1] In *ATD*, eventually, "the technique of synchronizing the popular genres being pastiched or appropriated with the era of the novel's storyworld" (2011: 20) is pushed to its limits. "Now single up all lines!" (*ATD*: 3), the novel's encouraging opening lines, do not only herald the Chums of Chance's next assignment but they anticipate that we're about to start reading an adventure novel whose most adventurous journey is a rollercoaster ride through sometimes obscure, mostly popular, and largely forgotten literary genres.

Complementing McHale's acute analysis of *ATD*'s dominant intertextual strategies, John Clute (2007) offers the most comprehensive list of the vast number of genres worked into the novel. Clute discerns four different generic clusters: the Airship Boys cluster, the Western Revenge cluster, the Geek Eccentric cluster, and the Flaneur Spy Adventuress cluster. More genres, both those contemporary to the book's setting and those that emerged only later, are interspersed within these large generic blocks. Most of those incorporated genres are decidedly "minor" and popular, although some are not without a certain high-literary reputation (*Vernean journey, steampunk*); others are not historically limited genres but rather transhistorical modes

---

[1] "Gravity's Rainbow, a novel about the 1940s, is cast in the form of a movie from the forties—or rather, it mingles several different genres of forties movies, including the war movie, the musical comedy, the romance, the horror movie, even the animated cartoon" (McHale 2011: 21).

of writing (*utopia*); others again are hilariously hyper-specific spin-offs (*Shangri-La thriller, Symmesian Hollow Earth tale, gaslight romance*); and some seem to be the original invention of a highly motivated reviewer (*mildly sadomasochistic soft porn tale*).

Besides the sheer delight that listing and clustering all these quaint and charming genres brings, Clute also has a few things to say about Pynchon's global strategy. As could be expected, the clusters do not appear in clearly distinguishable sections but mingle and merge, disappear and reappear "in occluded waves of unfolding," a mingling and merging that becomes stronger and stronger as the novel proceeds. More than pastiches, they are not narrated in their traditional key but, to use a musical metaphor, modulated into "an amalgam of styles" and idioms (2007). What we could call the phenomenality of Pynchon's historical genres, their mode of appearance, thus corresponds to the characters' erratic and flickering intermittence, their syncopated rhythm of appearing, disappearing, and reappearing in mostly unforeseeable ways. But despite the constant echo of those literary genres in *ATD*, the remarkable consistency of the narrative voice makes it impossible to read the novel as mere proliferation of pastiches. There is something else that holds Pynchon's uncountable stunts of distorting mimicry together, which Clute defines as follows: "The intervening filter is, of course, the literatures of the fantastic as they actually exist" (2007).

Less comprehensively than Clute, who sees *ATD* as a "pure science fiction novel" (2007), McHale adds a little more narratological nuance to the understanding of Pynchon's intertextual strategies and identifies another dominating filter at the core of the book—history, or rather: literary history. Not only does Pynchon compile "a massive anthology of popular genres, a virtual library of entertainment fiction" (McHale 2011: 18), he "appropriates the conventions and materials of genres that flourished at the historical moments during which the events of his story occur" (2011: 19). On a metaliterary level, then, *ATD* does two things at the same time: it mimics historical genres and realigns them within an overarching fantastic register; and it creates a maximalist anthology of fantastic genres to expand the expressive range of the historical novel.

This "logic of *synchronization*" of history, genre poetics, and narrativity motivates McHale to speak of the novel as "*mediated historiography*—the writing of an era's history through the medium of its popular genres" (2011: 25). If we have seen such strategies before, especially in postmodern literature, Pynchon's "sampling from the whole range of a whole era's popular genres" seems unprecedented, producing "if not genuinely exhaustive coverage, then at least a compelling illusion of exhaustiveness" (2011: 25).

This is where the logic of hyperbole comes into play. The novel does not merely repeat, sample and merge historical and historically fantastic genres, but uncovers the "repressed content of the genre[s] itself" (2011: 23), restores their "unspoken realities" (2011: 28) and, by simultaneously marking these retrospective interventions as (fantastic) exaggerations, exposes their limitations. A great example for such a complex interventionist behavior is the queer character "Cyprian Latewood, a flaming queen who uses his sexuality as a tool of the espionage trade." In a textbook-like act of outdoing, Pynchon "seizes the [spy] genre's intense homosociality and amplifies it into outright homosexuality" (2011: 24).[2]

Though contradictory at first glance, McHale's and Clute's analyses complement each other. *ATD* is in fact both a pure science fiction novel and an outstanding example of mediated historiography. Mimicking some of the characters' talent to be at two different places at the exact same time, the novel sets into motion a dizzying machine of (inter)generic bilocation.[3] This allows Pynchon to inscribe a vector of historical time and materialist vision into popular genres that traditionally work without a critical notion of historical, social, and political temporality.

This becomes all too clear toward the end of the novel when the Chums of Chance experience what the limits of their literary genre would normally not allow them to experience: they grow older. If most popular genres exempt their heroes from aging, a tendency prominently mocked in "high" literature as early as Voltaire's *Candide*, they are also ingenuously oblivious of (or at least implicit about) the larger political environment in which their heroes' adventures gain traction. Pynchon's revisionist strategies set out to correct that political aphasia of the popular genre. As the novel proceeds, it becomes clearer and clearer that the Chums are not as innocent as it seems; even if their intentions appear neutral or well-intentioned, even if they do not actively support the dark forces of history that contract them, they remain painstakingly aware of the fact that they "capture our [and their] innocence, and take it away with them into futurity" (*ATD*: 416).

Besides their inventive exuberance, the comic-like adventures in the sky and under earth foreshadow the emerging modern colonization of these realms beyond (and beneath) the earth's surface. No matter how remote the traveling boy group's fantastic destinations are, the messengers of Capital have always already been there. It comes as no surprise, then, that there are souvenir shops in Arctic Iceland foreshadowing the rapid commodification of the global economy and the domesticating miniaturization of an until recently untouched wilderness (*ATD*: 66; 188). And it is no more surprising that on their travels under sand to yet another impossible underworld, they bump into a couple of explorers on their search for what would become the most conflict-ridden material of the twentieth century: oil (*ATD*: 441).

---

[2] For a recent account on the spy genre's flirting with homosociality, see Bellamy (2018).
[3] "Bilocation" is the title of *ATD*'s third part and one of the major "themes" of the book. More on it in Chapters 5 and 6.

Pynchon's revisionist strategy strips off the innocence that is implied in popular literary genres. The colonial logic of occupation and the Capital logic of extractivism seep into the most seemingly fantastic and remote locales. At the same time, Pynchon's revisionism embodies a countercultural dimension of political resistance. In the heavy footsteps of Eve Kosofsky Sedgwick's seminal essay against paranoia (1997), one of the major intentions of the novel's intertextual behavior could be defined as redeeming the popular genres' (repressed) political potential, which turns Pynchon's genre-poaching into an exercise in reparative reading. Not merely merging the high and the low, the many metabolized genres are revamped as a time machine for the comprehensive understanding of a historical period, its genealogical importance for its immediate aftermath and its *longue durée* effects that last until today. The past, to remodel a famous phrase by Mike Davis, becomes visible not only from the disaters it produces but also "from the ruins of its alternative future[s]" (Davis 1990: 1).

Sedgwick presents reparative reading as a powerful alternative to both "the hermeneutic of suspicion" (Sedgwick 1997: 4) and "the state of complacent adequacy that Jonathan Culler calls 'literary competence'" (1997: 3). In the wake of Sedgwick, Pynchon's "queering" (McHale 2011: 26) of popular genre fiction aims for "a much more speculative, superstitious, and methodologically adventurous state" (Sedgwick 1997: 4), in which political resistance against the State like anarchism, union labor struggles, and a not party-oriented, horizontal Communism (Palmeri 2017), alternative belief systems against the official monotheistic religions (Coffmann 2011), and alternative epistemologies beyond the narrow boundaries of Enlightenment rationalism (Strandberg 2000)[4] are redeemed together with and within these very popular genres. The ostentatiously melodramatic, more-than-ironic, and operetta-like key in which these narrative alternatives are performed, supports a "seemingly perpetual digestion of Pynchon's telling" (Clute 2007), a cruft-tolerant aesthetics of *telling* ignorant of the dietetic demands of any craft-related economy of *showing*, which brings some passages of the novel close to what Gregory Woods has called "high camp" (Woods 1993).

This lack of seriousness often implied in reparative readings may lead to the suspicion that they invite uncritical and depoliticizing perspectives on history. However, Pynchon's genre-poaching arguably offers a more critical and politicizing take than any paranoid conjuring of global interconnectedness and its related economy of negative affects can provide. Working through *ATD*'s reparative adventures, readers are not only confronted with marginalized undercurrents of Western history, most prominently the history of anarchism and unionized resistance from Colorado to Naples;

---

[4]Which is in fact a running theme in Pynchon's fiction, most explicitly but not exclusively in his only novel set in the eighteenth century, *Mason & Dixon* (Pynchon 1997).

they also gain access to silenced histories at the peripheries of the West, in the so-called "East" and in a few locales of the Global South. From the picturesque and folkloristic background, marginal sites and historical events like the Mexican revolution, the confusing configuration of the Balkans, or imperial power struggles across Central Asia rise more and more to the fore to as the novel proceeds.[5]

If paranoid modes of reading tend to enact an epistemological and interpretative closure, reparative modes, at least the way Pynchon deploys them, militate in favor of a more complex and multidimensional understanding of history and thus reality as a whole. If Pynchon mobilizes marginal sites and remote systems of belief and knowledge production, this does not mean, however, that he adheres to a nostalgic re-enchantment of the world, where superstitious, anti-secular resentment is summoned to compensate for the well-known downsides to Enlightened rationality. Although the very last word of the novel, *grace*, leaves room for a religious interpretation, Pynchon's redeeming of fantastic, popular, and minor genres as well as his re-centering of subaltern modes of existence comes without any hope for salvation. Final redemption is not an option in Pynchon's cosmos; if only for the reason that nobody in his reparative politicization of popular adventurism is completely innocent—not even the dead (see *ATD*: 362).

Bolaño's Intertextual Name-Dropping

Not only in *2666*, but in Bolaño's writing in general, excessive intertextuality is the preferred milieu out of which emerge his text, his themes, motifs, formal inventions, and a large amount of gossip scooped from the "vast ocean" of literary history, an ocean richly populated with famous, illustrious, marginal, forgotten, and invented writers (Bolaño [2011] 2013: 3).[6] Encountering a text that seems to spring directly from the source of extensive and obsessive reading is not an untypical impression for readers of Latin American literature. Bolaño, however, takes this dynamic to the extreme, and projects it as a rather unhealthy habit on his fictional characters. Some of Bolaño's funniest imaginary additions to the history of literature, especially of the avant-gardes, are the *Barbaric Writers,* a fictional working-class avant-garde movement, active in Paris over a short period during the rebellious 1960s. They figure most prominently in *Distant Star,* but they also appear briefly

---

[5]However, the West remains clearly the center of Pynchon's historical vision (and his generic competence), which is probably the most powerful reminder that, pace John Clute, his genre-poaching, as excessive as it might be, cannot and does not claim to be exhaustive.
[6]This structure is masterfully elucidated in Loy (2019).

in *The Savage Detectives* as well as in Bolaño's splendid posthumous novel *Woes of the True Policeman*, which is partly an earlier version of what would later become Bolaño's magnum opus, *2666*.

Founded in 1968 by the concierge Raoul Delorme, the *Barbaric Writers* are driven by the avant-garde impulse to crush tradition and build a new form of art and life from its ruins: "The apprenticeship consisted of two apparently simple steps: seclusion and reading" (Bolaño [1996] 2004: 131). Their extravagant practice is to gather in week-long conspirational meetings, baptized by their charismatic leader as "communions," which culminate in the cathartic act of desecrating expensive editions of French classical writers.

> According to Delorme, one had to commune with the master works. Communion was achieved in a singularly odd fashion: by defecating on the pages of Stendhal, blowing one's nose on the pages of Victor Hugo, masturbating and spreading one's semen over the pages of Gautier or Banville, vomiting onto the pages of Daudet, urinating on the pages of Lamartine, cutting oneself with a razor blade and spattering blood over the pages of Balzac or Maupassant, in short, submitting the books to a process of degradation which Delorme called "humanization" (2004d: 131).[7]

The *Barbaric Writers* are part of a familiar pattern in Bolaño's literature: his fictional, narrative, and aesthetic exploitation of the long and complex history of the avant-gardes, mostly but not exclusively in literature. Having abandoned his own avant-garde ambition as a co-founder of the infrarealist movement in the Mexico City of the 1970s (Caro 2010), Bolaño saved significants parts of his youthful and rebellious avant-gardism as fuel to energize his stories and novels to come. Although we must keep in mind that his published work is not that of an avant-garde writer, but rather something we should describe as post-avant-garde (Loy 2019: 272), we can still draw some parallels between the cults of the *Barbaric Writers* and Bolaño's own practice.

First, Delorme and his gang submit to a visceral conception of literature as anti-literature. Their assault on literature is paradoxical, deliberately so, as literature is the major conveyor of Bourgeois ideals and therefore a privileged site from where to attack those same ideals. As the poet

---

[7] "Según Delorme, había que fundirse con las obras maestras. Esto se conseguía de una manera harto curiosa: defecando sobre las páginas de Stendhal, sonándose los mocos con las páginas de Victor Hugo, masturbándose y desparramando el semen sobre las páginas de Gautier o Banville, vomitando sobre las páginas de Daudet, orinándose sobre las páginas de Lamartine, haciéndose cortes con hojas de afeitar y salpicando de sangre las páginas de Balzac, sometiendo, en fin, a los libros a un proceso de degradación que Delorme llamaba humanización" (Bolaño 1996: 139).

Jules Defoe, another invented member of the group points out: "The corresponding revolution in writing [...] would, in a sense, abolish literature itself. When poetry is written by non-poets and read by non-readers" (Bolaño [1996] 2004: 135). Bolaño himself often plays with related ideas, in other texts or in his rare paratextual confessions, which has a certain familiarity with the familiar Latin American motif of literature as anti-literature (Shellhorse 2017) and of poetry as *antipoesía*. For Bolaño, but not only for him, *antipoesía* is inseparably associated with the Chilean poet Nicanor Parra whom Bolaño repeatedly called "the greatest poet alive in the Spanish language" (Bolaño 2004b: 144).[8] Naturally, Parra did not actually want to abolish poetry. This brings him closer to Bolaño's post-avant-garde persuasions than to the fervent creationism of a poet like Vicente Huidobro.[9] His mission was not to abolish poetry once and for all, but to exorcise its faux solemnity: *Hay que modernizar esta ceremonia*—"The time has come to modernize this ceremony" (Parra [1969] 1983: 28, my transl.).

One of Parra's most famous poems, quoted by Bolaño at various occasions, offers a hyperbolically condensed "complete" history of Chilean poetry:

Chile's four great poets
are three:
Alonso de Ercilla and Rubén Darío (Bolaño 2004b: 43).[10]

Experienced readers of our author should not be surprised that Bolaño must have been immediately attracted by such an efficient, epigrammatic, anti-climactic, metaliterary five-finger exercise, which reduces the four great Chilean poets (Gabriela Mistral, Vicente Huidobro, Pablo de Rokha, Pablo Neruda) to three—from which, under new names, only two are left at the premature end of the poem. To push the hyperbolic game to its limits, the two remaining poets were not even Chilean. Alonso de Ercilla y Zúñiga, author of the colonialist Chilean national epos *La Araucuana* (1569), a

---

[8]See Bolaño's promotion of Parra and his complementary dethronement of Neruda in an interview with Eliseo Álvarez: "For me, Chile's great poet is Nicanor Parra and after Nicanor Parra there are several others. Neruda is one of them, without a doubt. Neruda is what I pretended to be at age twenty: Living like a poet without writing. Neruda wrote three very good books; the rest—the great majority—are very bad, some truly infected" (Bolaño 2009: 81).

[9]Vicente Huidobro, a seminal Chilean modernist, is the target of Bolaño's scoffing humor in the same essay that lauds Parra as the greatest poet writing in Spanish: "Huidobro bores me a little. Too much trilling and tra-la-la-ing, too much of the parachutist who sings Tyrolean songs as he falls. Better the parachutist who plummets in flames, or the parachutist whose parachute simply never opens" (Bolaño 2004b: 358).

[10]"Los cuatro grandes poetas de Chile / Son tres / Alonso de Ercilla y Rubén Darío" (Bolaño 2004c: 44).

remarkable text for its sporadic compassion with its victims, was a Spanish *siglo de oro* aristocrat who spent less than ten years in the country; Ruben Darío was a Creole poet from Nicaragua, widely celebrated as the leading figure of *modernismo* in Latin America.

Defying logical coherence, good taste, and poetic nationalism are only a few pillars of Parra's poetic practice that made him to one of Bolaño's earliest and lasting influences (Loy 2015). Also typical in Bolaño's style of referring to Parra, is the fact that Bolaño often establishes a speculative and sharp relation not or not only to a single text or passage, but to the complete works of an author, an entire poetic movement or even the totality of literature. However, this relation to a whole is not imposed as a totalizing view from above, but smuggled in as a materialist and visceral contact from below, inscribing at the heart of Bolaño's writing the scatological and demonumentalizing desire for a "literatura del albañal" ("literature's bottomless cesspools") produced by a romanticized lumpenproletariat of marginal artist figures (Bolaño 1996: 129, Bolaño [1996] 2004: 72–6, *the story of Lorenzo*).[11]

So as not to anger the gods of narratology, we must not misread the *Barbaric Writer*'s intention to "commune with the master works" (2004c: 131) for a direct explanation of Bolaño's literature. But it may be allowed to see in it an exaggerated expression of his consistently irreverent metabolization of the totality of world literature.[12] Bolaño's primary intertextual operation is not to establish a single, hermeneutic relation to a limited section of a *hypotext*, but devours and incorporates a speculative totality of world literature in general. This dynamic produces a "desecralization of literature, but a desecralization that enabled a tremendously original and political, albeit non-humanist writing project" (Rodríguez Freire 2013: 67, my transl.).

It cannot be overestimated that the *Barbaric Writer*'s key avant-garde operation is presented as an act of reading. Accordingly, Bolaño's metabolization of his earlier avant-garde experiments into the post-avant-garde form of his published works is not so much occupied with the search

---

[11]Bolaño frequently uses *lumpen* as a descriptive term with a predominantly positive connotation. It points at an aesthetics originating in socially inferior spheres and directed against middle-class and petty-Bourgeois core values such as politeness and decency. Bolaño's last published novella uses the term in its title: *Una novelita lumpen* (Bolaño 2002). Together with another charged word of this chapter, *barbaric*, it is also used for Archimboldi who is described as "essentially a man of the lower orders [*esencialmente un lumpen*], a Germanic barbarian, an artist in a state of permanent incandescence" (2666: 839).

[12]For committed adherents of the doctrine of unbounded aesthetic autonomy, the use of literature might already represent an irreverent act in itself. For a theory of such a pragmatic and practical use of literature see Felski (2008).

for new and revolutionary writing scenes;[13] it is much more invested in inventing new and revolutionary reading scenes. On the subject of writing scenes, the literary scholar Sandro Zanetti says this:

> This diverse writing culture is not exhausted in the production of texts, nor even in the orientation toward interpretability or applicability. Rather, it outlines a field in which movements of the body, traces of writing and trains of thought can repeatedly form completely unexpected constellations (Zanetti 2009: 85, my transl.).

In Bolaño's universe, reading is one of the privileged scenes where those body movements and trains of thought interfere to produce new and unforeseeable traces of writing, which are only in a next step translated into a coherent text. But this reading as a concrete and situated practice is further characterized. His favorite reading scenario is not that of the sedentary act of converting signs into meaning, but places a living body in an environment that often seems hostile to reading. One of Bolaño's most eccentric reading scenes is certainly that of *The Savage Detectives* where Ulises Lima reads under the shower of his tiny and shabby apartment. Playing with the risk of the physical destruction of the material object, Lima exhibits a strangely ceremonial attachment to literature or, to be more precise, the book (Bolaño [1998] 2007: 218).

The act of destroying books could make us belief that Bolaño's characters seek to privilege the spiritual product over the physical object; but it is books (not texts) that usually adopt a truly talismanic quality for them. When preparing for his fateful reunion with the fascist poet Carlos Wieder, the first-person narrator of *Estrella Distante* does not merely read a text, but *tries* to read *in* the *obra completa* of Bruno Schulz, the important Polish modernist:

> From the front windows of the bar there was a view of the sea, with a few fishing boats at work near the coast, under an intensely blue sky. I ordered a coffee with milk and tried to calm down; I felt as if my heart was going to burst out of my chest. The bar was almost empty. There was a woman sitting at a table reading a magazine and two men talking or arguing with the bartender. I opened the book, the *Complete Works of Bruno Schulz*, translated by Juan Carlos Vidal, and tried to read.

---

[13] The concept of the writing scene was introduced in German, as *Schreibszene*, by Campe (1991).

The shifting modality is crucial: he *tried to* read—but failed:

> After a few pages I realized I wasn't understanding anything. I was reading, but the words went scuttling past like beetles, busy at incomprehensible tasks. I thought of Bibiano again, and Fat Marta. I didn't want to think about the Garmendia sisters, so distant now, or the other women, but I couldn't help myself (Bolaño [1996] 2004: 143).[14]

In quite typically melancholic fashion, a fateful encounter is embedded in a visceral reading scene whose hermeneutic effort fails as much as the effort to bring back biographical memories that are already as distant as the star that gives Bolaño's maximalist novella its name. But like Pynchon, albeit in a different key, Bolaño also offers us a reparative option because the failure of reading not only informs the writing scene of the very text in front of our eyes, *Estrella Distante*, but announces the final act of revenge of Wieder's crimes. What is more, the crucial act of hermeneutic deciphering had already occurred; it was close readings of Wieder's poems, after all, that helped tracking him down in Spain. Working together with the private detective Abel Romero, the narrator had used his philological capacities to work through large amounts of literary cruft, as Wieder's poems are written in pseudonyms and scattered across obscure and peripheral magazines and journals, a heroic act of maximalist reading that ultimately leads to the restoration of some kind of justice, even if this justice is only poetic (Sellami 2014: 134).

Across his entire body of work, then, Bolaño's excessive use of intertextuality oscillates between two poles. On the one hand, a pretty romantic involvement with *obras completas,* with books as physical and sensual objects open for creative use and reuse, and with a speculative and megalomaniac totality of (world) literature. On the other hand, we have the simple, almost trivial reference to authors, titles and poetic movements, the playful and frivolous act of intertextual name-dropping. Where intertextual allusions are reduced to long list and catalogues of names and titles, signatures almost empty of either content or form, intertextuality produces a nominalist noise as one of the fundamental conditions of Bolaño's hyperbolically realist fiction. Right from the first page of *Woes of the True Policemen,* to cite just one particularly drastic example among

---

[14]"Desde los ventanales del bar se veía el mar y el cielo muy azul y unas pocas barcas de pescadores faenando cerca de la costa. Pedí un café con leche e intenté serenarme: el corazón parecía que se me iba a salir del pecho. El bar estaba casi vacío. Una mujer leía una revista sentada en una mesa y dos hombres hablaban o discutían con el que atendía la barra. Abrí el libro, la *Obra completa* de Bruno Schulz traducida por Juan Carlos Vidal, e intenté leer. Al cabo de varias páginas me di cuenta que no entendía nada. Leía pero las palabras pasaban como escarabajos incomprensibles, atareados en un mundo enigmático" (Bolaño 1996: 151).

many others, readers are immediately thrown into a fury of categorization, a deliberately unserious categorization, however, which performs a queering of literary history against the learned seriousness of more mainstream ways of periodization and classification:

> According to Padilla, remembered Amalfitano, all literature could be classified as heterosexual, homosexual, or bisexual. Novels, in general, were heterosexual. Poetry, on the other hand, was completely homosexual. Within the vast ocean of poetry he identified various currents: faggots, queers, sissies, freaks, butches, fairies, nymphs, and philenes. But the two major currents were faggots and queers. Walt Whitman, for example, was a faggot poet. Pablo Neruda, a queer. William Blake was definitely a faggot. Octavio Paz was a queer. Borges was a philene, or in other words he might be a faggot one minute and simply asexual the next. Rubén Darío was a freak, in fact, the queen freak, the prototypical freak (in Spanish, of course; in the wider world the reigning freak is still Verlaine the Generous) (Bolaño [2011] 2013: 3).[15]

Such creative, irreverent acts of categorization, which bear some resemblance with Borges's fantastic encyclopedias and impossible libraries, disrupt the seriousness and positivism of canon building and turn reading into a performative and visceral act of "doing things with books."[16]

In part II of *2666*, Amalfitano performs one of the most eccentric reading acts of Bolaño's entire oeuvre when he reenacts the instruction to a ready made that Marcel Duchamp had once written on a postcard for his sister as a wedding present. On the postcard, Duchamp told his sister to fix a geometry book with a cord, hang it out of her window, and wait. When Amalfitano finds an obscure geometry textbook by the Galician poet Rafael Dieste, he hangs it on the clothesline in his backyard to let the wind *"go through the book, choose its own problems, turn and tear out the pages"* (*2666*: 191). The tension between the rigidity of the book's geometrical

---

[15] "Para Padilla, recordaba Amalfitano, existía literatura heterosexual, homosexual y bisexual. Las novelas, generalmente, eran heterosexuales. La poesía, en cambio, era absolutamente homosexual. Dentro del inmenso océano de ésta distinguía varias corrientes: maricones, maricas, mariquitas, locas, bujarrones, mariposas, ninfos y filenos. Las dos corrientes mayores, sin embargo, eran la de los maricones y la de los maricas. Walt Whitman, por ejemplo, era un poeta maricón. Pablo Neruda, un poeta marica. William Blake era maricón, sin asomo de duda, y Octavio Paz marica. Borges era fileno, es decir de improviso podía ser maricón y de improviso simplemente asexual. Rubén Darío era una loca, de hecho la reina y el paradigma de las locas (en nuestra lengua, claro está; en el mundo ancho y ajeno el paradigma seguía siendo Verlaine el Generoso)" (Bolaño 2011: 21) [and the list goes on].

[16] For an insightful account of how readers can do and have done things with books see Price (2019). I have not been able to find a similar study for the Latin American context.

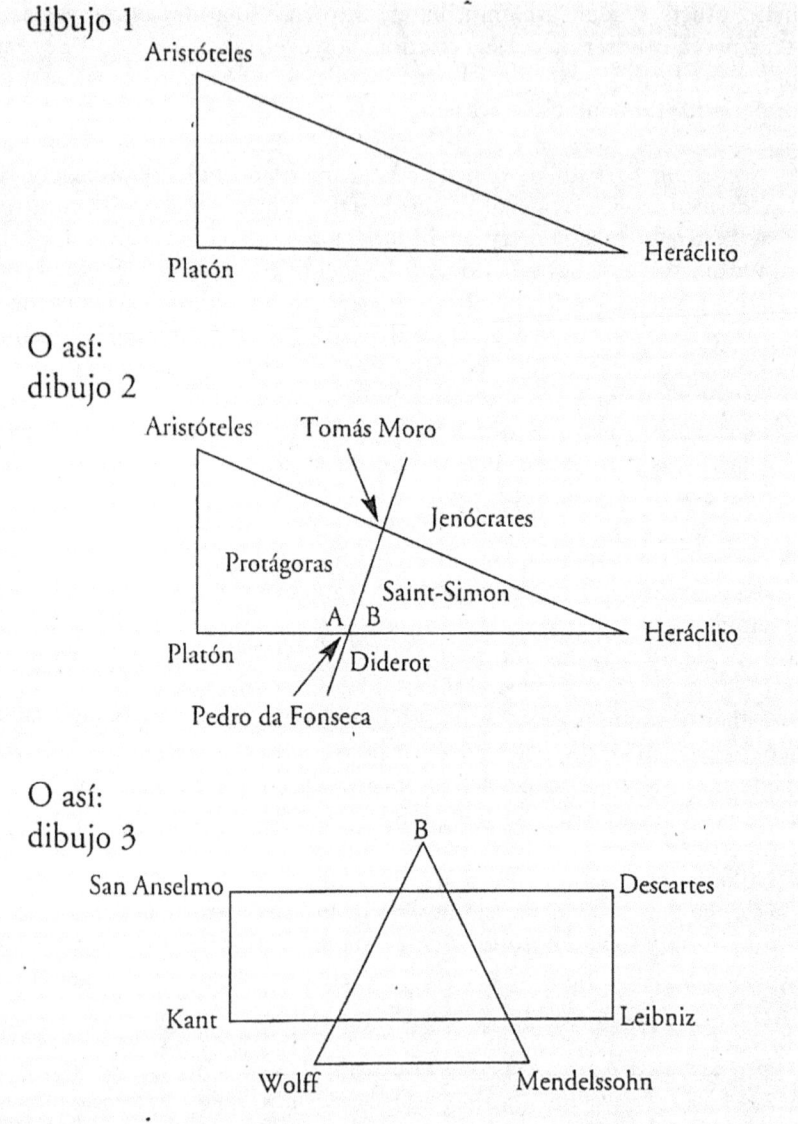

FIGURE 4.1 *2666*, p. 192.

content, the vagaries of nature, and the contingencies of reception provides the sad background for Amalfitano's gradual descent into madness. Shortly after hanging the book on the line "to see how it survives the assault of nature, to see how it survives this desert climate" (2666: 191), he starts to draw strange diagrams (see figure 4.1).

The diagrams are made of nothing but the names of writers, critics, and philosophers—and lines that draw confusing relations between them. Trying to make sense of these relations is certainly entertaining, but if we don't insist on them having any meaning at all, they witness to what we could call Bolaño's diagrammatic use of intertextuality. It is diagrammatic in that it privileges distant reading, name-dropping, the sheer pleasure of listing, counter-canonizing, and counter-categorizing over close readings and careful interpretations. It is therefore only natural that the authorial origins of the writing scene that created these diagrams remain in the dark (2666: 191–2).

Amalfitano is both the author, the reader and the critic of these "very simple geometric figures" that are at the same time hyperbolic in content and ambition. His authorship, however, is not an outcome of his conscious, rational decision, but emerges half-consciously from a complex interplay of Amalfitano's wild and eclectic reading biography, his crippled emotional state, the boredom of his working life, his alienated social environment and the challenging climate. A gothic element, expressed in a few laconic words, is added to the scene as Amalfitano only retrospectively recognizes himself as the author of his haunting creations: "Amalfitano found three more diagrams on his desk. It was clear he had drawn them himself" (2666: 193).

But let's be clear about one thing: If Bolaño's intertextual name-dropping creates a thick and noisy texture that seems to suspend interpretation, tracing back particular intertextual relations is nevertheless a valuable thing to do. Let us turn to the enigmatic Archimboldi as a last example of this section. Working as a domestic servant for a German aristocrat before the outbreak of the Second World War, he eventually gets to read his first book other than *Animals and Plants of the European Coastal Region*, which is the only book he ever read as a young adult (2666: 640). At that point, his name is still Hans Reiter, he is penniless, utterly uneducated, and can only read with a loud voice. As in Amalfitano's case, what guides his decision is pure chance or fate, which anyway seems to be more or less the same thing: "Chance or the devil had it that the book Hans Reiter chose to read was Wolfram von Eschenbach's *Parzival*" (2666: 658).

In the passages that follow, the narrator summarizes Wolfram's poetic vision and social status, which is remarkably similar to Archimboldi's—as far as the novel tells us. Reiter-Archimboldi, though initially cautious, is quickly seduced by Wolfram's anti-establishment pose, his violations of courtly etiquettes, and, most importantly, his self-cultivation as a writer who does not know "a single letter of the alphabet" [*ine kan decheinen buochstap*] (Wolfram 2006: 50) although he knows his way with words and "a little of singing" [*und kan ein teil mit sange*] (Wolfram 2006: 49). However, what in Wolfram's case is a staged dyslexia and performed stylistic clumsiness is a literal fact in the case of Reiter: "Hans Reiter said he didn't know the difference between a good refnits (reference) book and a good litchy (literary) book" (2666: 657).[17] If we believe the words of his later editor, that Archimboldi will be one of the few postwar writers who will profoundly change the German language, we are forced to agree with Bolaño that poetic innovation is achieved through auto-didactic bravery instead of diligent correctness.[18]

Wolfram's claim that he owns neither land nor house echoes Archimboldi's errant and nomadic life style, which directly translates into his errant and nomadic writing style.[19] Admiring Wolfram's "halo of dizzying mystery, of terrible indifference" (2666: 659) and his constant flirting with madness, he aims to step into the footsteps of this distant giant who claimed to sing adventures instead of writing scripts: "And what he liked most, what made him cry and roll laughing in the grass, was that Parzival sometimes rode (*my hereditary office is the shield*) wearing his madman's garb under his suit of armor" (2666: 659).

Inspired by such exciting intertextual possibilities, readers might read Wolfram's *Parsifal* not only as a fateful awakening of Archimboldi's literary vocation, but also as a hint toward Bolaño's own maximalist ambitions. Trying to find out more about Archimboldi through his relation to Wolfram von Eschenbach, we are almost inevitably reminded how strongly the metaliterary remarks in the opening of that astonishing novel from the twelfth century prefigure the poetic adventurism of *2666*. Looking for Archimboldi, we find, in part, Bolaño, "Inconstancy's companion" (Wolfram 2006: 3), zigzagging away from the reader's grasp like Wolfram's chatty magpie. ("There is both scorning and adorning when a man's undaunted mind turns pied like the magpie's hue" Wolfram 2006: 3.)[20]

---

[17]"Hans Reiter dijo que no sabía cuál era la diferencia entre un buen libro ditivo (divulgativo) y un buen libro liario (literario)" (Bolaño 2004a: 820).

[18]In his famous *Caracas Speech*, Bolaño deploys his enumerative and counterlogical style to attack cultural identitarianism in Latin American literature and elsewhere, assuming "that there might be a method hidden in my dyslexia, a bastard semiotic or graphological or metasyntactic or phonemic method, or simply a poetic method, and that the underlying truth is that Caracas is the capital of Colombia just as Bogotá is the capital of Venezuela, in the same way that Bolívar, who is Venezuelan, died in Colombia, which is also Venezuela and Mexico and Chile" (Bolaño 2004b: 31).

[19]On the parallelism between being and erring see Bolaño (2004a: 761): "Estar y errar es [...] una actitud tan congruente como agazaparse y esperar [*lurking and waiting*]."

[20]*2666* contains several processes of finding something without looking for it. Brought to Mexico by their obsessive goal to track down the reclusive writer Benno von Archimboldi, the literary critics "discover" the sad phenomenon of the *feminicidios* on behalf of the reader. They don't find what they were looking for, but they find something else, something infinitely more important. This discovery has, of course, neocolonial undertones—a reality that exists and could easily be known is only taken to be really true once it is sanctioned and recognized by European eyes.

Bolaño's ongoing intertextual excess, then, invites us to play that game as long as we do not forget that our intertextual constructions always remain embedded in the noise and cruft of endless lists of names, names that establish relations guided by nothing but chance or fate—which, again, seems to be more or less the same thing. Accordingly, as much as one might speculate about the relationship between Giuseppe Arcimboldo, the factual Italian Baroque painter, and Benno von Archimboldi, the fictional postwar German novelist, the moment where Reiter is turning into Archimboldi makes it clear that assuming a new name is, as formative as it may be, a headless *acte gratuit*. When asked for his name by an old accountant, "Reiter said the first thing that came into his head: 'My name is Benno von Archimboldi'" (2666: 784). An *acte gratuit*, however, that assumes more and more reality and is imbued with more and more meaning as it gets iterated and slowly integrated into the flesh of the real. Thus, when the old man shows his perplexity in the face of the grotesque name, Reiter reinforces his act of spontaneous renaming: "'My name is Benno von Archimboldi, sir,' said Reiter, 'and if you think I'm joking I'd better go'" (784).

Metabolic Intertextuality, Anthropophagic Form

Letzler's adaptation of the term "cruft" to the discourse of literary criticism echoes the widely shared belief that digitalization profoundly changes how we write and read. As far as the long and difficult novel is concerned, the change is expected to be even more drastic. The most obviously digital of all maximalist novels is arguably David Foster Wallace's *Infinite Jest*, with its tech-savvy playfulness, rapid changes of direction, permanent interruptions, extensive footnotes, nerdy digressions, and bizarre apocalyptic vision of a boundless and distanceless digital consumerism.

In *ATD* and *2666*, on the contrary, the digital rarely becomes an explicit thematic concern. As usual, Pynchon puts a lot of narrative effort into technological inventions, scientific discoveries, and the mise-en-scène of media that have today become obsolete. But his exploration of "technomodernism" (McGurl 2009: 37–46) plays in a much more nostalgic key than in a futuristic one, which has to do, in part, with his aforementioned mimicry of once popular genres and their tendency to paint a quaintly romanticized tableau of technological progress.[21] Bolaño's approach to technology, on

---

[21] Reading Paul Scheerbart against Jules Verne in *Experience and Poverty*, Walter Benjamin suggested that popular Bourgeois genre fiction, in contrast to what Quentin Meillassoux ([2013] 2015) has aptly called extro-science fiction, often reunites scientific curiosity with cultural nostalgia and backwardness: "No one has greeted this present with greater joy and hilarity than Paul Scheerbart. There are novels by him that from a distance look like works

the other hand, is ascetic, and his scarce references to technical systems and technical objects reveal a preference for the analog and for outdated media such as phone calls, typewriters, video tapes, and conversations.

On the surface, *2666* and *ATD* seem to adhere much less to the frantic circulation of digital data than a novel like, say, *Infinite Jest*. The rhythm of their slow adventures conveys an ostentatiously calmer and steadier feeling than the "textual zaniness" (Grausam 2011: 44) of Foster Wallace's end-of-millennium narrative or Pynchon's and Bolaño's own earlier maximalist efforts, *Gravity's Rainbow* and *The Savage Detectives*.[22] However, as emancipated readers well-equipped with digital sensors, we can certainly hear echoes of our contemporary media environment in the ways in which Bolaño and Pynchon metabolize and mobilize intertextual cruft in their late maximalist novels. By way of conclusion, I want to describe their genre-poaching and name-dropping as metabolic intertextuality, a concept trying to make sense of a digestive intertextual approach that relies on a visceral contact with the literary tradition. Two seemingly unrelated theoretical positions will frame my conclusive remarks: media theorist Shane Denson's notion of metabolic images and Brazilian modernist Oswald de Andrade's concept of cultural cannibalism.

In his essay *Crazy Cameras, Discorrelated Images, and the Post-Perceptual Mediation of Post-Cinematic Affect*, Denson writes that with "the shift to a digital and more broadly post-cinematic media environment, moving images have undergone what I term their 'discorrelation' from human embodied subjectivities and (phenomenological, narrative, and visual) perspectives" (Denson 2016: 193). As human sense organs are increasingly outperformed by cameras, sensors, and other digital enhancers, the standard perceptual scene is no longer that between a perceiving organic subject and a perceived image-as-object. Instead, the "interpassivity" (Pfaller 2017) and "interfacticity" (Richir 2004) among images-as-flows, apparatuses, and organisms become the perceptual norm; perception (and, according

---

by Jules Verne. But quite unlike Verne, who always has ordinary French or English gentlemen of leisure travelling around the cosmos in the most amazing vehicles, Scheerbart is interested in inquiring how our telescopes, our airplanes, our rockets can transform human beings as they haven been up to now into completely new, lovable, and interesting creatures" (Benjamin [1933] 1999: 733).

[22]In the middle of the two lies perhaps a novel like *Underworld*, a maximalist novel that in a spectacular epilogue points at the passage from analog reciprocity to digital interconnectedness: "There is no space or time out here, or in here, or wherever she is. There are only connections. Everything is connected. All human knowledge gathered and linked, hyperlinked, this site leading to that, this fact referenced to that, a keystroke, a mouse-click, a password-world without end, amen" (DeLillo 1997: 825).

to Pfaller and arguably Foster Wallace: enjoyment) is delegated from human subjects to post-cinematic machines. The amount of recorded material that is not crafted and remains largely unseen exceeds by far any content that could be grasped by a human subject. With the rise of big data, recognition software and AI image modeling, the idea that it is the video recorder that is watching on our behalf is gradually shifting from metaphor to reality.[23] Media are no longer merely prosthetic extensions of men, but give birth to "new forms of life by modulating the metabolic processes through which organisms [...] are structurally coupled with [...] ecospheres" (Denson 2016: 216).

If an earlier version of this take on digitalization stands behind Riffaterre's fear that hypertextuality might ultimately abandon a disoriented reader in the wilderness of cyberspace, Denson, unsurprisingly, offers a much more positive perspective on what he calls the discorrelation of images from the human senses. If metabolic images tend to be discorrelated from meaning, perception, human experience, narrative, and memory, this doesn't mean they are exempt of agency and responsibility. What they do instead, is to shift the focus toward scales that operate on both micro and macro levels outside of the realm traditionally defined by the grasp of human subjects:

> Finally, these techno-organic processes point us beyond our individual experiences, towards the larger ecologies and imbalances of the Anthropocene. Ultimately, we might speculate, what post-cinema demands of us by means of its discorrelated images is that we learn to take responsibility for our own affective discorrelations—that we develop an ethical and radically post-individual sensibility for the networked dividualities through which computational, endocrinological, socio-political, meteorological, subatomic, and economic agencies are all enmeshed with one another in the metabolic processing and mediation of life today (2016: 216).

Almost a century earlier than Denson, the influential Brazilian modernist poet Oswald de Andrade already explored a metabolic approach to culture, known today under the name of cultural cannibalism: "Cannibalism only unites us. Socially. Economically. Philosophically" (Andrade [1928]

---

[23] "For example, the way some people use their video recorders: they programme these machines with great care when leaving the house in the evening, in spite of the fact that interesting movies are being shown on TV. Back home, the video freaks anxiously check to see if the recording has taken place, and then, with a certain relief, they put the tape on a shelf—without ever watching it. But they have already experienced a deep satisfaction the moment the tape with the recorded movie was taken out of the machine: it was as if the video recorder had watched the movie in their place" (Pfaller 2017: 18–19).

1991: 38). Ironically adopting the perspective of the predator, not the prey, cultural anthropophagy according to Oswald represents a symbolic counterreaction to European settler colonialism. It exploits and appropriates the foreigner to the extent that the cannibalist seeks to become one with her prey in an act of metonymic-metaphoric incorporation: "I asked a man what the law was. He answered that it was the guarantee of the exercise of possibility. That man was called Galli Mathias. I ate him" (1991: 41). If colonial appropriation aims to accumulate possessions, cannibalistic inoculation strives for a physical and spiritual communion with the other, with the crucial difference of incorporating instead of exploiting its otherness, articulating "a participatory consciousness" (1991: 39) "only concerned with what is not mine" (1991: 38). Attacking Occidental values such as thinly disguised rivalry and halfheartedly sublimated violence, Oswald's cannibalism respects the radical difference of its prey, but thinks of it as weaved into one and the same cosmic texture, poking holes into the impermeable "raincoat placed between the inner and outer worlds" (1991: 38). It promotes a face-to-face encounter of predator and prey in which the digestive performance is not only a one-sided act of violent consumption, but transforms both parts of the equation through a complex metabolic process. The anti-occidental values propagated by Oswald, then, are magic, subsistence, ancestrality, and the carnival; his preferred mode of social relation is kinship instead of competition.

In line with the programs of comparable avant-garde writers, one of the manifesto's pinnacles is Oswald's attack on the concept of *memoria*: "Down with memory as a source of custom" (1991: 43). If this does not mean a complete dismissal of historical thinking, it is nevertheless directed against the monumentalization of official history as it is written by its victors. That historiography of the colonial gaze shall be replaced by history as carnivalesque travesty, which operates in the name of a radical political vision defined as a proto-Communist "science of distribution" (1991: 42) and directed against all forms of institutional authoritarianism: "We were never catechized. What we really made was Carnaval. The Indian dressed as senator of the Empire" (1991: 40).

Reading Pynchon's and Bolaño's strategies in this light of metabolic intertextuality and anthropophagic form, they appear as acts of self-delivery, exposing themselves and their semiotic universes to the "vast ocean" (Bolaño [2011] 2013: 3) of literary history and to its contaminatedness with the noise and emissions of intertextual cruft. As such, they transcend the anxiety of influence, replacing the "horror of contamination" (Bloom 1997: xxiv) with a fearless "ecstasy of influence[s]" (Lethem 2007). Intertextual hyper-connectedness, here, is much more invested in reparation than in paranoia; and according to yet another of Bolaño's aesthetic appeals, the only poetic project that deserves to survive is one that lets go of itself to slide "into an asymmetrical well, the well of the great poets, where all that can be heard is [the] voice gradually mingling with other voices" (Bolaño 2004b: 73).

Although working against a background of discorrelation and metabolic images, Pynchon's and Bolaño's aesthetics of intertextuality reveal an even stronger affiliation with Oswald's fantasies of amalgamation than with Denson who writes elsewhere:

> As a "unidirectional change that leaves no memory of its passing", metabolism "does not honor the thresholds that protect the identity of neighboring domains. Instead, it destroys all distance and difference between them as it turns the one into the other". The industrial revolution, as a metabolic transformation, "eroded distinctions between animals and human beings and between living beings and inanimate things", thus outstripping the discursive or "metaphorical" categories by which humans position themselves in the world (Denson 2014: 258).[24]

As we have seen, Oswald too, "does not honor the thresholds that protect the identity of neighboring domains," but his metabolic logic does not efface *all* "memory of its passing." While it is true that metabolic processes outstrip metaphorical interpretations in *2666* and *ATD*, they do not completely abandon the metaphoric and even the mimetic mission of traditional literature. Not exclusively directed against representation nor interpretation, they inject metabolic energy into mimesis and representation, pushing its Euclidean habits toward the fourth dimension (Daalsgard 2011).[25] If those novels reveal a thorough realist tendency as they unfold, it is a realism not satisfied with trusting the laws of classical physics and three-dimensional geometry. In what almost appears as a nostalgic regression, Pynchon and Bolaño, unlike digital natives such as David Foster Wallace, cling to an almost anachronistic concept of literature, making of the novel a shelter for what is threatened with obsolescence in Denson's post-cinematic, post-perceptual world, which is also ours. Their hyperbolically realist aim is thus not merely to mimic the metabolic environment of our digital age, but to reconstruct an eclectic afterlife of analog, metaphoric, and hermeneutic potentials within the new ecological era of the Anthropocene.

---

[24]Denson's quotations refer to Jager (2004).
[25]I adopt the fitting critical metaphor of mimesis in the fourth gear from Rinck (2015: 13).

5

The Visible and the Invisible

The night was an exceptional possibility.
CLARICE LISPECTOR

It's Always Night, or We Wouldn't Need Light

Besides the materialist abundance of signs and things, of the staggering diversity of characters, sprawling plot lines, minutiae-obsessed fabulation, endless name-dropping, enumerative mourning, the proliferation of specialized knowledge and the constant making of worlds, underworlds and counterworlds—*2666* and *ATD* are no less fascinated with darkness, absence, nothingness and negativity, the gaps of perception, knowledge, and even reality itself. Darkness in a very literal sense—as an atmospheric element and light effect that contains a secondary, metaphorical, potential of darkness. A large number of the events in *2666* happen at night;[1] and a search for words would most certainly lead to the result that *dark* is one of the most frequent adjectives in Pynchon's *ATD*.

In both novels, light and darkness or, more generally, the visible and the invisible, as I want to show in this chapter, are placed within remarkably similar economies. Yet, if in both novels obscurity is reliably associated with secrecy, barbarism, violence, and death, it is difficult if not impossible to reconstruct a coherent semantic or symbolic system around the opposition of

---

[1] The most evident example of the night as a privileged time of day in Bolaño's fiction is, as the title already suggests, *By Night in Chile* (Bolaño [2000] 2003). Night, darkness, and darkening as structural metaphors are explicit in Bolaño's story *Last Evenings on Earth* (Bolaño 2006: 131–57).

darkness and light. On first view, Bolaño's obsession with disappearance, both on the semantic and the agential level, strongly resonates with the horrible Latin American phenomenon of the so-called *desaparecidos*, the victims of kidnappings, torture, and assassinations mainly carried out by Right-wing military governments with the support of a complicit social fabric and an aggressively anti-Communist political climate. Elsewhere, however, the act of disappearing as an existential and even ethical mode of entering the dark figures as the last available exit strategy, as a minor act of survival, as a source of temporary relief, and sometimes even as a potential for political resistance.

In *ATD,* the novel's motto, a slightly altered quote from famous jazz pianist Thelonious Monk, anticipates the unequal distribution of light and darkness throughout the book. *It's always night or we wouldn't need light—* according to Monk's motto, most of the novel's events occur in the realm of the dark, the almost invisible, above the clouds and under the surface, *off scene,* beyond, beneath, and besides the well-lit theater of our daily lifeworld.

Another paratext, the novel's title, supports the centrality of light as a theme. It points to a certain privileging of darkness, too. At first glance, the opposition seems to be unequivocal—against the day and in favor of night. But the word *against* plays a much more complex and ambiguous role in the novel. Its oppositional meaning is attenuated where it indicates only resistance, not contrast or contrary; and in a now uncommon usage it can refer to a forward-looking, almost hopeful connotation in the sense of *towards*. And even if it seems a bit exaggerated, one can discern an element of repetition (*again*) in the leading preposition of the title (*against*).

Apart from the title, *ATD* as an explicit expression appears only twice in the whole novel. The first occurrence refers to the ambivalence of sunlight, which is on the one hand a necessary condition of appearance and perception, but can also serve as perceptual obstacle; for example, when one tries to take a photograph against the light. In a turning of the phrase with obvious Melville-inspired undertones, the narrator lays out Frank's difficulties to Stray's "face veiled in its own penumbra" as it is set "against the daylight flowing in off the plain ... afraid somehow of misreading it, the brow smoothed by the uncertain light" (*ATD* 205).

The second occurrence (from a purist's perspective the only one) is much more mystical than this one, which is not really in danger to mistake an illuminated brow for a full-fledged human face. It is tied to the ecological climax of the novel, the Tunguska event, which hovers like a bad omen over the end of the nineteenth century. Embedded in late colonialist competition and geopolitical turmoil, the so-called Tunguska event will soon release the century's accumulated energies into a magnitude of violence that was previously unheard and unknown. As the ominous weather phenomenon slowly fades out, "most had difficulty remembering the earlier rise of heart, the sense of overture and possibility, and went back once again to seeking only orgasm, hallucination, stupor, sleep, to fetch them through the night and prepare them against the day" (*ATD*: 805).

There's a crucial change of direction in this second paragraph: not simply against, but toward the day—the day understood as an existential unit of measurement in which the characters must prove their ground. Late in the novel, the night has lost its earlier aura as a kairotic state of exception in which a "sense of overture and possibility" reigns. Instead, it becomes the part of the day one needs to survive with the help of sexual debauchery, mental deviation, and corporeal shutdown (stupor, sleep). At the same time, it remains a source for some of the characters to recharge their energy reserves, which they need to "prepare them against the day."

We should not halt at this fundamental symbolic and semantic ambiguities of light and darkness, day and night in both novels, but examine the poetic infrastructure underneath the ways in which this ambiguity unfolds. Adopting a phenomenological mode of analysis, then, promises a better grasp of the complex relation between the visible and the invisible in *2666* and *ATD*. In this chapter, my aim is therefore to do more and less than a more orthodox hermeneutic approach would probably attempt to do. More modestly than hermeneutics, I want to retrace the qualities and forms, temporalities, and rhythms according to which the visible and invisible is organized and distributed across these poetic texts. But beyond the hermeneutic task and with the help of *phenomenological* nuance, I will try to formulate a few *speculative* hypotheses about the embedded *realism* in Bolaño's and Pynchon's evocation of flickering lights in an otherwise pitch-black universe.

Flickering Lights in Otherwise Perfect Darkness

Let us begin with a few eye-catching examples from *2666*: One character makes out "three shadowy figures" in "semidarkness [*semioscuridad*]" (*2666*: 168), two others make love "at her express request, in semidarkness [*semipenumbra*]" (424). When Morini and Johns sit down for their showdown in the strenuously sublime ambience of the Swiss alps, they are "rodeados de penumbra" (2004a: 124), encircled by darkness. Assisting to a box fight in Santa Teresa, Oscar Fate, the main protagonist of Part III, tries to get a clear look at the opponents, "but the lights, focused on the ring, left the upper part of the hall in darkness" (*2666*: 308). A bit earlier in the novel, he had been struck by a hyperbolic tattoo depicting a scene where "at least ten angels in female form came flying out of ... darkness and vague shapes" (*2666*: 274). And quite a bit later, rushing through the nights with Chucho Flores and Rosa Mendez, Fate is more and more overcome with nausea and exhaustion, but "he didn't want to close his eyes and instead he kept scanning the lot, the two streetlights in front of the motel, the shadows dispersed by the flashes of car lights like comet tails in the dark [*semejantes a colas de cometas, en los alrededores oscuros*]" (2666: 340).

This short and gleefully incomplete selection contains predominant elements of the typical lighting conditions in 2666. Darkness and shadows are ubiquitous, but even where they dominate the visible scenery to the extreme, "vague forms" and weakly flickering lights persist. Darkness is not the abstract opposite of brightness, but surrounds the visible as a pulsating halo, constantly reminding us that there is so much more out there than what we actually see. More importantly, darkness is the fundamental condition that something becomes visible in the first place. What appears, does not necessarily appear to someone (at least not in the sense of a full-blown, conscious subjectivity), but often as if autonomously, abruptly, and ephemerally, like "comet tails in the dark," before it disappears again or gets replaced by new appearances.

The high frequency of words like *semioscuridad* and *semipenumbra* in 2666 indicates that instead of complete presence or total absence of light, it is the twilight which is the novel's preferred mode of illumination. Sure, 2666 does provide exemplary moments of epiphany, as the one experienced by Oscar Fate during a jazz concert in Santa Teresa (2666: 308), but the same or even more attention is usually spent on the darkness surrounding those epiphanic moments of time-freezing *evidentia*.

The similarities to the lighting conditions in Pynchon's *ATD* are striking. Not only characters, but items as insignificant as a telephone cord are said to trail "out the door into the scarcely lit darkness" (*ATD*: 107). In the twilight of the Belgian city of Bruges, street lamps are lit up "against a hovering shadow of beleaguerment by forces semi-visible" (*ATD*: 529). Even in daylight, most figures and shapes look "sinister" (*ATD*: 329) or want to disappear from the realm of visibility "to rejoin the Invisible" as nameless remembrances (*ATD*: 107). Lew, the talented spy, displays "a keen sympathy for the invisible" (*ATD*: 43) whereas for Merle, photography and alchemy belong to each other as they are "redeeming light from the inertia of precious metals" (*ATD*: 80). Hunter argues that people come to Venice because of nothing else but the city's "'chiaroscuro'" (*ATD*: 582), Lindsay—cold, frugal, and austere—lets himself be carried away by the mystical idea "that light might be the *secret determinant of history*" (*ATD*: 431). And not only during their polar mission do the Chums of Chance confirm the novel's nocturnal phenomenology and its surplus of everything unseen: "Whatever it was, it was invisible" (*ATD*: 142).

It is not hard to recognize in these and innumerable other examples that night and darkness are the rule to which light is clearly the exception. As Pynchon's narrator (like elsewhere in his work) often adapts to the conditions of the setting and atmosphere from which the characters emerge, the reign of the almost-invisible seems less consistent than in Bolaño's case where similar phrases and turns often appear at different and seemingly unrelated moments in the narrative. But in *ATD*, too—no matter if we are in a foggy and mysterious Venice, or in Mexico where rumoring sounds from the invisible parts of the city allude to the revolutionary underground, or in a spectacularly wired and electrified Chicago during the World's Columbian Exhibition in 1893—the novel demonstrates the same "sympathy for the invisible" (*ATD*: 43) that Lew Basnight, the British private detective who works for the infamous spy agency called Pinkertons, needs for his profession.

Lew is one of many characters who are intimately linked to the topic of light and who prefer invisibility to presence and positivity. As an assistant of Nikola Tesla, Kit Traverse is fascinated by the invisible forces behind the electric impulse; Merle Rideout compares photography to alchemy, knowing that the creation of photographic immateriality depends on the very material use of "precious metals" (*ATD*: 80); and the painter Hunter Penhallow fittingly describes Venice in art-historical terms as *chiaroscuro*, a painting technique that hyperbolically amplifies darkness to produce an even sharper lighting effect.

Things, characters, or even entire cities and islands suddenly disappear, first from the map, then from the world itself—only to "*emerge...* [again] *from invisibility*" (*ATD*: 62), often unintentionally, before they "rejoin the Invisible" (*ATD*: 107) again until further notice. This fate also befalls a short-living character fittingly called Blinky. He disappears right at the time the scientists Michelson and Morley run their famous, eponymous experiment, which proved that light is not dependent upon a substance or specific medium to spread and radiate.

From a cosmological point of view, the Michelson-Morley experiment marks the end of the ether (*ATD*: 62) as a generally accepted medium of physical process and is thus a landmark moment in the transition from classical to modern physics. After the death of the ether, there is nothing left but light, albeit in its by now familiar dual character as waves and particles. The mystery is thus not completely abolished, as showed by the penultimate quote on my list above. Esoteric convictions, superstition, and the search for the transcendent, the secret, the magical, and the mystical stubbornly persist within the more and more fact-oriented fabric of the modern world and shape the characters' deepest desires and motivations.

The last quote, finally, corresponds to a structure mentioned earlier in this book, the fact that something is happening, *somehow, anyhow* (Rosset 1977; Lowry [1947] 1971), although it is not altogether clear what is happening and how it is happening. Spectral presence in *ATD* certainly relates to some of Pynchon's exploited literary genres, especially the already familiar gothic and the horror genre, which was only emerging at the time. Whateverness, especially in its invisible form, becomes a source of reality in its extremes, connecting the sublime and transcendent with the seemingly opposite pole of the uneventful banal.

In a first attempt of summarizing, Pynchon's and Bolaño's remarkably similar vision of light and darkness can be described as stereoscopic. It is a vision that juxtaposes enigmatic and mystical elements that contain a deep metaphoric potential with extremely casual, seemingly banal, and trivial occurrences. The word *semipenumbra* in *2666* can thus be used to describe both a fateful turning point and a ridiculously prudish sex scene: "They made love, at her express request, in semidarkness" (*2666*: 424).

Light in *ATD* and *2666* flickers not only through darkness and the invisible as its general medium, but also between the phenomenal and the ontological realm, between being and appearance. The erratic distribution of the visible in both novels constantly alludes to a profound discontinuity in the realms of perception, matter, and existence. In *ATD*, the shift from phenomenological irregularity to ontological discontinuity is most clearly performed at the passage from the second to the third part of the novel, from the doubling of perception through the powerful *Iceland Spar* to the gift or curse of *Bilocation*, the dubious talent to appear at two different places at the exact same time.

The Visible and the Invisible in Richir and Merleau-Ponty

Conceptions of presence and absence in philosophy and theory often seem to be caught in a one-sided preference for one of both sides. At best, they search for some kind of dialectical solution, which, as I shall argue, fails to come to terms with the fine-grained textures that the visible and the invisible weave in our lifeworld. In his final project, interrupted by his unexpected death in 1961, Maurice Merleau-Ponty thus pursued a decidedly non-dialectical strategy. As we work ourselves through the four completed chapters and some 200 pages of working notes of his posthumously published *The Visible and the Invisible*, we assist to the fascinating genesis of a project that had "the origin of truth" (Merleau-Ponty [1964] 1968: 164) as one of his working titles; a project that is not only simultaneously interested in phenomenological and ontological issues, but resonates in remarkable ways with the conditions of light and (in)visibility in *2666* and *ATD*.

In Chapter 4, *The Intertwining—The Chiasm*, for many commentators the most important chapter of the book, Merleau-Ponty states that our body as well as other things in the world all "involve clear zones, clearings, about which pivot their opaque zones, and the primary visibility, that of the *quale* and of the things, does not come without a second visibility, that of the lines of force and dimensions" (1968: 148). Just like in our novels' phenomenology of light, the visible in Merleau-Ponty is surrounded by darkness; darkness not as an unchangeable substance, but as a productive medium. The possessive pronoun is a crucial detail, as Merleau-Ponty's invisibility does not merely mean the absence of phenomenality, but is an integral part of the dynamic process of phenomenalization. What surrounds the "clear zones [of] primary visibility" is thus not invisibility as such, but *their* invisibility, not absolute emptiness, but "specific voids" (1968: 239). By way of temporalization and spatialization, these voids and spots of absence can be turned into new foci of visibility, which in turn create new and varied "opaque zones." Any invisible can thus chance its character to become a center of visible presence, but—beware—the invisible is still "not another visible … a positive only *absent*" (1968: 251). It is an independent force instead, a conveyor of "lines of force and dimensions," which is nevertheless always related or at least relatable to the world of appearances. What is invisible now, may become visible in the next moment, but not without producing its own new invisible environment. No act of vision can thus abolish the invisible, but nothing exists, which is invisible in itself; there is no absolute or metaphysical *Verborgenheit* that is not in one way or another affected by phenomenalization.

The invisible that Merleau-Ponty is trying to come to terms with is therefore

> not a *de facto* invisible, like an object hidden behind another, and not an absolute invisible, which would have nothing to do with the visible. Rather it is the invisible *of* this world, that which inhabits this world, sustains it, and renders it visible, its own and interior possibility, the Being of this being (1968: 151).[2]

Neither merely empirical ("a positive only *absent*," 1968: 151) nor absolute transcendence, but dwelling beyond, beneath, and in-between, Merleau-Ponty's figuration of the invisible comes very close to this book's conception of the hyperbolic. Both figures point toward a register that exceeds the visible in all possible directions and dimensions ("the visible is pregnant with the invisible," 1968: 216) by surrounding and conditioning it. Both figures gesture beyond language, but from the field of language itself—not into an abstract realm of mystical anti-language, but toward a concrete pre-linguistic or proto-linguistic *khôra* out of which radiates articulation, a space whose task "consists in restoring a power to signify, a birth of meaning, or a wild meaning" (1968: 155). This space comes close

---

[2] "non pas donc un invisible de fait, comme un objet caché derrière un autre, et non pas un invisible absolu, qui n'aurait rien à faire avec le visible, mais l'invisible de ce monde, celui qui l'habite, le soutient et le rend visible, sa possibilité intérieure et propre, l'Être de cet étant" (Merleau-Ponty 1964: 196).

to the space of fiction, understood as the preferred milieu and laboratory of "unemployed" (Bataille [1937] 1988: 90) figuration: "Literature, music, the passions, but also the experience of the visible world are—no less than is the science of Lavoisier and Ampere—the exploration of an invisible and the disclosure of a universe of ideas" (Merleau-Ponty [1964] 1968: 149).

Writing, art, desire, physics, chemistry, and lived experience drawn together on one and the same level, weaved into a texture where the invisible, the intellectual, and the adventurous play leading roles—one can hardly think of a better context to circumscribe the hyperbolic modes through which a hyperbolic reality is made tangible in 2666 and *ATD*. Here and there, invisibility is not fetishized as dark irrationality, but exerts a constant and powerful influence on the visible world. It challenges the concept of presence in philosophy and that of representation in literature in order to make space for an articulation of experience from the perspective of experience itself, a perspective that reflexively integrates "our own obscurity" and the "opacity of my life" (1968: 39 and 56). As opposed against every discourse of the absolute, Merleau-Ponty's project should neither be confounded with the existentialist celebration of nothingness—Sartre is a constant adversary especially in the *notes de travail*—nor with a dialectical negotiation of the visible and the invisible, positivity and negativity. Between these two alternatives, Merleau-Ponty's late phenomenology maps out a fluid and self-reflexive system of constant displacement, an integral composition of decentered sequences that fall out of sight, but never disappear fully and without leaving a trace (1968: 193).

However, to get to the point that Merleau-Ponty could only suggest, we need to go one step further. Despite its audacity, especially considering the historical moment, Merleau-Ponty's project is still seeking for closure and some kind of organic totality, aiming eventually at "a sort of *hyper-reflection (sur-réflexion)* that would also take itself and the changes it introduces into the spectacle into account" (1968: 38).

It is precisely such an organic—or even romantic—conception of philosophy that the Belgian phenomenologist Marc Richir criticizes and transcends in his radicalization of Merleau-Ponty and the rest of the phenomenological tradition. According to Richir, accessing "the brute thing and brute perception" (1968: 38) is not as evident as it seems for his older predecessor precisely because there are no such things as purely given phenomenality and immediate, undistorted perception. Instead, a crack runs through appearance and phenomenality itself, as "every phenomenon is affected by an *originary distortion*" (Richir [1982] 1993: 69):

> If there is being, it can only be in a sort of originating mingling with non-being (cf. VI 89), which constitutes perceptual faith as much as what we have called the feint of the phenomenon in itself, where truth and error are intrinsically tied and mixed together. To change the phenomenon into

a full, wild being is to cut it off from its irreducible share in non-being and non-truth, to make an *ontological fiction* of it insofar as the truth of the phenomenon is changed into fiction as soon as its share of truth is taken unilaterally, without its share of non-truth, which, being embedded in it, brings alive and gives consistency to its share of truth (1993: 66–7).

We do not need to make sense of each and every turn in Richir's highly speculative, technical, and often tedious reflections. However, if one is ready to plunge into his philosophical cosmos, the rewards are substantial. In the passage above—apart from the promising reconceptualization of the phenomenon as wild being (*être brut et plein*) and ontological fiction, which I will explore more in depth in a later stage of this book—the take on both nature and appearance (which is, of course, a part of nature) is still more radical than in Merleau-Ponty's late works. More radical because the phenomenon in Richir's philosophy is not merely conditioned by its invisible surroundings, but internally tied to what is non-existent and untrue *inside* them.

Within the phenomenological tradition, Richir marks a fourth decisive stage in the evolution of the concept of the phenomenon itself (Gondek & Tengelyi 2011). If Husserl saw the phenomenon as that which is unmistakably present to a consciousness stripped of all contaminations by its natural attitude, if Heidegger saw the phenomenon basically as an ontic illusion that veils the true ontological being that must be uncovered by the analytic of *Dasein*, and if Merleau-Ponty finally, described the phenomenon as complex intermingling of the visible and the invisible, Richir's conception of the phenomenon is modeled on a type of representation that is even wilder and even more brute. For Richir, the model of appearance is not that of a troubled vision or a vision enriched by the imagination, that is, the nonseen. Instead, Richir's preferred phenomenalization is located in a register he calls *phantasia* (Schnell 2011: 97), where the phenomena are almost irreal, subjected to a largely unpredictable rhythm of appearance, disappearance, and re-appearance, "erupting in discontinuous manners" (Richir 2000: 312), flickering as "Protean, fleeting, fluctuating and intermittent flashes [*clignotement*]" (2000: 148) through otherwise perfect darkness.

Santa Teresa as *Centro Intermitente* of *2666*

In *2666*, intermittent appearance is not only an important feature of the novel's compositional rhythm, it has one early moment of glory in the spotlight of the long and winding course of events. At a congress in Bremen, the four protagonists of the first part, experts of Archimboldi's literature from non-German-speaking countries, finally all meet, sharing gossip and speculations "about the secret of the great writer's whereabouts and life like people endlessly analyzing a favorite movie," strolling through "the wet, bright streets (bright only intermittently, as if Bremen were a machine jolted every so often by brief, powerful electric charges)" (2666: 13).

Bolaño does not wait until the novel moves to Mexico to introduce us to intermittence as a dominant mode of appearance in his novel. In retrospect, this introduction will seem even more effective as it is embedded in a scene and setting determined by an almost extreme form of ordinariness. The fact that intermittence is brought to our attention in a mid-sized city in Northern Germany during a seemingly uneventful night suggests that semidarkness and semivisibility are not limited to the description of a specific milieu, but play a structuring role for the novel's implicit phenomenology and even its underlying ontology. Even in Bremen, light is flashing and flickering, hectically, as the bold and somewhat strained metaphor of the city as "a machine jolted every so often by brief, powerful electric charges" establishes an early ambience of uncanniness. Even within the most peaceful situations in 2666, there is a remaining potential that what is supposed to be normal and ordinary is suddenly interrupted, suspending, at least intermittently, its ordinariness and normalcy.

Intermittence as dominant mode of appearance evokes another world than the reign of total absence or darkness, which is all too often suggested by Bolaño's commentators to be the favorite atmosphere of his narratives. In his influential afterword to the novel, Bolaño's editor at Anagrama, Ignacio Echevarría, speculates about a note left by the author:

> In one of his many notes for 2666, Bolaño indicates the existence in the work of a "hidden center," concealed beneath what might be considered the novel's "physical center." There is reason to think that this physical center is the city of Santa Teresa, faithful reflection of Ciudad Juarez, on the Mexican-U.S. border. There the five parts of the novel ultimately converge; there the crimes are committed that comprise its spectacular backdrop (and that are said by one of the novel's characters to contain "the secret of the world"). As for the "hidden center" … might it not represent 2666 itself, the date upon which the whole novel rests? (2666: 896–7).

It is tempting to fully subscribe to Echevarria's witty description, but we have good reasons to be cautious about it. First, if Santa Teresa is indeed an only thinly veiled version of the real Ciudad Juárez, the mere fact that it is renamed indicates at least a minimal distance from the physical site at the Mexican-US border. Also, Santa Teresa is not merely the "spectacular backdrop" (*telón de fondo*) of the novel's events, but moves in and out of the narrator's focus in an almost agential fashion, flickering between appearance and disappearance just like any other character of the novel.

Concerning the enigmatic number that gives the novel its title, to say that "2666" is the novel's hidden center (*centro oculto*) does not have a lot of analytical value. Sure, in Bolaño's novella *Amulet,* the hyperbolic number indicates a dystopian date (Bolaño [1999] 2006a: 86), but there is no textual evidence that it is used with the same intention in his maximalist masterpiece. The meaning of 2666 remains mysterious, so much so that we should probably not see it as a metatextual promise holding together the five disparate parts, but more as a reminder that every effort to subsume the novel's heterogeneous material under a common denominator must inevitably fail. Besides, there are other centers, physical and hidden at the same time, in 2666: Archimboldi, most importantly; the *feminicidios* and their breeding ground, patriarchy; art, literature, and the possibility of writing; or less obvious candidates such as the long history of colonial oppression and its continuation through neo-colonial practice, to which Bolaño obliquely alludes at various occasions.[3] Yet, as even the fifth part is loosely connected to Santa Teresa, it makes indeed sense to speak of it as *a* center of the novel, though not as its *centro oculto,* but as its *centro intermitente.*

This makes even more sense if we look at how Bolaño narrates the disappearance and re-appearance of the women's murdered bodies all across Part IV. With a surprisingly reliable frequency, they are found in conditions of *semioscuridad*, in scarcely lit, peripheral areas of the city—areas where the hostile Sonoran Desert gnaws at urban construction. Those bodies are not completely hidden from public sight; they are often rather easy to spot—at the end of a street or next to the road where they have been dumped with little effort by their perpetrators. That they remain nevertheless undiscovered, often for a considerable amount of time, alludes to the atmosphere of fear, intimidation, and sometimes blunt ignorance that reigns in Santa Teresa, which also suggests that intermittence and flickering phenomenality are not merely "natural" modes of appearance, but intensified by "culture" and specific socioeconomic conditions.

When the corpses are found by the police, they are "half hidden behind some cardboard boxes" (2666: 461) or "half buried in a decumbent position" (2666: 462) and often almost completely naked. Found "in a complex state of decomposition" (2666: 549) or with a "mutilated face" (2666: 507), the corpses are notoriously hard to identify. Both the investigating detectives and the novel's readers, two roles often identified in Bolaño's work, do not face complete invisibility or absence. Instead, they are confronted with the challenge to reconstruct from extremely precarious traces the approximate

---

[3]Most prominently in two memorable scenes: 1) in the passages about the hyperbolic/impossible, but actually existing book of a racist Chilean writer (2666: 216–25), and 2) in the passages narrating the sad family tree of Lalo Cura whose female ancestors are all called *María Expósito* and have all been raped by Europeans or descendants of Europeans (2666: 554–8).

circumstances of the events. The phenomenal material from which this reconstruction must depart is precisely that of Richir's wild beings, flickering phenomena in otherwise perfect darkness.

The responsible authorities, the investigating detectives, the media, and the larger public all fail to come to terms with these crimes as they refuse to see them as the visible outcome of an underlying systemic violence. The ridiculous search for a single serial killer reduces the *feminicidios* to a spectacular singularity that will be solved once the suspect is arrested. But since the crimes are intermittent outbursts of a rotten systemic structure, this is not how the problem is solved. The failure to acknowledge the complexity of the reality behind the murders plays into the hands of those with an interest to cover up its real causes. As the novel unfolds, almost everybody seems to be part of a huge cartel of accomplices: not only the notorious *narcos,* but also politicians, both local and national, multinational concerns, the police, the press, the law, the university, cultural institutions and even the art world, and, finally, literature.[4]

In fact, 2666 itself should not be freed from the charge of complicity, and we should not too hastily dismiss expressed concerns about the novel's exploitation and reproduction of violence and suffering as spectacle. But no matter how one might feel about those reservations, we can also understand such a risked complicity as a crucial element of the novel's performative strategy. Seen in that way, it would be one function of that hyperbolic accumulation of female victims, that tedious enumeration of murder cases, to make those crimes painfully tangible to an extent that they test and eventually exhaust the reader's patience. To make the reader stop reading must then be seen as one among many aesthetic dimensions offered by this novel and especially its fourth part. The enumerative mode is aptly called hyperbolic because it only seems endless, but makes unmistakably clear that there are always more crimes, more violence, and more murders outside of its scope. The feeling of endlessness combined with the evidence of finitude and limitedness is one of many signatures of the hyperbolic. From the very beginning of Part IV, Bolaño makes it unmistakably clear that this is the mode in which he tries to come to terms with the overwhelming phenomenon of the *feminicidios*:

> This happened in 1993. January 1993. From then on, the killings of women began to be counted. But it's likely there had been other deaths before. The name of the first victim was Esperanza Gomez Saldana and she was thirteen. Maybe for the sake of convenience, maybe because she

---

[4] The tragic complicity of literature with structures and systems of violence is a major theme of Bolaño's work, most prominently in *Nazi Literature in the Americas* (Bolaño [1996] 2008), but almost as intensely in *Estrella Distante* (Bolaño 1996) and *Nocturno de Chile* (Bolaño 2000).

was the first to be killed in 1993, she heads the list. Although surely there were other girls and women who died in 1992. Other girls and women who didn't make it onto the list or were never found, who were buried in unmarked graves in the desert or whose ashes were scattered in the middle of the night, when not even the person scattering them knew where he was, what place he had come to (2666: 444).[5]

The beginning of the list is as arbitrary as its end. The visible part of the registered violence seems already excessive, almost overwhelmingly so, and no documentary act, no effort of recording, could ever hope to fully comprehend the extent of its horror. Nevertheless, we must begin with the scarce visibility that is given to us, even if those who have scattered the victims' ashes across the desert seem to ignore where to find the unmarked graves of those who did not make it onto the list.

Despite their tediousness, Bolaño's epic repetitions reserve a space for the singularity of each crime and each victim. One method to ensure such a singularity lies in the use of horrible details even if they are often mentioned casually and *en passant*: "Her body had been dropped into a fifty-gallon drum of corrosive acid. Only her hands and feet were still whole. Identification was possible thanks to her silicone implants" (2666: 516). Immediately afterwards, we learn that the victim in question has been raped and murdered by no less than seventeen men. After they killed her, the perpetrators tried to destroy her organic shape by dropping her body into a large container filled with acid, but the serial number of her inorganic silicone implants makes it possible to identify her in the end. In an almost unbearably acerbic way, Bolaño alludes to an economy thriving on institutionalized sexism that is one of the major factors driving the profoundly misogynistic violence in Santa Teresa.

If it seems already difficult to increase the extent of cruelty evoked in this scene, another case poses an even tougher challenge to the tolerance level of the reader. It is the case of an unnamed girl, "ten years old, more or less" (2666: 501). Her fragile corpse is retrieved from a small valley, dumped like so many others after having been "stabbed eight times, three times in the chest"; one police officer, in a moment of rare compassion, starts to cry, while others speculate that the brown-haired girl, "lighter where it fell over

---

[5]"Esto ocurrió en 1993. En enero de 1993. A partir de esta muerta comenzaron a contarse los asesinatos de mujeres. Pero es probable que antes hubiera otras. La primera muerta se llamaba Esperanza Gómez Saldaña y tenía trece años. Pero es probable que no fuera la primera muerta. Tal vez por comodidad, por ser la primera asesinada en el año 1993, ella encabeza la lista. Aunque seguramente en 1992 murieron otras. Otras que quedaron fuera de la lista o que jamás nadie las encontró, enterradas en fosas comunes en el desierto o esparcidas sus cenizas en medio de la noche, cuando ni el que siembra sabe en dónde, en qué lugar se encuentra" (Bolaño 2004a: 444).

her forehead, as if it had been dyed" (501), may not be from Santa Teresa after all. Her description is sent to police stations in Mexico, but without any result, the case like the overwhelming majority of all cases, soon gets closed.

So let us hold on for a moment. The dead girl is ten years old; she is therefore the youngest victim of Bolaño's dismal catalogue of murdered women. If her unbelievably low age and the fact that she was stabbed no less than eight times before being dumped into some deserted valley was not enough, one by then familiar sentence conveys what is perhaps the most horrifying scrap of information of the whole novel: "Nadie fue a reclamarla" (Bolaño 2004a: 627). The narrator is stating this with the same tranquility familiar for his forensic expression. But how can we accept that among all those unclaimed bodies there is a ten-year-old girl with no name and no identity? "What was she doing there? How had she come there? That they didn't say." The answer is: we cannot and should not accept it. Bolaño seems to present this particularly horrendous case as one among many others to urge us to actively seek out its singularity. In his typical use of intermittent appearance, the case of the ten-year-old girl is hiding out in plain sight within the narrative, overshadowed by the stultifying repetitiveness of an endless sequence of misogynistic *feminicidios*.

By his masterful use of minutiae, Bolaño creates intimacy in the midst of forensic impersonality. The detailed description of the girl's hair color, the allure of her transparent plastic sandals as if she had been playing in a backyard or on a playground before she was kidnapped, the crying policeman, and, eventually, the use of the diminutive in the Spanish original (*cuerpito, zapatillas*), all those elements conspire to produce a subtle deviation from the narrator's apparent neutrality. It is this intermittent yet shocking appearance of minutiae which produces the dismal epiphany of a fragile corpse, now aggressively tied to a stretcher in order to be retrieved from its ignoble grave.

Such examples demonstrate that 2666 aims both beyond strictly documentary procedures *and* beyond narrative strategies that limit themselves to illustrate collective tragedies through individual destinies. Instead, Bolaño's preferred type of a maximalist novel attempts to account for both: the abundant and systemic violence, on the one hand, *and* the singularity of each event and victim, on the other. Bolaño's narrator moves both ways: either they start from the general picture and go on to insert little details; or they start with a few visible traces and try to rescue as much as possible from what remains. Both ways, the distribution of the visible and the invisible is both a hindrance and a condition of coming to terms with the complexity of this task.

The novel thus makes room for a reality beyond immediate and subjective experience and moves beyond the classical mode of narrating violence in Latin America, namely the tradition of *testimonio*. *Testimonio* presupposes the existence of a witness; on her survival, her presence and her ability to speak. In Santa Teresa, many times these preconditions are not met. The recurring formula "there were no witnesses" (*2666*: 392, 455, 583) almost reads like a fatalist mantra that accompanies the failure of the legal system as it tries or not tries to deal with the hyperbolic problem of the *feminicidios*. A lawyer complains about "trials ... being postponed, about the evidence lost, the witnesses coerced" (*2666*: 603), and most of the forensic reports conclude with some version of another mantra: "and the case was soon closed" (*2666*: 390, 501, and many more). But while legal cases can be closed, no meaningful closure can be enacted on what goes on in real life.

In that sense, the tedious repetitiveness and tiring abundance of Part IV is not only a stylistic choice, but touches the reader with the authority of an epic necessity. In his book about the genocidal regime of the Khmer Rouge, Cambodian filmmaker Rithy Panh writes: "I'm repeating myself, but repetition is indispensable when the subject of your investigation is a great crime" (Panh 2013: 132). If the extreme monotony in *La parte de los crímenes* challenges the reader's patience to the extreme, it is because it attests to a sublime manifestation of the real and forces us to pay attention to it with an intensity by far exceeding that of watching the news or listening to individual stories and witness reports. The danger of the numbing effects of the repetitive style is always there, but maximalist reading makes of the chapter a performative experience against the normalization of horror. In a short, typically casual conversation, two policemen come to the conclusion that the smell of "blood and semen" is indeed pretty bad, but one still ends up getting used to it. That makes it altogether different from "the smell of decomposing flesh, which you never get used to and which worms its way into your head, even into your thoughts" (*2666*: 531).

Conversations like this one, often wantonly or inadvertently cynical, frame the police reports. This one reads like an oblique appeal to the reader: don't get accustomed by the smell of blood, semen, and alcohol; read on, be patient, and stay attentive to both the systemic structure and the individualizing details of these hyperbolic crimes.

In her programmatic essay to which I referred in Chapter 1 of this book, Spivak claims that without a broad view on both past and present "we can neither mourn nor judge" (Spivak 2012: 6). Bolaño's aim in *2666*, not only in Part IV but throughout the whole book, is to create the conditions that enable such a broad view on the events in Santa Teresa. The violence behind the *feminicidios* is not explained away through a vague gesture toward a near-metaphysical outburst of barbaric energy, but intricately tied to the conditions of life and production under late millennial capitalism at a prominent global (semi)periphery (Deckard 2012).

The *copia* of Part IV, which is only the most visible part of a general overabundance at the heart of this poetic project, is not the outcome of a hysterical subject's urge to over-perform, but the compelling result of the novel's epic commitment to near-completeness. At the same time, this epic obligation is transplanted into a post-metaphysical, post-classical environment where closure is no longer an option. The exhaustive description of a global whole is replaced by the broad engagement with the planetary past, present, and future—if there is one.

In *Totality and Infinity,* Emmanuel Levinas, another phenomenologist on good terms with hyperbole (Fifield 2013: 141–59), writes: "If totality can not be constituted it is because Infinity does not permit itself to be integrated" (Levinas [1961] 1979: 80). We can read this as both a mathematical claim and an aesthetic one. Bolaño's specific use of detail in conjunction with exhausting repetitiveness allows glimpses into a larger structure of violence, which is produced by an alliance of global corporate capital, culturally anchored *machismo,* dysfunctional institutions, and the complicit silence of the public sphere. But the whole reality in which this larger structure is embedded remains ultimately uncontainable, larger than what an act of narration could ever hope to grasp. Hyperbole is the aesthetic and ethical figure of this complex cosmology; intermittence, in Richir's radicalization of Merleau-Ponty, its phenomenological mode of appearance. Together they create more than a "literature of exhaustion" (Barth [1967] 1995b: 161–78); they create a literature that exhausts us: cognitively, emotionally, and morally.

Perfect Darkness and Capitalist Sorcery in *ATD*

Let me conclude this chapter with Pynchon's insight that the act of synchronizing with the rhythms of intermittent appearance not only leads to a more complex view of reality, but also promises to provide tools to control it. The second part of *ATD, Iceland Spar,* is particularly committed to models of perception that reach beyond the classical paradigm of linear experience in a well-lit, three-dimensional world. Halfway through the chapter, we meet a minor but eccentric character, the Italian magician Luca Zombini, in his New York apartment where he initiates his kids into the phenomenology of wizardry.

According to Zombini, God's first act was not to make light, but "to *allow light in* to what had been Nothing." As he unrolls an expensive fabric of "absolute fluid blackness," he urges his kids to always remember to "work with the light." The pitch-black blanket soon appears as a perfectly inverted mirror that fully absorbs instead of reflecting everything back. "Because if the smallest amount of light you can think of bounces off one single thread, the whole act—*affondato, vero?* It's all about the light, you control the light, you control the effect, *capisci?*" (*ATD:* 354).

In this giggly little scene, neither the references to God and the Old Testament nor the allusions to capitalism (import of commodities, trade secrets, factory inspections, cheap invisible labor underlying the production of luxury goods, etc.) are coincidental. But what seems even more conspicuous is the fact that here the one who's sovereign over the light effect is not a typical Pynchon villain (elusive, charismatic, and vicious characters like Pierce Inverarity in *Crying of Lot 49* or Weissmann/Blicero in *Gravity's Rainbow*), but the minor and rather lovable trick wizard Luca Zombini. In *ATD*, that role is occupied by Scarsdale Vibe, a New York-based tycoon and relentless entrepreneur (any resemblances to a contemporary businessman and wannabe president are of course purely accidental). Among Scarsdale's eccentric hobbies are the collecting of rare Italian Renaissance art objects and the waging of war against insubordinate anarchists in mining areas like Colorado. He is the epitome of a capitalist wizard who masters the art of intermittent disappearance with the help of Foley Walker, a talented stooge who also serves as Scarsdale's temporary doppelganger (*ATD*: 724).

Early on in the book, Vibe and a complicit professor at Yale discuss ways of neutralizing Nikola Tesla's plans to make electricity a freely available public good, a project he defines as "the most terrible weapon the world has seen, designed to destroy not armies or matériel, but the very nature of exchange, our Economy's long struggle to evolve up out of the fish-market anarchy" (*ATD*: 34). Scarsdale points at one of the most dominating themes of the novel: the conflict between anarchism denounced as irrational and the various interlocking mechanisms of control, disguised as rational systems of order.[6] As the action unfolds, it becomes more and more clear that those systems of control and subjugation are not only based on multi-dimensional violence, structural deprivation, and colonial-imperialist patterns of exploitation, but they also depend on a wide range of secret micro-operations. Against Scarsdale's praise of global capitalism's rationality, the novel exposes the malicious orchestration of the illusionistic light effects enacted by a whole "system of sorcery without sorcerers (thinking of themselves as such), a system operating in a world which judges that sorcery is only a simple 'belief,' a superstition that therefore doesn't necessitate any adequate means of protection" (Pignarre & Stengers [2005] 2011: 40).

As we all know, capitalism loves to portray itself as a rational, enlightened, and enlightening system against all forms of backward superstition and for the benefit of all; the famous trickle-down effect is also supposed to work in the realm of cognition and knowledge. Yet, in *ATD* capitalism and its allied subsystems of control are much closer to structures that the Iranian philosopher Reza Negarestani calls *occultures* (2008: 26–7). The

---

[6]Toward the end of the novel, however, the contrast between anarchism and corporate control is almost dissolved when Scarsdale predicts a future of capitalism as the dark realization of a radical anarchist's wet dream, where "race will degenerate into silence" and "money will beget money ... and bring low all before it" (*ATD*: 1001).

phenomenology of intermittence allows us to describe this structure as a network of mostly anonymous but dense infra-relations, not as a mere collection of isolated malicious acts. And although everybody is to a certain extent subjected to the same anonymity of that system, it is biased toward the needs and schemes of the corporate venture capitalists, Capital's most committed sorcerers.

Concealing the magical ontology of their own system, powerful accumulation artists like Scarsdale Vibe act as closeted magicians who know how to exploit the effects of those velvet mirrors that absorb more than what they reflect. Put to a much wider use than that of cheap legerdemain, Zombini's "perfect black velvet" (*ATD*: 351) comes closer to the ideal of perfect crime than to the concept of perfect invisibility. In the passage quoted above, the megalomaniac Scarsdale plans to use his money and network of semi-illegal agents and seized resources to neutralize another megalomaniac project, that of Nikola Tesla's socialist dream of electricity as a common good, which he sees as one of the greatest conceivable threats to a system based on principles of maximum privatization and maximized profits.[7]

In light of the dominance of corporate occultures disguising themselves as benevolent rational systems, an eternal question returns: What are the prospects for a politics of resistance? And where and how should it intervene? Pignarre and Stengers never get tired of emphasizing that rehearsing the worn-out rituals of denouncing capital as a bad ideology is of little help for the project of confronting the power structures which hold us as captives:

> [I]t is not enough to denounce a capture the way one might denounce an ideology. Whilst ideology screens out, capture gets a hold over something that matters, that makes whoever is captured live and think. To come back to those things of which we are so proud—for example, scientific knowledge, and more precisely those sciences that are inventive and transform the world ... each of us can recognise that these sciences play roles that cannot in the slightest be described in terms of the pure advance of knowledge. One may then be tempted to call those scientists who refuse to accept all the consequences of these roles "blind," only to go on to discuss the possibility of defining a difference between "true knowledge" and what certain people have called "the spontaneous

---

[7]Electricity is an important ontological frame in *ATD*. Stuff happens as "unseen—though easily enough and sometimes dangerously felt—electrical events" (*ATD*: 98). Scarsdale and other capitalist sorcerers are eager to control the currents of electricity, which, in the early days of its discovery, is perceived as a mysterious, occult power that invites all sorts of manipulative ambitions.

ideology of scientists." To affirm that there is capture instead implies, for its part, a double movement: a suspension and an exposing to risk (Pignarre and Stengers: 43).

Like Pynchon, Stengers and Pignarre are not satisfied with merely debunking capitalism as sorcery (*suspension*); they also conjure practices of resistance associated with alter-modernity, anti-globalization, and counter-enlightenment (*exposure to risk*). Not only does corporate violence, always in close cooperation with the avant-gardes of science and academia, seize the material conditions of life and production, it also enacts an ongoing attack on epistemological variants inhibiting their unrestricted development. This is the political ambition behind Pynchon's fascination for "obscure mathematics" (Leise 2011: 2, Engelhardt 2018), forgotten or violently eradicated epistemologies (Sousa Santos 2014), subaltern belief systems, and transformative spiritualties (Coffman 2011). Like the two philosophers' pragmatic and speculative alliance with ecosophy, protest culture, radical feminism, and indigenous forms of knowledge, Pynchon's obsession with obsolescent epistemologies in *ATD* is not a celebration of irrationalism, but rather an acknowledgment of all those modes of thinking and being in the world oppressed and eradicated by so-called Enlightened modernity, modes of (wild) thinking and being that some proponents of Anthropocenic thought, for better or for worse, want to resuscitate (Stengers 2012; Viveiros de Castro 2002). Against the Cartesian terror of *clara et distincta perceptio*, Pynchon redirects our ontological and phenomenological sensibilities toward all that is "invisible but felt" (*ATD*: 753). Through an attitude that Stengers (2012) could describe as *radically pragmatic animism*, Pynchon expands the range of agency and stages an implicit plea for the uninhibited unleashing of a widely disseminated general intellect.

As so often in Pynchon's post-counter-cultural approach, some of the ways in which standard Enlightenment and down-to-earth realist solutions get challenged are presented in the most outrageously unserious and silly scenes. In Part III of *ATD*, after having suffered from a drug overdose at a party among math nerds in Göttingen, Kit Traverse finds himself locked up in the *Klapsmühle,* the local loony bin, where he meets a patient who believes he is a jelly doughnut, which he illustrates with a statement that, as we all know, John F. Kennedy would pick up many years later in a famous speech: "*Ich bin ein Berliner!*" (*ATD*: 626).

The treating clinician, Dr. Willi Dingkopf (literally: "thinghead"), tries to make sense of the patient's metamorphosis into pastry by taking it more seriously than most of his colleagues of the time or even today would do, explaining to Kit that here one "must resort to Phenomenology, and accept the literal truth of his delusion bringing him into Göttingen, to a certain *Konditerei* [sic] where he is all over powdered with *Puderzucker* and allowed to sit, or actually recline, up on a shelf ordinarily reserved for the pastries"

(626). We should resist the temptation to take scenes like these at face value bearing in mind that Dr. Dingkopf's reliability may at least be affected by the fact that he is himself part of a paradigmatically modern system of control, the psychiatric hospital. Seen from the perspective of *ATD*, however, it is always recommendable to rely on a certain kind of "Phenomenology" that not only accepts the literalness of delusion but constantly hyperbolizes it to invent literary shock treatments with an inexhaustible appetite for dramatic subtlety and nuance (note that the patient not only sits, but *reclines* on the shelf).

As pure reason is not enough to escape from the material and metaphoric capture enacted by capitalist sorcery, some sort of counter-sorcery is needed for "breaking the spell" of that seemingly absolute order. Yet, it seems that both Pynchon and Bolaño are less optimistic when it comes to the realist prospects of revolutionary action than Pignarre and Stengers who write with the expressed hope that "another world is possible" ([2005] 2011: 4). More cautiously, they focus on material and metaphorical practices of survival and endurance within the enemy lines of what Elizabeth Povinelli (2011) has described as "economies of abandonment."

Through one of Pynchon's characteristic fabrications of resonant parallelisms among distant scenes, we learn that a minor character's aesthetics of survival might profit from roughly the same art of (intermittent) disappearance that acts on behalf of malicious capitalist sorcerers like Scarsdale Vibe. Among so many things, the scene offers us a privileged glimpse into the core of *ATD*'s vision of history. Through the eyes of young Bria and by way of an inherited memoir ("an ancient volume, bound in shark leather, *The travels and adventures of Niccolò dei Zombini, Specchiere*"), the narrative jots down a few biographical remarks about said Niccolò who lived in the seventeenth century and worked as an apprentice in a manufactory of Venetian mirror-makers "who like the glassmakers on Murano were fanatically protective about their trade secrets. Corporations today are gentle and caring compared to those early factory owners, whose secrecy and obsession just got meaner and meaner as the years and generations passed" (*ATD*: 569). Niccolò manages to escape from the cruel regime of forced labor, apparently taking with him at least some of those secrets that will be conserved and passed on by later generations. Bria's father Luca loves to read to his kids from the courageous ancestor's journey "across the map of Europe and through the Renaissance, no telegraphs, no passports, no international spy networks, all you needed to stay ahead was better speed and some imagination. Niccolò managed to disappear into all the noise and confusion, which is what Europe was then" (569).

A hidden continuity between corporate practices from the Renaissance all the way through to the late nineteenth century is suggested. But within this continuity, some things have drastically changed. However, the impression of modern capitalists as a little bit gentler than their predecessors can only be related to the fact that they've come up with subtler forms of hiding their violence. In the larger context of the novel, the scene suggests that while outbursts of direct physical violence seem to have decreased in modern times, the power mechanisms responsible for the continuous transformation of that violence are getting stronger and stronger. And yet, both sides—the corporate pigs *and* the resourceful anarchists—make use of the same techniques of mirroring and disappearance to make their way across the map and through the ages. As the novel moves deeper into the twentieth century, however, doubts increase whether those techniques will suffice, given the unprecedented magnitude of noise and confusion the future has in store for them—and us.

6

Flat Fictionality

But what I saw that afternoon reduced all my ideas, all my imaginative possibilities, to the point where the unreal outweighs the real and gives it something like a pair of feet to walk on.

JOSÉ LEZAMA LIMA

Métaphores Filées

As the topic of this chapter is metaphor, I shall begin with a metaphor:

> Mrs. Bubis's eyes lit up. *As if* she were at the scene of a fire, Pelletier told Liz Norton later. *Not* a raging blaze, *but* a fire that was *about to* go out, *after* burning for months (2666: 28, my emphases).[1]

A typical Bolaño metaphor—even in the English translation which despite its sophistication cannot convey its full drama. Let's take a very close look at the operating rhetorical infrastructure. It begins with a rather hackneyed image: the flashing eyes of the widow of Archimboldi's German publisher, Mrs. Bubis. But Bolaño's metaphors are never static, they follow an often remarkably similar dynamic pattern, a pattern that our example embodies in its almost purest form. In a first step, Bolaño makes it explicit that we find ourselves in a metaphoric register by introducing the conjunction *as if*—an

---

[1] "Los ojos de la señora Bubis se iluminaron. *Como si* estuviera presenciando un incendio, le dijo después Pelletier a Liz Norton. *Pero no* un incendio en su punto crítico, *sino* uno *que*, *después de* meses de arder, estuviera *a punto de* apagarse" (Bolaño 2004a: 46, my emphases).

additional emphasis is given by placing it at the beginning of a sentence. In a second step, the already less common image is corrected and nuanced with the help of one of Bolaño's all-time favorite operators: *pero no, sino que* ("not this, but that"). The seemingly inconspicuous phrase performs several functions at the same time: it zooms in on a specific detail from a larger metaphorical context; it lists a variety of connotative possibilities, most of which are dumped again; it substitutes those dismissed elements with elements that better fit; it involves the initial image in a process of open and ongoing metaphorization. From this moment on, the metaphorical content of the initial image can be further enriched by all imaginable kinds of narrative, spatial, temporal, atmospheric, or other adverbial modifications.[2]

Bolaño's metaphors are constantly under revision. There is hardly a metaphor that is not subjected to a larger scene of figurative unfolding, to a process through which layer upon layer of figuration is amassed. A comparison, often inconspicuous at first, is progressively defamiliarized; different versions and nuances are tested; most of them dismissed and discarded again; suggested relations are spatially amplified, contracted, or woven into confusing temporal entanglements. The outcome is ambivalent: on the one hand, the initial image becomes more and more concrete as more and more figurative and imaginary material is added to the figurative origin; on the other hand, the accumulation of figurative data tends to challenge our sensory and aesthetic apparatus to keep hold of all the elements pertaining to the process of metaphorization.

Bolaño's protruding metaphorical scenes negotiate between affirmation and negation; but this does not produce a secure middle ground because negation usually outperforms the remaining "positive" elements by far: "[Archimboldi found] the path neither flat nor flat with hills nor flat with switchbacks, but vertical, a prolonged fall toward the bottom of the sea" (2666: 649).[3]

Bolaño is fond of strong images, but there is almost always more that his metaphors withhold than what they express. Theorists of figurative language have highlighted the fact that metaphors are not only deviant forms of

---

[2] Another example from one of Bolaño's stories demonstrates that while the order of these little operators can of course change, a very similar dynamic is in play: the beginning with a conventional image (*atmósfera fúnebre*), the delimiting specification in two steps (*pero no, sino de*), the offering of alternatives (*o*), and the making explicit of the metaphorical scene (*como si*): "La atmósfera que se respira en la casa de sus amigos es fúnebre. El ambiente, los movimientos que se registran, son de conciliábulo, *pero no* de conciliábulo general, *sino de* conciliábulos en petit comité o conciliábulos fragmentados en las diferentes habitaciones de la vivienda, *como si* una conversación entre todos estuviera vedada por motivos indecibles que todos acatan" (Bolaño 2010: 271, my emphasis).

[3] "[E]l camino ... para él [= Archimboldi] no era horizontal o accidentadamente horizontal o zigzagueantemente horizontal, sino vertical, una prolongada caída hacia el fondo del mar" (Bolaño 2004a: 810).

language, but are also highly condensed, representing a use of language that is economic, epiphanic, elliptic, and enigmatic.[4] Accordingly, the standard model of metaphor assumes that its most important information remains unsaid, which turns metaphor into a *pars pro toto* for poetry as a whole. According to most of its renowned analysts, metaphor always hides more than what it reveals and "leaves a good deal to be supplied at the reader's discretion" (Black 1979: 142).

Bolaño, however, is anything but discreet. His constant inventions of alternatives, specifications, and nuances, which remain part of the process of metaphorical phenomenalization even as they get dismissed, produces a wonderfully unapologetic mannerism. Until his stubborn attempt of finding the right image finally comes to rest, it must undergo a long preparatory phase that often borders on the absurd and ridiculous.

In the little example quoted just above, a condensed metaphor might have said that being on the road was like a long fall downwards to the bottom of the sea. Bolaño's narrator, however, is haunted by the obligation and, why not, the pleasure to provide a mannered and deliberatively cumbersome account of any situation. In a way, then, this sinuous and laborious search for the right image mimics or anticipates the sinuous mode in which the novel's events unfold, a mode that metaphorical expression seems to dislike or at least not to encourage.

In Bolaño's short but magnificent novel *Amuleto*, apparently excluded elements exert their ongoing power on the text as remaining insinuations. We can exemplarily see that in a key moment of the novel, which deals with the 1968 student massacre in Mexico. In her description of a certain part of Mexico City by night, the first-person narrator Auxilio Lacouture writes that "[the Avenida] Guerrero, at that time of night, is more like a cemetery than an avenue, not a cemetery in 1974 or in 1968, or 1975, but a cemetery in the year 2666, a forgotten cemetery under the eyelid of a corpse or an unborn child" (Bolaño [1999] 2006a: 86).

Trying to unpack this passage, we are faced with a variety of riddles that seem impossible to solve. First, why exactly those three dates: 1968, 1974, and 1975? If we might relate 1968 directly to the tragedy of Tlatleloco, the referents of 1974 and 1975 are much less obvious. Are they referring to the direct aftermath of Pinochet's coup in Chile, an event that Bolaño has repeatedly described as one of the lowest points in a series of political defeats for what he has called the lost or defeated generation of Latin

---

[4]As far as Christopher Johnson is concerned, even in its accumulative and hyperbolic use, metaphor enacts such an effect of condensation: "Metaphor and metaphoric hyperbole can be employed judiciously to balance the far off and the familiar, thereby producing knowledge. They also produce such knowledge more swiftly than more discursive language" (Johnson 2010: 54).

American writers and intellectuals (Bolaño 2004b: 34)? But why not mention the year 1973 instead, which marks the exact date of Pinochet's seizure of power? Why the odd order of 1974, 1968, 1975; and why that mannered separate naming of two consecutive years? Why no year from a more distant past or another closer to the narrator's (and the author's) present; for example, the year 1998? And what should we make of the preliminary outcome of this metaphorical process, the terrifying, hyperbolic number 2666? Is it an allusion to the devil's numeric signature, 666, to a lurking danger of apocalypse, the final extinction of human life; or nothing more but an example of the eccentric temperament of Auxilio Lacouture, the "mother of Mexican poetry" (Bolaño [1999] 2006a: 1)?

No matter how we might decide on those riddles, which Bolaño hides within larger metaphorical scenarios, it is evident that the cumbersome way in which they are introduced, prepared, and worked through represents a rejection of both classical and modernist models of metaphoric usage. If the classical approach seeks to balance *energeia* and *enargeia*, *dynamis* and *stasis*, or liveliness and clarity with the aim to produce a homeostatic harmony between the centrifugal and centripetal tendencies of metaphor, modernism seeks to push the energetic and productive side of metaphorization further and further to its limits. The rift between classical and modernist approaches to metaphor is succinctly summed up in a book by the Argentinian cult writer César Aira on legendary Argentinian poet Alejandra Pizarnik: "One could say that in classical art, there is a harmony between process and result, and the classical is defined by this harmony. In the modern era, this dialectic is exacerbated; the avant-gardes of the twentieth century push it to the fore, embarking on a journey towards an art that is all process" (Aira 1998: 11, my transl.).

But neither harmony nor pure process is a fitting term to make full sense of Bolaño's use of metaphor. If Bolaño has little intention to create an organic economy of image and meaning, it would be just as wrong to see him as the orthodox representative of a modernist (or even postmodernist) literature of process, where precious epiphanies provide rare moments of highly improbable aesthetic truth. Instead, in Bolaño's long and winding metaphorical scenes, heterogeneous forms of metaphorization—explosive epiphanies; explicit comparisons; mannered explications and proliferations; negotiations between wrong or right, true or false; revitalizations of worn-out expressions; and dead, forgotten, or "sunken metaphors" (Küpper 1988: 161, my transl.)—co-exist within an ostensibly non-figurative textual environment. Bolaño's metaphorical moments, as hyperbolic as they may be in themselves, are surrounded by long passages of plain language; and yet they do not merely arise as epiphanic states of emergency gesturing toward a transcendental vantage point from which the rest of the text receives its final orders.

Marked as temporary and open to revision, Bolaño's adventures to find a metaphorical solution often appear as a result of the narrator's laborious effort. At the same time, the search for them reveals the sheer pleasure of *telling*. Constantly re-arranging their figurative material, Bolaño's narrators as well as many of his characters dive into wild and uncontrolled forms of digressive exuberance, which regularly includes the careless production of textual redundancies and even monotony.

In most cases, the labor of negation (and the pleasure produced by negation) by far outweighs the positive parts, although there is always something positive that remains. No matter how exhausting a specific metaphorical proliferation may seem, there are always more things that will remain unsaid. Bolaño's metaphorology is thus reminiscent of what Georges Bataille famously called *unemployed negativity*:

> If action ("doing") is—as Hegel says—negativity, the question arises as to whether the negativity of one who has "nothing more to do" disappears or remains in a state of "unemployed negativity." Personally, I can only decide in one way, being myself precisely this "unemployed negativity" (I would not be able to define myself more precisely) (Bataille [1937] 1988: 90).

Marc Richir has his own phenomenological version of such an emphatically non-dialectical,[5] autonomous form of negativity. Beyond Husserl's fascinating concept of *Durchstreichung* (crossing out), a form of negativity that despite its graphic phenomenality remains dependent from a pre-given positivity, Richir assumes a "true negativity ... neither Hegelian negativity, nor Sartrean negativity" (Richir 2000: 302); that is, a form of negativity different from Hegel's antithesis and Sartre's nothingness. In the tradition of Bataille's unemployed negativity, Richir's negativity represents an independent form of agency, not just the absence of it, and a "positive" and autonomous mode of phenomenalization. Just like in Bolaño's complex metaphorical proliferations, unemployed negativity not only represents an intermediary and auxiliary state, but acts as an emancipated and egalitarian element within a series of horizontally juxtaposed symbolic decisions.

A Facilitator of Passages

Co-existence, juxtaposition, and "adjacency" (Serpell 2014: 119–52) are some of the terms that apply to the fundamental architecture of Bolaño's use

---

[5]Note that Bataille coins this term in a letter to Alexandre Kojève, considered by many to be the most important lecturer on Hegel of his period.

of metaphor. In Chapters 3 and 4, I've discussed *2666* and *ATD* as works of art that conjure a totality without closure (Ercolino 2014: 30). While others have described the intention of such works of art as a dialectical mapping out of contradictions (Andersen 2016; Toscano and Kinkle 2015), a Hegelian approach is not very helpful when trying to understand Bolaño's and, as I will show now, Pynchon's metaphorologies.

Like Bolaño, Pynchon does not allow his metaphorical scenes to come to a closure. We should be cautious, however, to see this as the outcome of an orthodox postmodern sentiment that tends to think of (post-)history as a space of mutually reversible relations. Against such a post-historical tendency, Pynchon exploits history to gain insights into the very nature of metaphor and vice versa. One of the major sites of this mutual fertilization of metaphor and history in *ATD* is, interestingly, mathematics. Revisiting the open and often sectarian debates on what was then the future of mathematics, Pynchon locates questions of sense and signification within a larger environment where different conceptions of time, space, truth, and experience converge and compete.

If in *2666* strong images are comparatively rare and deeply embedded into large passages of seemingly plain and non-figurative speech, metaphors abound in *ATD*, which produces an altogether different type of mannerism. This brings us back to the concept of *cruft* discussed in Chapter 3. The overabundance of metaphors challenges the reader to select, synthesize, and recombine the metaphorical material at hand to wrestle away a bit of sense and sound from the overwhelming noise of the mega-novel's zeal and ambition. How do we know, for instance, which metaphors are more relevant for the novel's way of worldmaking and its implicit (or should we rather say: intermittent?) cosmology? How do such moments of figuration depend on the specific contexts in which they are used and the characters who use them? And to what extent do they transcend their immediate context? One thing that is certainly true for *2666* and *ATD* is the fact that both books use metaphor in an emphatically trans-contextual way. Recurring phrases and similar figurative operations are highly disseminated across the long novel, appearing, disappearing, and re-appearing according to the same erratic and flickering rhythms that we encountered in Chapter 4.

As Amy Elias and others have observed, Pynchon's longest novel "is replete with metaphors of duality: light refraction, bilocation, mirroring, multiple time and space dimensions, and metaphysical duality" (Elias 2011: 31). One important material agent through which duality is produced is "Iceland spar, a rock crystal that splits light to reveal multidimensionality" (Elias 2011: 29). Its importance is stressed by the fact that it gives the novel's second part its title, whereas the third part, *Bilocation*, makes the idea of duality unmistakably explicit. In the wake of its transition from *Iceland Spar* to *Bilocation*, a passage from a crystal that splits light to a multidimensional embodiment of such a splitting, the novel also shifts from duality as an effect of perception and perspective to the somehow more radical idea of duality as a serious ontological option.[6]

Keeping in mind these preliminary remarks, let's have a look at the very beginning of Part III:

> While the *Inconvenience* was in New York, Lindsay had heard rumors of a "Turkish Corner" that really was supposed, in some not strictly metaphorical way, to provide an "escape nook to Asia." Like, "One minute you're in a horrible high-bourgeois New York parlor, the next out on the Asian desert, on top of a Bactrian camel, searching for a lost subterranean city."
>
> "After a brief visit to Chinatown to inhale some fumes, you mean."
>
> "Not exactly. Not as subjective as that."
>
> "Not just mental transportation, you're saying, but actual, physical—"
>
> "Translation of the body, sort of lateral resurrection, if you like."
>
> "Say, who wouldn't? Where is this miraculous nook?"
>
> "Where indeed ... behind which of those heaped thousands on thousands of windows lighted and dark? A formidable quest, you'd have to say" (*ATD*: 431).

Introducing Part III, the short dialogue announces the transition the novel is about to perform—a transition from bi-perception to bi-location. If Pynchon's narrator had been demonstrating from the beginning how swiftly they can jump from one setting to another,[7] this somewhat supernatural ability is now transferred to the characters themselves. Metaphor becomes liberated from its narrow limitations as a cognitive figure and is turned into a processual operator capable of intervening directly into the fabric of the world. In the short passage above, the possibility of immediate teleportation from a "high-bourgeois" New York to the Central Asian desert is pondered as a real possibility of experience and embodiment, not only as a drug-induced, subjective hallucination. The metaphorical signature, however, is not completely lost, but only hyperbolically expanded. Hyperbolically applied to nature, metaphors tend to realize themselves, but the reality that ensues continues to oscillate between fantasy and nature, "rumor" and fact.

---

[6]Bilocation is of course an echo of the popularizing discourse on quantum physics, which refers to the possibility that one and the same entity can be at two different locations at the same time (Rovelli 2017). The relationship between modern physics and time in Pynchon's later novels is analyzed in Bourcier (2013). A thoughtful discussion of some of the relations between mathematics, fiction, and the concept of reality in *ATD* can be found in Engelhardt (2013).

[7]The comic-like character of such a sudden change of place is not only amplified by the goofiness of the plot. Smaller textual elements like *meanwhile*, which is repeatedly used (*ATD*: 21; 259; 493), also evoke the frame of the comic genre.

To compare seemingly disparate elements is not so much what is at stake in such a use of metaphor. Instead, and somehow closer to the etymological roots of *metaphorá*, the focus lies on metamorphosis and transmission of bodies and objects and their passing through disparate environments. Metaphor is not an ornament, it is a vehicle.

In *ATD,* metaphor undergoes a material twist that reconfigures it as a drug-like "facilitator of passages between the worlds" (*ATD*: 433), as a poetic figure with shamanic abilities. Like Bolaño, Pynchon diverts our attention from the single image, its function and meaning, and redirects it toward the figurative drifts and streams that run through the whole novel. The standard model of metaphor suggests a "vertical" structure that interrupts the text's continuous flow and forces the reader to explore secondary meanings and resonances on a paradigmatic level. What we witness at the beginning of *Bilocation,* however, is a rather "horizontal" conceptualization of metaphor. Instead of a tension among conflicting semantic options, the text foregrounds simultaneity, co-existence, juxtaposition, adjacency, and lateral displacement. Being attentive to the distribution of figurative energy throughout the text rather than to every single metaphorical moment, readers of hyperbolic realism become aware of a smoldering possibility of metaphorization, which only from time to time breaks through the text's surface in erratic, intermittent ways to ignite its epiphanic fires.

The Secret Trade of Metaphor

Merleau-Ponty's remarks on Bergson in *The Visible and the Invisible* provide an astonishing echo of Pynchon's metaphorological modus operandi:

> One has to believe, then, that language is not simply the contrary of the truth, of coincidence, that there is or could be a language of coincidence, a manner of making the things themselves speak—and this is what he seeks. It would be a language of which he would not be the organizer, words he would not assemble, that would combine through him by virtue of a natural intertwining of their meaning, through the occult trading of the metaphor—where what counts is no longer the manifest meaning of each word and of each image, but the lateral relations, the kinships that are implicated in their transfers and their exchanges (Merleau-Ponty [1964] 1968: 125).

Merleau-Ponty's "occult trading of the metaphor" aims at a structure in which the poetic function is not taken as auxiliary or ornamental, but as a field of forces in which language is questioned, reoriented, and re-energized both in relation to itself *and* in its relation to the real. As it shifts away from the "manifest meaning of each word and image" and toward the lateral connections among word and image, family resemblances, and semiotic circulation, metaphor is embedded in a thick and messy milieu in which its entanglements with matter, flesh, and other modes of extra-linguistic reality prevail over its semantic performance. The creation of meaning and sense is thus not overseen and controlled by a sovereign subject; the subject is seen as a medium in and through which the linguistic event occurs as a mostly autopoietic process. In such an optic, literal and figurative elements are less hierarchically organized, but rather horizontally arranged and composed, "by virtue of a natural intertwining of their meaning [*sens*]."

To critical ears, such a conception may sound highly suspicious. For is it not the eternal mission of critical theory to denaturalize and deconstruct, to disentangle and discorrelate in order to reveal the false naturalness of any social, linguistic, or epistemological system thought as an organic whole? In the realms of critical theory, nothing more but mentioning the word "natural" already amounts to a sacrilege, at least if it is done without quotation marks. In Merleau-Ponty's late philosophy, we encounter an unfashionable insistence on nature, an insistence, however, which presupposes an altogether different notion of nature than the one targeted by critical theory. In Merleau-Ponty's understanding, nature is not what Timothy Morton describes as "Easy Think Substance," a "bland lump of whatever decorated with accidents" (Morton 2016: 47). It is a productive force, constantly producing and re-producing an intricate web of relations largely independent of subjective experience.

There is an irony here that shouldn't be lost: one of the leading voices of a philosophical tradition, which has been reduced to the role of a more or less systematic elaboration of first-person experience (Sparrow 2014: 156), is one of the rare voices to promote a "return" to nature that is in fact its radically new conception. Against the modern consensus that sees nature as unchanging and passive background (Bryant 2013: 14), Merleau-Ponty's nature, further radicalized by Marc Richir, assumes a wild and anarchic movement of matter and meaning, brimming with contingencies, ruptures, surprises, unexpected encounters, and sudden turns. Much closer than expected to the agenda of a book like *After Finitude* whose author, Quentin Meillassoux, is an outspoken critic of what he sees as phenomenology's strong correlationism, Merleau-Ponty's ontological return does not intend to make nature rotate around a gravitational center of human beings, their abilities and institutions, but views it as the field of interrelating processes and intra-actions of which the relation between man and nature is just but one very specific case. Such a passage from correlationism to relationism (Shaviro 2009: 79, Stengers [2002] 2011: 386) has some astonishing similarity with the shift enacted in *ATD*. Pynchon's constant flirting with animism, which breathes life and agency into inorganic materials (ice, light, minerals, sand, opium, etc.), is exemplified in a passage in which the photographer Merle

Rideout understands that human life is shaped by "productive nature" (Grant 2006: 1) long before we are capable of shaping nature.

Merle, the narrator tells us, "had been visited by a strange feeling that 'photography' and 'alchemy' were just two ways of getting at the same thing—redeeming light from the inertia of precious metals" (*ATD*: 80). Immediately, the mystic functional parallelism between photography and alchemy is projected onto Merle's and his partner's life and proposed as a more compelling explanation to their erratic wanderings than "the result of any idle drift." To some extent, at least, the more compelling explanation is derived from the materials itself, that is to say, in the case of photography, "from all the silver he'd been developing out into the pictures he'd been taking over these years—as if silver were alive, with a soul and a voice, and he'd been working for it as much as it for him" (80).

As always, the devil is in the details. *As if,* which signals the dominant metaphorical context, undergoes an existential twist as it comes to mark the zone of uncertainty between the actual liveliness of the silver plate and its merely metaphorical animation.[8] As this uncertainty remains largely undecided, *ATD* makes use of a relation to the real that we could qualify as *radically pragmatic animism* (Stengers 2012). It therefore remains open to which extent silver and other materials are actually alive and agential. But what is certain is the fact that matter emits a "Force of Gravity" (Pynchon 1973: 639) that shapes the conditions of labor and, consequently, the fate of Merle and his wife Dally who will later leave him for the Italian magician Zombini, another eccentric character who, as we have seen in the previous chapter, shares Merle's professional intimacy with light.

The parallelization of alchemy and photography feeds into Pynchon's attack against the Enlightenment whose echoes can already be heard in the title of the novel. Alchemy as well as photography exploit animism to defy orthodox Enlightenment convictions: one as a mystic craft successfully delegitimized by science-confident rationalism as dangerous sorcery; the other as the state of the art of mimesis at the threshold to the twentieth century. Both practices confront the rationalist tendency to neutralize light,

---

[8] Pynchon's animistic poetics is neatly summed up in Tiina Käkelä-Pumula (2017: 55): "The material world—objects, physical phenomena, nature—and its eventual uncontrollability constitute a pervasive element in Pynchon's prose: the earth appears as a 'living critter' (GR, 590), objects are given a life of their own, and they turn into sublime beings that are far above the comprehension of men; the attributes of animate and inanimate are blurred. Living objects or personified natural phenomena are, of course, very literary beings, usually situated under the rubric of 'fantasy,' which gestures to something essentially different from realism. In Pynchon's prose, however, realistic accuracy and fantasy appear superimposed, impossible to separate. What is thematized in such a mode of writing is the distinction itself—the distinction between real and unreal, human and non-human, organic and inorganic—and thinking that proceeds by making such distinctions. In short, rationalism."

to make it completely transparent, to turn it into the source of universal knowledge (*lumen naturale*), but flirt with mysticism to redeem light from inertia and to rescue grace from gravity.

Seen in that light, the natural intertwining of words and images proposed by Merleau-Ponty appears as a bold attempt to imitate the dynamic and intra-active *poiesis* of nature itself. If Marc Richir speaks of a contact of language with itself, a "contact from oneself to oneself—through distance" (Richir 2015: 151), he tries to account for a sphere of linguistic activity that precedes the semantic production of meaning, but that is not necessarily more authentic or natural than a sphere where language is used with clear intention and purpose. Like this variant of phenomenology, hyperbolic realism turns our attention toward those registers before, beyond and beneath linguistic certainties, recognizable images, fixated meanings, and tightly knitted narratives. But it does so from within the fields of representation, imagination, semantics, and narrativity. Its aim is not simply to deconstruct, unmask, or debunk the false ideology behind representation, mimesis, intentionality, or meaning, but to ground those "symbolic institutions" (Richir 2018) in a proto-categorical, "pre-predicative" field (Husserl [1939] 1975), which is not completely allergic to form and recognition, but always preserves a certain distance to them.

The critique of what Marc Richir, with a term adopted from anthropology, describes as symbolic institution demands of its critic a more nuanced approach than the critique of ideology. Like "real" institutions, symbolic ones do not magically disappear once you start to realize their constructedness, nor is any meaningfully social, cultural, or political life possible or desirable without them. Symbolic institutions are cultural sub-systems based on institutionally regulated and socially rehearsed practices. If they provide an essential grid through which we make sense of the world and ourselves, they also have an in-built function that tends to fixate, reinforce, and naturalize the status quo. In other words, symbolic institutions are conservative structures, both in a political and intellectual sense. At first glance, Richir's anarchic (or, to be more precise: *anarchitectonic*) critique of symbolic institutions seems much less radical than more familiar attacks of critical theory and post-structuralism. But in his commitment to contingency and to the openness of the situation lies also a chance to defamiliarize some of the familiar habits and solutions of more canonized forms of critique.[9]

---

[9] Nevertheless, it is hard to deny that "actually existing phenomenologists" have hardly exhausted their tradition's potential for radical political critique. All too often, their commitment to the concrete has led to a devastating ignorance and avoidance of political issues. An obvious case of phenomenology's apolitical tendency is what has been described as its theological turn (Janicaud 1991).

In hyperbolic realism, a similar dynamic is in play. It outlines an aesthetic program, which is neither interested in restituting a direct and unproblematic relationship between words and things, nor does it promote yet another avant-garde project whose main concern is to destabilize the relation between signs and some kind of autonomous realm of the real. Hyperbolic realism comes both *after* realism and *after* the avant-gardes. Related to the concern of this chapter, metaphor, it marks a moment in which both realism and experimentalism have become equally futile as readymade solutions. As a result, the focus shifts from the production of singular and thus unique poetic images to what we could call an ecology of images. Among the metaphorological cruft of *2666* and *ATD*, we find a general dynamic that we could describe, with Merleau-Ponty's words, as a chiastic intertwining of metaphor and metonymy. According to this model, which we should not confound with dialectics, metaphor and metonymy are not clearly distinct types, but co-emerge in mutual entanglement. Metaphor creates "horizontal" continuity among mutually substituted elements; metonymy has more to do with the "vertical" transfer qua resemblance. But both operations meet in their intention to create "a language of coincidence, a manner of making the things themselves speak" (Merleau-Ponty [1964] 1968: 125). Let us have a closer look now on our role novels, *2666* and *ATD*, and on the concrete ways in which metaphors appear, disappear, and, as one of Pynchon's characters would say, how they get *laterally resurrected*.

Flat Fictionality

As if, como si. The inconspicuous little phrase abounds in Pynchon's and Bolaño's aesthetics of mannerism. Its effect is highly paradoxical. On the one hand, it frames a specific context as specifically metaphorical and prompts the reader to be aware of what exceeds the mere transmission of information. On the other hand, as it is so excessively used in both *2666* and *ATD*, it somehow loses its distinctive quality, which creates a diffuse atmosphere of uncertainty, irreality, and creates an additional fictional fold within an already fictional world (Bunia 2007; Deleuze [1988] 1992). In a way, then, all elements are placed under a common sign of the fantastic, the extraordinary, "the weird and the eerie" (Fisher 2016) and, not to forget, the hyperbolic. As Pynchon's and Bolaño's metaphorical scenes are expansive, prolific, and decidedly non-epiphanic, readers easily lose track of where they begin and where they end.

As we have seen in Chapter 4, Pynchon jumps back and forth between the fantastic and historical genres like a trickster. Something similar occurs between the factual and fictional, with the important difference that the whole action of a book is of course always already fictionalized action[10]—no matter if narrated in a historical or fantastic register, no matter if articulated in ostensibly metaphorical or seemingly plain language.

I want to propose the notion of *flat fictionality* as a name for such a dynamic, which folds every element of the text into a protective husk of pervasive fictionality, uncertainty, or even irreality. On the one hand, flat fictionality is a general feature of the structure of every literary text, an intrinsic quality of its ontology. On the other hand, hyperbolic realism dwells and insists on this feature, expands on it, exaggerates it and makes it thereby explicit. Despite Bolaño's accumulative, anaphoric use of *as if* and *como si*, however, their exposure of fictionality is a bit more relaxed than those from earlier postmodernist writers that come to mind, where the metaliterary character of a text often appears as its dominant function and quality.

The notion of flat fictionality hints at an altered adoption of a popular term within Anthropocenic thought, more precisely the controversially discussed branch of object-oriented ontology. Influenced by the works of Bruno Latour, theorists like Graham Harman, Levy R. Bryant, or Ian Bogost have introduced the notion of flat ontology to promote a re-organization of matter and being along the lines of a more horizontal, juxtaposed co-existence of organic, inorganic, and cultural entities. Flat ontology places things, beings, ideas, values—basically everything—on one and the same level, which claims to attack the privileged position of the *anthropos* as well as to contest the separation of subject and object, nature and culture (Descola [2005] 2013).

Flat fictionality plunges all elements of the poetic text in the same light of contingency, fantasy, and unreality, no matter if those elements challenge a hard-boiled realist's worldview or not. But there is more to my conceptual adoption than a mere play with similar sounds as flat fictionality, contrary to an influential view, does not abandon its groundedness in the world, but produces another ontology. To use the words of Merleau-Ponty once again, the local ontology produced by flat fictionality is not that of an entirely bodiless world, but of a world similar to the one of our dreams, a world of bodies "without weight" (Merleau-Ponty [1964] 1968: 262), a world of *corps sans poids* (Merleau-Ponty 1964: 310).

If flat fictionality points at a general ontological condition of the novel, it obviously makes itself felt under different shapes and modes of appearance. In *ATD* and *2666*, excessive fictionality is a salient signature of the textual universe while excessive metafictionality is not. Mitigating the weight of self-referentiality known from committed postmodernists, hyperbolic realism

---

[10] "Whatever makes it into a book is fantasy, as far as I'm concerned" (Alexis 2019: 206).

tends not to separate its meta-fictional musings from mimetic concerns. Representation of the real is often achieved by way of meta-fictional detours, and what appears as a merely meta-fictional comment of the text on itself can contain a surprisingly tangible, material dimension. In *ATD*, this is made unmistakably clear from the very beginning, that is at least from the moment on the Chums of Chance start their first surveillance job at the World's Columbus Exposition of 1893 in Chicago.

The Chicago fair, introduced as a territory that is both temporarily and spatially limited (six months, 280 hectares), offers "the exact degree of fictitiousness to permit the boys access and agency" (*ATD*: 36). It is isolated from the "harsh nonfictional world" outside and ruled by a mechanism in close resonance with what has just been presented as flat fictionality. The clearly delineated territory is both more than a physical thing and a simulacrum, it is an aesthetic zone, artificial yet materially meaningful, a world apart in which some natural and social laws are temporarily and spectacularly suspended while others remain untouched or all the more powerful. Dwelling into that "exact degree of fictitiousness" offered by the World Fair, the Chums of Chance optimize their game after leaving the lofty heights of air-travelling to set their feet on the ground. As fictional entities, they use a second-order flat fictionality, folded into the already fictional space of the novel, as camouflage to mingle with the "real" world's population who can and cannot see them at the same time.

As the novel unfolds, what seemed to be nasty tricks or little miracles confined to the White City's fairground more and more become the rule on a shrinking "World-Island" (*ATD*: 567) in constant crisis. Despite the late colonialist hyperbolic frenzy of drawing new colonial borders, the decline and dispersal of imperial power at the end of the nineteenth century leaves formerly colonized and clearly demarcated territories open for geopolitical contest; states of exception and lawless territory becomes increasingly the norm. As *ATD* jumps in frequently hilarious fashion from one exceptional situation to the next, the underlying material, historical and political conditions remain mostly in the dark, but exert an undeniable influence on the novel's jolly surface.

As flat fictionality takes over, not only do the borders between fact and fiction, between the imaginary and the real, and between genre convention and genre transgression become more and more porous. The fantastic and documental elements start to complement, substitute, and stand in for each other. What is introduced as fantastic turns out to be a scarily fitting description of reality while what comes from recorded history sounds elusive and incredible. Fact and fiction intermingle in a way that Merleau-Ponty would describe as chiastic. Instead of the suspicion that what we perceive as reality is merely the product of a powerful simulation machine, we are gradually initiated to an expanded sense of the real in which imaginary and speculative realities co-exist alongside more mundane experiences. In *ATD*, mathematics is a major site of such an expansion of what could possibly be or become real. In one of the novel's many moments that rescue metaphor from mathematics, a mathematical genius and committed yogi from India directly applies the "discovery of Imaginary numbers" (*ATD*: 133) to an understanding of human existence as a whole. By way of conclusion, he directs his speech at a young woman, confronting her with the slightly indecent idea that if "you were a vector, mademoiselle, you would begin in the 'real' world, change your length, enter an 'imaginary' reference system, rotate up to three different ways, and return to 'reality' a new person." But the woman, who shares some of Dr. Rao's talents, replies: "Fascinating. But … human beings aren't vectors. Are they?" (*ATD*: 539).

For all we know, humans are not vectors, but what if literary characters are? Is this part of a half-hidden message that the most important family name of the novel, *Traverse*, is trying to convey to us? No matter how we might feel about this, Ganesh's musings exemplify a crucial method of *ATD*: to make mathematical models serve as metaphors for an expanded and expanding sense of reality. In the passage above, imaginary numbers describe an action that originates from three-dimensional, Euclidean grounds from which it is extended into an imaginary space beyond the usual laws of experience. What is crucial is that the action does not remain in the imaginary space separated from the daylit world, but runs back to it as an altered state. The way the Belgian phenomenologist Marc Richir thinks about hyperbole is remarkably similar to the logic of Rao's "imaginary reference system." Hyperbole, as suggested by its etymology, casts a thought beyond what is immediately plausible with the hope that a part of hyperbole's notorious excess energy can be rescued once that thought returns to a zone of shared perceptions and social compromise (Richir 2014). Hyperbole loves to dwell on the side of what is difficult to imagine without methods of defamiliarization, suspension, and an expansion of the perceptual scene. At the same time, it comes with the danger that its projection does not meet any ground and dies away in the empty space of speculation. Finally, and perhaps even worse, there is the danger that one does not return from hyperbole's provisional and self-induced madness, the danger that one gets lost in exaggeration.[11]

It is along these lines that the reader may be gradually drawn into the same constant sense of unreality that many of Pynchon's and Bolaño's characters feel. As the African American sports reporter is more and more sucked into the vortex of Santa Teresa's night life, Bolaño writes a remarkably (but characteristically) non-metaphorical sentence: "La sensación de la irrealidad que le perseguía aquella noche se acentuó" (Bolaño 2004a: 407). (The sense of unreality that dogged him that night was heightened (*2666*: 322).) Through

---

[11]For Richir, Antonin Artaud is the evident example for an artist who ventured too far into hyperbolic spheres and never really came back (Varela 2010: 451).

the excessively recurring formula *as if*, an atmosphere of constant hyperbole is created exerting its influence on even the most inconspicuous scenes. On the one hand, this could simply be seen as a more explicit commitment to flat fictionality, which is an ontological feature of every novelistic discourse. On the other hand, it points to a specific conception of the real, according to which the most fateful events and encounters occur under the hyperbolic sign of pervasive unreality.

Timothy Morton's term of hyperobjects seeks to express a similar structure: "The feeling of being inside a hyperobject contains a necessary element of unreality—yet this is a symptom of its reality" (Morton 2013: 146). As the world at the beginning of the twenty-first century is becoming weirder and weirder, as Morton and others (Fisher 2016; Harman 2012) never tire of emphasizing, humans are losing their self-assigned superior status and becoming reintegrated into a shared environment, where all organic and even inorganic beings appear on one and the same ontological level. At the same time, humans are re-centered as the key geological factor of our age, the Anthropocene. If human hubris against interspecies coexistence, corporate violence against social emancipation, and industrial extractivism against the environment had already ruled the previous two centuries, at least, the disastrous consequences of these practices are now becoming unmistakably clear. However, as most of the developments that have led to the imminent possibility of ecological collapse operate on extremely macroscopic and/or microscopic levels, the classical apparatuses of human-scaled attention, perception, and knowledge production are thrown into deep crisis.

Hyperbolic realism names the ambition to translate the new/old authority of hyperobjects into literature. The sense of unreality, flat fictionality, and the intermittent entanglement of factual, counterfactual, and fantastic elements are deployed to point at a new configuration of the real that is already in itself strange, distorted, fantastic, excessive, and, in one word, hyperbolic. As Sharae Deckard writes about 2666: "This work does not deal in supernatural events narrated in a naturalist style but appropriates a language of the spectral or supernatural to narrate a totality experienced as irreal" (Deckard 2012: 355).

Hyperobjects relegate human agency and, accordingly, narrative form in a constitutive belatedness in relation to the real they try to deal with. In *2666* and *ATD*, this constitutive lateness or, as we could say, this transcendental trauma constantly haunts the narrative unfolding of the novels' events. If retrospection is usually supposed to bring order into chaos, in Bolaño's fictional world the sensation of unreality radiates beyond the actual event to make any hopes for an act of final appropriation look futile: "Con la luz diurna los sucesos de la noche anterior parecían irreales, revestidos de una gravedad infantil" (Bolaño 2004a: 434). ("In the light of day the previous night's events seemed unreal, invested with childish gravity." (2666: 344).)

Despite the partial impression of an omniscient narrator, both novels refuse an Archimedean "view from nowhere" (Nagel 1989) from where the sensation of unreality can be integrated once and for all into a normalizing empirical framework. Or as Chris Kraus would have it: "You never sense the 'aftermath' because always, something else starts up along the way" (Kraus 1997: 75). And just as there is no aftermath, through which the alienating events from the past can be entirely controlled, it is notoriously unclear where the sequence of a particular section of reality begins and where it ends. 2666 makes this unmistakably clear in the framing of the hyperbolic catalogue of the victims of the *feminicidios* in Santa Teresa, which begins with the first victim in 1993; "[B]ut it's likely there had been other deaths before," and then "surely there were other girls and women who died in 1992" (2666: 353). The necessity to begin somewhere faces the impossibility of a beginning that is not always already thwarted by reality itself. *Hyperbolic realism,* as most modern literature, has resigned from any hopes for a view from nowhere that could retrospectively tame previous encounters with the strangeness, the weirdness and the unavailability of the real. But this does not mean that it merely celebrates the fact that reality is forever unattainable through signs and language. Instead, the diachronic hiatus between reality and narrative, event and retrospection, and being and appearance is put to use for a new understanding of the real embedded in the sprawling narratives of these late maximalist novels.

Hence, the sense of unreality often leads to situations of perceptual claustrophobia, as is made clear from the early beginnings of 2666. When Pelletier and Espinoza meet, they soon agree on their shared respect for their older Italian colleague's work, "but Pelletier's words (spoken as if from inside an old castle or a dungeon dug under the moat of an old castle) sounded like a threat in the peaceful little restaurant on the Rue Galande" (2666: 11).

What is said in brackets anticipates what will be gradually realized by the general metaphorical language of the novel: it speaks as if from inside the echo chambers of an old castle to accommodate the "ritual reluctance" (Pynchon [1965] 2000: 51) with which the events in and around Santa Teresa unfold. At the same time, we get an early glimpse of one of Bolaño's favorite literary strategies at work, the accumulation of variants and alternatives that further specify, negate, correct, and hyperbolically expand the initial image. Most of us might have a more or less clear idea of the sound of threatening words echoed by the vast halls of an old castle. It is a lot harder to imagine how those words sound when uttered in a dungeon excavated from under the moat of that castle.

In two widely separated, seemingly unconnected passages in 2666, the metaphorical view from within is associated with the cultural imaginary of Aztec culture: the first passage looks at "the Aztec ruins springing like lilacs from wasteland ... stone flowers among other stone flowers [*flores de piedra en medio de otras floras de piedra*], a chaos that would surely lead nowhere, only to further chaos" (*2666*: 103); the second one narrates how a girl Reiter/Archimboldi meets during the war envisions Aztec waterbodies: with "no mosquitoes, nice weather all year round, and lots of pyramids, so many and so big it's impossible to count them all, pyramids on top of pyramids, pyramids behind other pyramids [*pirámides superpuestas, pirámides que ocultan otras pirámides*], all stained red with the blood of daily sacrifices" (*2666*: 697).

In another instance, reality itself is described with an image of immersion: "La realidad es como un padrote drogado en medio de una tormenta de truenos y relámpagos, dijo la diputada" (Bolaño 2004a: 765). Once again the riddle is hard to solve: reality is a pimp who's high on drugs—what on earth is this supposed to mean? And what are the equivalents of the sex workers, the suitors, the police, and the guardians of public morals? Or is the metaphor completely meaningless and nothing but a trite cliché, an expression of the trivial inner life of the local female politician who is its subject of enunciation? There is often a thin line in Bolaño's metaphors between *pathos* and *bathos*, between an overwhelming force of the image's fateful effect and the imminent danger of the image's relapse into the quotidian, the literal, the non-figurative, or even banal.

Much more than in *ATD*, which Kathryn Hume has aptly called Pynchon's "least paranoid novel" (Hume 2011: 168), metaphoric claustrophobia is an important feature in *Gravity's Rainbow* where not only Slothrop but many other characters live under a constant paranoid fear, the fear of being captured by surveillance systems they can neither decipher nor control. "Slothrop's Progress: London the secular city instructs him: turn any corner and he can find himself inside a parable" (Pynchon 1973: 25) is a cynical statement since Slothrop is neither doing progress nor does he really find himself as independent from the hidden forces that control him.

According to the famous initial phrase of *Gravity's Rainbow*, progress and/or progression in this novel (as much as in the rest of Pynchon's work) are usually not emancipatory, working not as "a disentanglement from, but [as] a progressive knotting into" (1973: 3) the structures of bio-political control and surveillance. On the other hand, the novel intimates that insights into one's own fate are only, if at all, possible when characters risk to penetrate the inner circle of the structures that hold them captive.

As a consequence of Slothrop's constant horniness, his perceptual adventures are often closely tied to his experiments with extraordinary sexual conduct. Among his many encounters, one that is particularly unsettling is that with "little Bianca," the minor daughter of the famous German actress Greta Erdmann. The scene's reality status, which takes place in the Zone and mid-way through the novel, oscillates between actual event and hallucinatory fantasy. In this probably pedophiliac moment of intimacy, the interiorization of metaphor is pushed to the extreme when Slothrop suddenly experiences the world from inside his erection:

> Now something, oh, kind of *funny* happens here. Not that Slothrop is really aware of it now, while it's going on—but later on, it will occur to him that he was—this may sound odd, but he was somehow, actually, well, *inside his own cock*. If you can imagine such a thing. Yes, inside the metropolitan organ entirely, all other colonial tissue forgotten and left to fend for itself, his arms and legs it seems *woven* among vessels and ducts, his sperm roaring louder and louder, getting ready to erupt, somewhere below his feet ... maroon and evening sunlight reaches him in a single ray through the opening at the top, refracted through the clear juices flowing up around him. He is enclosed. Everything is about to come, come incredibly, and he's helpless here in this exploding *emprise* ... red flesh echoing ... an extraordinary sense of *waiting to rise* (1973: 469–70).

The scene condenses many elements that we've mentioned so far: the retrospective view that makes the event increasingly stranger than it initially seemed; the lack of straightforwardness in the delivery of the metaphor; its "not strictly metaphorical" (*ATD*: 431) character as an actually embodied state of perception; the structure of correction, self-commentary, and self-reflection; the pushing of the image to the edge of the plausible; the sense of confinement, helplessness, and capture (*emprise*); and finally a somehow heightened contact with the world, even if the sudden intimacy with the real is not immediately translated into more "access and agency" (*ATD*: 36).

As usual in *Gravity's Rainbow*, Slothrop's encounter with Bianca will remain enigmatic and resist a final interpretation either by the reader or Slothrop himself. This leaves us with the characteristic sense of wonder in relation to both the eccentric event and the eccentric language used for its narrative representation. But while Slothrop's question—"What happened back there?"—remains unanswered as Bianca's real shape is hidden in the text ("I'm a child, I know how to hide") just as much as she promises to hide him (Pynchon 1973: 470), Slothrop will continue his erratic pilgrimage deeper and deeper into the Zone. Bianca, on the opposite, will slowly vanish into the "textual unconscious" (Duyfhuizen 1991: § 13). But as we have seen in the previous chapter, disappearance within the matrix of hyperbolic realism never simply means going away, but often serves as a condition for the characters to enter another or perhaps even a true state of existence: "Right here, right now, under the makeup and the fancy underwear, she *exists,* love, invisibility ... For Slothrop this is some discovery" (Pynchon 1973: 470).

The Dismal Metonymies of the Dead

In the poetic world of hyperbolic realism, unreality or at least a heightened sense of it is waiting for us behind every corner. *As if* plunges the discursive whole, through excessive and often mannered repetitions, into a pervasive atmosphere of figurativeness. Metaphors are constantly replaced and displaced, they reproduce themselves metonymically, so to speak, allowing only punctually and sporadically the striking "lateral resurrections" (*ATD*: 431) of metaphorical epiphanies. At the same time, this very constant sense of unreality, as it is so coherently there, often points toward traces of emphatic events and a quite new concept of how reality is itself composed. What seemed initially exaggerated, stilted, pretentious, untrustworthy, and so on, becomes suddenly or gradually reintegrated in a larger ontological picture of the world and reality itself.

Pynchon and Bolaño make a specifically hyperbolic use of metaphor by venturing deep into the fantastic and the metaphorical, but they do so within a poetics that is deeply grounded in and oriented toward a recognizable, "earthly" reality—even where it clearly contradicts our laws of nature and experiential expectations. Most importantly, their expansion of the sense of reality does not halt at perception, but tries to bring home something of the eccentricity of the event and "productive nature" (Grant 2006: 1, Barad: 2003, 811) itself.

Metaphor infused with hyperbole produces sinuous, mannered proliferations of not always spectacular initial images; proliferations full of redundancies, the overflowing pleasure of figuration, and "catachrestic usurpations" (Butler 1993: 37) of rhetorical harmony and *decorum*. Since the days of Quintilian, at least, hyperbolic metaphors represent the pinnacle of risky discourse, always in danger of aiming too high, of becoming too frivolous, too hypertrophic, and too much of everything. Yet in the act of enunciation, we often find hints to a worldly texture that legitimizes and motivates the hyperbolic expression to save it from the reader's ridicule. A similar structure is aimed at in Timothy Morton's concept of hyperobjects, where a heightened sense of unreality in the way a phenomenon expresses itself is meant to hint at an extreme and emphatic reality that produces it. But in the end, Morton offers not many convincing criteria that help us to distinguish between a hyperobject produced by reality itself and a hyper-illusion produced by esoteric projection and unacknowledged magical thinking. This may have something to do, in part, with Morton's seductively suggestive style, but also with the fact that he misses to draw from the long tradition of hyperbolic thought and methodology, which foregrounds the risk of hyperbolic speech itself.

About Slothrop's encounter with Bianca, Bernhard Duyfhuizen writes: "If we grant that we cannot know Bianca because of the narrative filters of fetish and hallucination, can we even be sure—in a perfectly pynchonian paradox—of the certainty of our fantasy?" (Duyfhuizen 1991: § 14). With Pynchon and his partner-in-arms Bolaño, we can definitely answer: no—at least not for each and every case. More consistently than *2666*, *ATD* strains our tolerance for the supernatural to the extreme, as it places the most improbable phenomena and the most common experiences on one and the same ontological level. It is the very uncertainty about any rigid distinction between the real and the rest, between fantasy and history that drives the narrative and its human and not-so-human characters forward. Surrounded by apocryphal interpretations of obsolete mathematical theories, eccentric manifestations of political extremism and cutting-edge capitalist management strategies, the majority of *ATD*'s characters struggle hard to survive in a widely imperturbable reality. It is only the happy few who have amassed enough power to manipulate the real for their antisocial purposes, while only a few gain enough power to manipulate the real for their mostly evil needs.

Linked to the characters' trajectories, metaphor not only works as an expansion of what can be said, but gives way to meta-metaphorological reflections that often include an agential dimension. In the third part of *2666*, Barry Seaman, the Black editor-in-chief of a Harlem-based sports magazine, offers a succinct version of such a micro-metaphorology, when he says that "[M]etaphors are our way of losing ourselves in semblances or treading water in a sea of seeming" (*2666*: 254) (Las metáforas son nuestra manera de perdernos en las apariciones o de quedarnos inmóviles en el mar de las apariencias) (Bolaño 2004a: 322). Existentially twisted, metaphor does not serve as an approximate attempt to express the otherwise ineffable, but as a strategy of survival in the vast and overwhelming sea of appearances, a form of survival that like so often in Bolaño (and Pynchon) involves an element of disappearance and self-forgetting. Metaphor is here represented as a brave and adventurous act, but the adventure mainly consists in remaining passive, immobile, and imperceptible.

What metaphor teaches to characters and readers alike, is, to say it with the words of Morton, a theory of urgent action in the mode of *as if*. Facing the personal, political, and ecological challenges of the twenty-first century, as the endpoint of modernity, we cannot afford to wait for full statistical evidence, but should instead act "as if the threat was real" (Morton 2013: 182). Something of that ethos is encoded in the novels of *hyperbolic realism* where even the most supernatural thing is treated as if it was real—or could be real, at least. Metaphor becomes thus a vehicle for a temporary and always precarious access to or contact with all forms of parallel universes that seem to have always existed alongside the visible world, but the two only sporadically intersect.

The notorious ambivalence of metaphorical expression simultaneously veils and unveils this flickering appearance of alternative universes in the plain of the visible world that is constructed through our perceptual routines. Bolaño and Pynchon emphasize this ambivalence by not conceiving the concealing part as a lack, but often as a condition that something can survive within the *sea of appearances* in the first place. The work of their hyperbolic metaphors can thus be compared to *Iceland Spar,* the powerful mineral in *ATD* that first serves as an opener for the doors of perception *(bi-perception)* to then become the entry point for alternative ontological forms of existence *(bi-location)*. "Iceland spar," says a knowledgeable librarian early in the novel "is what hides the Hidden People, makes it possible for them to move through the world that thinks of itself as 'real,' ... so they can exist alongside our own world but not be seen" (*ATD*: 134).

The several underworlds, counterworlds, and alternative modes of existence and knowledge evoked in Pynchon's and Bolaño's novels have long seemed to exist as untouched from the "daylit" world (*ATD*: 566). If such a marginalization has perhaps not fully denied their existence, it has at least kept them safely away in some sort of "ontological quarantine" (Franke 2016: 8). But instead of merely blurring the boundaries between the visible and the invisible, the dominant and the alternative, *hyperbolic realism* plays on their permeability and porosity in often exhilaratingly funny ways. Take as an example the scene where a character jumps from his residing "severe ice-scape" to the "luxuriant world" of a parrot contemplated on the label of a bottle of liquor. Both worlds seem unbridgeably far away yet are in fact "separated from [each other] by only the thinnest of membranes." The method for traveling between the worlds is somewhat mystical as one has to "fill one's attention unremittingly with the bird's image," repeating its cheeky advertising slogan—"¡*Cuidado cabrón!*"—over and over again until it loses its meaning (*ATD*: 130).

All this seems as far away from reality as one can possibly imagine. But even in the most hyperreal and fantastic setting, we always seem to hear a version of Slothrop's question in the face of his liminal encounter with Bianca: "What happened back there?"—back there, where we cannot even be sure "of the certainty of our fantasy" (Duyfhuizen 1991: § 14)? If a certain grounding in the material structure of the real seems always at hand, flat fictionality constantly reminds us of the novel's consistent metaphorization and plunges the whole action into a dreamlike atmosphere. In *Paradiso,* one of the most exciting and challenging maximalist novels of modern literature, José Lezama Lima finds timeless words to that moment where the borders between the worlds become porous as flat fictionality rises to the fore and *as if* temporarily kidnaps the whole discourse:

> Now, at the bottom of the drain, José Eugenio Cemí was lifting the pitcher curving it over a glass, as his hand increased the parabola of the falling water with that dream-like elasticity that erases distances between objects, lacking temporal chiaroscuro, matter surrendered to the penetration of waters into the dream. A spongy world, indistinct, where

undifferentiated, concentric rosettas emphasized the contractions of their plucking, a non-existent realm of color like a shadow that bites as it retreats, the biting also useless, beginning to set (Lezama Lima [1966] 2000: 93).[12]

Against a strong tendency of paranoid readings, which might as well be called postmodernist, Lezama's onto-poetic model of the "spongy world" does not necessarily picture the real as a conspiratorial network of simulations, although it acknowledges and even emphasizes extreme degrees of unreality. Much more nuanced than that, the sponge represents a weird entity, oscillating between the organic and the inorganic, releasing its stored materials in relation to the pressure that is exerted on it, inviting more options for the ways in which the new, the fantastic, and "that dream-like elasticity that erases distance between objects" become eligible to permeate our daily lives.

In moments that appear extremely unreal, the hyperbolically real paves a way through the spongy world and reveals itself at the intersection of (im)possible worlds. To the extent that alternative ontologies of these worlds can be vicariously approached through metaphor, metonymy, and the combination of the two, strange and fateful encounters across conflicting realities become possible, although the outcome and reach of these encounters remain almost always uncertain.

In their most radical consequence, these trans-mundane encounters almost entirely collapse the difference between metaphor and metonymy to become negotiations between the worlds of the living and the dead. He "coalesced slowly into the dark institutional hour" (*ATD*: 673); the phrase prepares the intersecting of two worlds that are usually separate, so that a short encounter between Kit Traverse and his murdered Anarchist father becomes possible. Again, it is the night, that "exceptional possibility" (Lispector 2015: 491), that puts Kit in a liminal state where he can hear the "voices and flows and mechanical repetitions he was forbidden to hear in daytime," even if he cannot free himself completely of the claustrophobic "thinking [that] he was somehow in jail" (*ATD*: 673).

The encounter is framed as a life-changing, epiphanic moment as Kit feels a "terrible certainty he couldn't immediately name but which

---

[12]"Ahora en el fondo del tragante, José Eugenio Cemí levantaba la jarra, curvándola sobre un vaso, que a medida que su mano acrecentaba la parábola de la caída de las aguas, por esa elasticidad del sueño que borra las dimensiones entre los objetos, llegando a convertirse en una cascada rodeada de una naturaleza detenida, congelada, sin claroscuro temporal, donde la materia se había rendido a la penetración de las aguas en el sueño. Mundo espongiario, indistinto, donde las concéntricas rosetas indiferenciadas, señalaban las contracciones de su desprendimiento, inexistente la región donde el color, como una sombra que muerde al retroceder, también inútil sus mordeduras, comenzó a fijarse" (Lezama Lima [1966] 2011: 125).

he knew he had to live under the weight of now" (*ATD*: 673). But the mutual feeling of guilt and failure prevail: on Webb's side, the failure of not having provided enough fatherly care due to his Anarchist adventures; on Kit's side, the guilty feeling of receiving financial support from his father's assassin, Scarsdale Vibe. The bitter lesson of this scene, then, is that post-mortal communication cannot compensate for what has been missed in life. If flat fictionality works like a "drug-like facilitator between the worlds" (*ATD*: 433), it cannot lead to a real resurrection beyond the metaphorical ones, and no one is saved, neither the living nor the dead. Despite the trans-mundane contact briefly established between Kit and his father, then, what prevails in the end is insurmountable distance and a melancholic acceptance that what should have clearly been spoken out once can now only be indirectly implied through the extremely elliptic form of metonymic allusion:

> He must have wanted all along to be the one son Webb could believe in—no matter what kind of trouble Reef might be rambling around out there looking to get into, or how pro-or anti-Union Frank's engineering ambitions might turn out to be, Kit had always thought he would be there for his father no matter what, if only because there was nothing in the way of it, nothing he could see. But then just like that there he was, out of the house and down in the meanest part of the U.S., and before he could even remember who he was, Webb was gone. If he could only've been surer of Kit, maybe when the awful hour came to claim him, he could have fought back by just enough extra will to survive after all. Restricted now to séances and dreams, he could no longer say this to Kit in so many words but must use the stripped and dismal metonymies of the dead (*ATD*: 673).

7

Sed Tamen Effabor

My doubt is a petition for more certainty.
JOÃO GUIMARÃES ROSA

Practical Disbelief

Toward the end of Part I of *2666*, the two European literary critics Pelletier and Espinoza arrive in Mexico where they start searching for traces of their favorite writer, the mysterious Archimboldi. Driven by their literary obsession to the Latin American continent, they do not find what they are looking for. But instead they find something else: "la historia de las mujeres asesinadas" (Bolaño 2004a: 181). From the very beginning, this unbelievable story is surrounded by oblivion, rumor, and disbelief. One night, Spinoza, suddenly and randomly, remembers the conversation with a boy who had told him and Pelletier of more than two hundred female victims, a fact he had "to repeat … two or three times because neither Espinoza nor Pelletier could believe his ears" (*2666*: 137).

The critics' first reaction to their conversational encounter with the *feminicidios* is incredulous astonishment. As professional readers, their routinized doubt makes it hard for them at first to believe in such brutal news, which pose a threat to all usual forms of symbolic appropriation. But while Espinoza starts a romance with Rosa Amalfitano, the daughter of the second part's main protagonist, Pelletier, after a brief hesitation, puts Archimboldi's books aside and turns his attention to the newspaper. Literally lifting his head to return to the world from his immersion into Archimboldi's aesthetics of marginality, Pelletier starts to make use of his poor Spanish "to find out what's going on in this city" (*2666*: 137).

As Pelletier is trying to break through the sealed surfaces of words and signs, Espinoza meditates on the seemingly inconspicuous phrase *no dar crédito,* used by the narrator to express the critics' skepticism:

> Not believing your ears, though, thought Espinoza, is a form of exaggeration. You see something beautiful and you can't believe your eyes. Someone tells you something about ... the natural beauty of Iceland ... people bathing in thermal springs, among geysers ... in fact you've seen it in pictures, but still you say you can't believe it ... Although obviously you believe it ... Exaggeration is a form of polite admiration ... You set it up so the person you're talking to can say: it's true ... And then you say: incredible. First you can't believe it and then you think it's incredible (2666: 137).[1]

The narrative voice oscillates between an extensive, if not unrestrained omniscient view from above and an internal focalization on the character. It also shifts back and forth from almost unintelligible banality into highly charged metapoetic reflection. If we take Espinoza's daydreaming seriously, we can see in it the staging of a conflict between disbelief and exaggeration, or, to put it differently, of doubt and hyperbole.

No dar crédito invites two paradoxes. The first one is rather harmless. Confronted with an overwhelming manifestation of the real, we casually say that we cannot believe what we experience, even if we've seen it before and even if, *en realidad,* we actually do believe it. However, what begins as a merely rhetorical routine—the insinuation of doubt and disbelief in the face of extreme reality—can suddenly get out of control: *First you can't believe it and then you think it's incredible.* This second paradox is much trickier than the first one, but as pathos and bathos in Bolaño are often separated by only the thinnest of membranes, we should not see them as absolutely different from each other. What they both intend to show is that the routinized uses of exaggeration and disbelief, which mainly serve to strengthen the phatic relation between speaker and listener, are always in danger of relegating into oblivion and nothingness what is an extreme and therefore emphatic expression of the real.

In the context of the *feminicidios,* we could read Espinoza's words as a subtle and almost cynical hint to the profound abyss that separates theoretical knowledge from political action. Everybody in Santa Teresa knows and believes more or less what is going on there, yet most actors don't seem

---

[1] "No dar crédito, sin embargo, pensó Espinoza, es una forma de exagerar. Uno ve algo hermoso y no da crédito a sus ojos. Te cuentan algo sobre ... la belleza natural de Islandia ... gente bañándose en aguas termales, entre géiseres, en realidad tú ya lo has visto en fotos, pero igual dices que no te lo puedes creer ... Aunque evidentemente lo crees ... Exagerar es una forma de admirar cortésmente ... Das el pie para que tu interlocutor diga: es verdad ... Y entonces dices: es increíble. Primero no te lo puedes creer y luego te parece increíble" (Bolaño 2004a: 181).

to believe it strongly enough or in a way that makes them engage in truly political acts of resistance, and not only symbolic ones. Placed in the realm of politics and social conflict, then, *no dar crédito* sounds like the society of spectacle's infinitely repeated standard reaction to incommensurate violence and inequality, a standard reaction qualified by the British filmmaker Adam Curtis as *Oh dearism* (Curtis 2009). *Oh dearism* is a media-oriented form of permanent indignation that refuses to get at the core of the problem and leaves the spectator with a feeling of complete powerlessness. Instead of assessing the systemic condition of violence, of calling out names and institutions, and assuming political and economic responsibility, the public, the media, and even the responsible institutions (the police, the justice, the politicians) produce and reproduce spectacular "unbelievable" stories about a serial killer roaming the streets of Santa Teresa, raping and killing working-class women at random.

But *no dar crédito* can also be used as an opposing strategy to the official histories and narratives that shape public opinion and our present at large. Radical skepticism concerning any kind of *grand narrative* is of course the quintessential trademark of postmodern literature and culture, so it seems hardly worth mentioning. Yet in Bolaño's and Pynchon's late maximalist novels 2666 and *ATD*, doubt and uncertainty are not always foregrounded, less ostentatiously exposed but rather elegantly incorporated into the calm flux of the narrative voice(s). In earlier fiction of these authors such as *Crying of Lot 49* or *Estrella Distante,* linguistic, perceptual, and ontological skepticism catches the eye from even the smallest details, as we can see in the following example: "Off the coast of either what is now Carmel-by-the-Sea, or what is now Pismo Beach, around noon or possibly toward dusk, the two ships sighted each other. One of them may have fired, if it did then the other responded; but both were out of range so neither showed a scar afterward to prove anything" (Pynchon [1965] 2000: 33). *Around noon or possibly towards dusk*—a hilariously elastic time indication serving as a perfect frame for the novel's consistent atmosphere of doubt and uncertainty.

In times of dwindling confidence in postmodern routines, 2666 and *ATD* refuse to put their narrative doubt into the service of a hermeneutics of suspicion. Their narrative doubt usually remains a discrete potential of the text's unconscious, only rarely and erratically pushing through its surface.[2] As much as hyperbole itself, doubt in Pynchon's and Bolaño's

---

[2] My (phenomenological) understanding of doubt as latent or rather intermittent potential of the text comes close to Namwali Serpell's conception of uncertainty developed in *Seven Modes of Uncertainty*. Unlike Empson's seven types of ambiguity, Serpell's vagueness and uncertainty refer not so much to a punctual stylistic event, but rather to a mode of composition, an atmospheric *Stimmung* of the text. They are distributive phenomena rather than fixated entities. About the irreducible multiplicity of perspectives juxtaposed in what she fittingly calls the *Rashomon effect*, Serpell writes: "If we view multiplicity under a phenomenological lens, we see that its various literary manifestations possess varying degrees of doubt about 'what really happened.' These degrees of doubt depend as much on the thickness and intensity of the text's mode of uncertainty as on where we land at its end" (Serpell 2014: 116).

late maximalist novels functions as an intermittent *figura* that impregnates the whole narrative universe while often remaining discretely in its background.

At first glance, it might seem strange to view doubt and hyperbole as related phenomena or even homologues. We could even see them as complete opposites in the sense that radical doubt interrupts discourse and narrative to widen the chasm between words and things whereas hyperbole is engaged in a constant effort of bridging the semiotic rift through the use of speculation, superlative, and abundant description. Such a binary and static view of doubt and hyperbole, however, is misleading, as we can easily see if we go back to a famous example. In Descartes's methodological skepticism, doubt itself becomes hyperbolic, and together they do not inhibit but condition knowledge, reason, and experience. In their interrelatedness, doubt becomes much more than an interruption of the flux of meaning; whereas hyperbole can overcome its triumphalist tendency by exposing its excesses and limitations.

Extravagant Doubt and the Suspension of Mimesis

In his seminal book on hyperbolic thought and writing in the Baroque, Christopher Johnson keeps returning to the complex relation between doubt and hyperbole. Across the varying cases, it becomes clear that radical doubt is not an unequivocally defensive strategy but that it can be extremely combative. In Sor Juana's *Sueños*, for instance, doubt is intimately connected to desire and the risk of self-exposure (Johnson 2010: 268). In Chapter 9, which analyzes the relation between skepticism, stoicism, and hyperbole's "provisional violence against belief" (2010: 291), Johnson introduces the notion of "extravagant doubt" (2010: 309) to highlight the affective pathos dwelling "between saying and meaning" (2010: 281), in the gaps created by poetic disbelief. In the chapter on Descartes, eventually, Johnson reads the rationalist's notorious use of hyperbolic doubt as both an attack on the dogmatic certainties of scholasticism and as an attempt to overcome the one-dimensional skepticism that has led to a *crise pyrrhonienne* (2010: 413). Before Descartes eventually reaches what he sees as a final truth—the discovery of the cogito by way of eliminating any options for the bad influence of a *deus malignus*—he first needs to fight off a number of specters and illusions. This entails the possibility that if his final solution won't be convincing, those illusions and specters come back to claim their haunting presence at the heart of the epistemological scene. Revealing an extremely versatile and stubborn nature, hyperbolic doubt becomes a constant challenge to the hopes and ambitions of the rationalist philosophers.

If Johnson demonstrates how doubt and hyperbole interact in poetry, rhetoric, and philosophy, Elizabeth Levine adds a narratological dimension to the problem. In a short chapter of her book *The Serious Pleasures of Suspense*, Levine (2003) reads George Eliot's story *The Lifted Veil* from 1859 and the use it makes of narrative doubt as a clever attack against two pillars of nineteenth-century realism: mimesis and suspense.

Responding to the century's waning reliance on literature as an instrument of suspenseful representations of the world, Eliot's first-person narrator turns inward. In the short autobiographical narrative, both explicit and implicit doubt surrounding mimesis and suspense serve as a springboard for the escape of a rich banker's son from business life. Secluded from the public sphere, his restless mind wanders "uncertainly in search of more vivid images" and "clairvoyant" moments (Levine 2003: 131; Eliot [1859] 1999: 10, 37).

One of the crucial passages on doubt in *The Lifted Veil* is revealing:

So absolute is our soul's need of something hidden and uncertain for the maintenance of that doubt and hope and effort which are the breath of its life, that if the whole future were laid bare to us beyond to-day, the interest of all mankind would be bent on the hours that lie between; we should pant after the uncertainties of our one morning and our one afternoon; we should rush fiercely to the Exchange for our last possibility of speculation, of success, of disappointment: we should have a glut of political prophets foretelling a crisis or a no-crisis within the only twenty-four hours left open to prophecy (Eliot [1859] 1999: 29).

Without entering too deeply into the intricacies of this peculiar text, one major thing to retain from the quote is the fact that just as epistemic doubt does not erode the soul, but breathes new life into it, narrative doubt does not merely interrupt the text's progress, but drives it forward—by way of interruption. The fact that doubt is mentioned in one breath with "hope and effort" has at least two implications for a phenomenology of literary doubt. First, instead of being mutually exclusive, doubt and hope—uncertainty and belief—join forces to defend the enigmatic nature of life against the terror of hyper-rationalism and full transparency. Second, connecting doubt with effort suggests that both the soul's and the text's lives cannot be organized once and for all, but that they are the result of an ongoing, laborious practice. If both the text and the soul depend on ongoing labor, doubt is no longer a problem to be overcome, but becomes an important factor that drives the narrative and spiritual effort to their non-conclusive ends.

Lucretius Reacts to the Myth of the Ineffable

Lucretius, *De Rerum Natura,* Book 5. We have arrived at a significant moment in the epos, right before Lucretius starts to present the main assumptions of his materialist cosmology. But before that, we come across a rather peculiar passage that I want to quote in full length:

> To proceed, and to delay you no longer with promises, first of all, Memmius, consider the sea, the earth, and the sky: their triple nature, their three bodies, their three different forms, their three huge fabrics, a single day will consign to destruction; and the massive structure of the world, sustained for countless years, will collapse. I am well aware how strange and stupendous to the mind is the notion that heaven and earth are destined to be destroyed, and how difficult it is for me to win belief by words alone. This is always the case when one brings to people's ears something hitherto unfamiliar, without being able to set it before their eyes or place it in their hands the two highways that give belief easiest access to the human breast and the precincts of the mind. Nevertheless I will speak out. Perhaps the actual event will confirm my words, and you will see the whole world shattered in a brief space of time by violent earthquakes. But may piloting fortune steer this catastrophe far from us, and may reasoning rather than reality convince you that the whole world may give way and collapse with a horrendous crash (Lucretius 2011: 139).

In this turbulent passage, Lucretius confronts his friend Memmius and the reader alike with a "strange and stupendous" idea, the idea of the certainty of the world's future collapse in one single day. Reading the passage in its entirety gives us a sense of the rhythmic environment in which "something hitherto unfamiliar" finally comes to expression. The difficulty "to win belief by words alone" is countered with the resolute rhetorical gesture that I adopt as a title for this chapter: *sed tamen effabor*—"nevertheless I will speak out." In Lucretius's articulation of his view of the cosmos, *sed tamen effabor* marks the moment when radical doubt about the possibility of any discourse on nature comes to the fore, surprisingly, to motivate the speaker's speaking and not to plunge his speech into powerless silence.

The passage starts with a characteristic reminder to not further delay the beginning or continuation of the narrative and to move from rhetorical promise to actual linguistic fulfillment. Against the backdrop of mankind's certain extinction—actually not only mankind, not even the gods will be spared by the end of the world—Lucretius will develop a cosmology based on the idea that the whole universe and the formation of matter are a result of purely contingent processes. Such a hitherto unfamiliar thought inevitably provokes astonishment, wonder, and anxiety among the audience, and, as Lucretius anticipates, it will take a considerable effort to convince his listeners of the truth of his materialist vision.

Lucretius clearly flirts with the topos of the ineffable, but his materialist take on both language and nature has no patience for the metaphysics of absolute inexpressibility.[3] Instead, he ventures into a space where "something hitherto unfamiliar," a "not-yet-thought" (Morton 2016: 1) cosmological truth, inaccessible for sight and touch, is voiced in a highly speculative manner. It is a linguistic situation that invites intuition, metaphor, analogy, and, of course, hyperbole.

It is in this atmosphere of extreme linguistic difficulty that the crucial phrase is uttered: *sed tamen effabor*. As the verse continues, the authority is transferred to the "actual reality," *ipsa res*, which will or will not confirm the speaker's "oracles" (Lucretius 2011: 139). The subject is decentered to make way for language itself as it becomes an auxiliary medium for the "piloting nature [that] steers the courses of the sun and the motions of the moon" (2011: 139). In almost exemplary hyperbolic manner, Lucretius tries to produce a somehow paradoxical *evidentia* ("and you will see"), culminating in the bold confirmation that "the whole world may give way and collapse with a horrendous crash."

Like every totality, the cosmos as a whole is ineffable. Nevertheless, says Lucretius, here I am, speaking it out. In his prologue to *Dark Ecology*, Timothy Morton does something strikingly similar: "There is not-yet-thought that never arrives—yet here we are thinking it in the paradoxical flicker of this very sentence" (Morton 2016: 1). Speaking about that which is not yet thought—nature, the cosmos, and the end of the world—is a risky act. Its only measure of success lies on the side of nature itself, of *res ipsa*, which is the thing that never arrives, for speech and expression at least. So here we are with not much more than the labor of language. Lucretius therefore proposes a decidedly materialist approach to totality, an approach that always knows and exposes both its limits and its excesses. Just like Lucretius and Morton, Pynchon and Bolaño are always aware of their hyperbolic ambitions and the impossibility to come to a complete description of nature, the cosmos or the real. Yet their reaction is not infinite suspension, indifference, resignation, or the endlessly self-reflective play with signs and references. Knowing all too well that the real is ultimately ineffable, they speak it out, nevertheless. Against the day, against the grain, and against all odds.

---

[3]In his comprehensive study of Lucretius's influence on Western writing across the countries and centuries, Jonathan Pollock writes: "There is no absolute zero in the Epicurean world" (Pollock 2010: 147)—good news for the hyperbolist who always prefers the beta and psi to the alpha and omega.

Sin Embargo: Ontological Simulacrum and Hyperbolic Stubbornness

With Johnson, Levine, and Lucretius in mind, let's go back to 2666 at the end of Part I. "Not believing your ears, though, thought Espinoza, is a form of exaggeration" (2666: 137). Espinoza's idle thought intimately connects doubt, defiance, and hyperbole. As literary critics, Espinoza and Pelletier are trained to view nature and so-called reality as a construction. Nothing could be more familiar to them than to raise constant linguistic and epistemological doubt in the face of the official versions of history. Yet, if we belief what the narrator tells us (a belief that is not self-evident, obviously), the critics fail to apply their literary competences to existential and social questions that are quite basic. In their immersive search for a voluntary *desaparecido*, not only did they lose connection with the brute facts in front of their eyes, they are equally oblivious of the hyperbolic and mysterious realities produced by the material conditions of millennial capitalism.

Their discovery of the *feminicidios* brutally interrupts their ontological slumber, as the narrator emphasizes in a rare moment of declarative explicitness: "After that moment, reality for Pelletier and Espinoza seemed to tear like paper scenery" (2666: 179), a description embodying almost perfectly the well-known postmodern devaluation of empirical reality as ontological simulacrum. But Bolaño is not satisfied with just another reiteration of skeptical resignation or ironic detachment in face of the real. Instead, what follows up on interruptive event is a typically hyperbolic image of what reality looks like once its texture is torn apart like a sheet of paper: "and when it was stripped away it revealed what was behind it: a smoking landscape, as if someone, an angel, maybe, was tending hundreds of barbecue pits for a crowd of invisible beings" (2666: 179).

Against the postmodern standard scenario, the deconstruction of reality naively seen from the "natural attitude" (Husserl [1913] 1983: 51–62) as simulacrum does not produce an effect of derealization, but provokes a hyperbolic counter-reaction, a "plunge into reality" (O'Connor [1957] 1970: 78) by way of fiction and risky metaphor.[4] Richir (2015: 133) makes it very

---

[4] The whole passage in O'Connor's essay about her craft is also a polemic against the middle-brow complaint that modern and difficult writers cultivate despair and negativity: "People are always complaining that the modern novelist has no hope and that the picture he paints of the world is unbearable. The only answer to this is that people without hope do not write novels. Writing a novel is a terrible experience, during which the hair often falls out and the teeth decay. I'm always highly irritated by people who imply that writing fiction is an escape from reality. It is a plunge into reality and it's very shocking to the system. If the novelist is not sustained by a hope of money, then he must be sustained by a hope of salvation, or he simply won't survive the ordeal" (O'Connor [1957] 1970: 78–9).

clear that this understanding of the ontological simulacrum is quite different from a Baudrillardian view that tends to turn all experience into the product of a large and delusional machine that produces nothing but simulations. However, hyperbole in Bolaño's as well as in Pynchon's narrative systems is not meant to overcome and abolish doubt and uncertainty once and for all. To say the least, we are not sure how lasting the effect of the critics' discovery will be as they are abandoned by the narrator after the first part.

On the one hand, then, the hyperbolic image is a daring attempt to produce images for a reality that is given under the sign of unreality and inexpressibility. On the other hand, it does not hide the riskiness of its attempt, the fragility of every act of expression that tries to evoke some sense of totality or wholeness, its contingent character, and its temporary validity.

Pynchon's Hyperbolic Carnival

One of the funniest and most inventive episodes in a book full of funny inventions takes place at the margins of Venice and is narrated in the fourth part of *ATD*. During the official carnival period, a "secret counter-Carnevale known as Carnesalve" takes place at the outskirts of Venice, a hyperbolic feast, outplaying and outdoing Carnevale (*ATD*: 880). The ground for transgressive behavior could hardly be more fertile. A remote underworld, an island at the outer limits of the Venetian Lagoon, a "slowly drowning palazzo," and midnight as the ominous part of the day provide the setting for the "secret life of Masks" ruling over the following couple of pages. Substantial constraints are suspended, identities are loosened up, and masks are put and passed on. But similar to our examples above, Carnesalve is not simply another occasion to escape reality, but provides a springboard to plunge deeper into the complex texture of the real, "not a farewell but an enthusiastic welcome to flesh in all its promise" (*ATD*: 880).

Three characters from the main cast of the book are part of the happy few who get invited to Pynchon's hyperbolic carnival: Cyprian Latewood who is dressed in drag,[5] "in a black taffeta ball toilette borrowed from the

---

[5] Let us remember that drag is not (just) disguise, as demonstrated by Jennie Livingston's movie *Paris Is Burning* and most other examples of drag culture that is keeping it real. The difference between drag and disguise pretty much describes the difference between carnevale and carnesalve. Drag is not escapist; *keeping it real* is a major quality standard in drag culture. To be in drag not only means to buy yourself a brief moment of liberation from everyday life. Instead, drag creates a real-time fictional zone that enables the invention of new aesthetic forms, the creation and tightening of social bonds and the building of communities.

Principessa, an abbreviated mask of black leather over his eyes" (*ATD*: 881); Reef Traverse, a Colorado gunslinger and showpiece of macho masculinity, who is wearing a tight and glaringly out-of-character Pierrot costume; and, finally, Yashmeen Halfcourt, "in satin domino, speaking from behind a lace veil that covered her face from hairline to just below her chin" (881). After Cyprian illicitly touches Reef's genitals and arouses him almost against his will, Yashmeen abducts the two into "an upper room" (881) decorated with velvet furniture and frescos whose putti "over the generations had seen it all" (*ATD*: 882). Hidden in the decadent scenery, the unusual trio engages in an exquisite threesome, which ends with a remarkable scene of insemination: Yashmeen forces Reef to come into Cyprian's mouth who then impregnates Yashmeen by spitting Reef's sperm into her vagina.

Carnesalve ends as abruptly as it began, with an aposiopesis that leaves the outcome of the scene in suspension until a little later when Yashmeen's pregnancy is revealed. The narrative cut is striking, not at least because it involves one of the very few direct explicit appearances of the narrator on the narrative surface. Having indulged in pornographic play, the narrator suddenly (and somewhat ironically) shifts into a prudish register, as if reminded of the rules of conduct of their historical age. The reader is asked to grant the quirky threesome their intimacy, with Reef and Yashmeen "smiling too directly at one another," holding an "absurdly grateful" Cyprian between them like a baby for whom "the vigorous seeing-to he was now receiving seem[s] almost—though only almost—incidental" (*ATD*: 883).

The move away from Carnesalve could hardly be more anti-climactic considering how effervescently Pynchon had introduced the event to its readers. "With no interference from authority, church or civic," he writes, "all this bounded world here succumbed to a masked imperative, all hold on verbatim identities loosening until lost altogether in the delirium" (*ATD*: 879). After a transitional period of immersion, the feeling or, more precisely, the certainty emerges "that there had always existed separately a world in which masks were the real, everyday faces, faces with their own rules of expression, which knew and understand one another—a secret life of Masks" (879). The event is thus clearly distinguished from Carnevale where the partygoers are "allowed to pretend," where they can cultivate a "privileged indifference to the world of flesh" whereas at Carnesalve "as in espionage, or some revolutionary project, the Mask's desire was to be invisible, unthreatening, transparent yet mercilessly deceptive, as beneath its dark authority danger ruled and all was transgressed" (879).

As Carnesalve, like fiction, represents a "bounded world," it creates a fictional fold within an already fictional universe. It is a separate realm, yet accessible through a physical and ritual transition from a better-known point of departure (historical Venice), although it takes "a day or two" to perform this transition to really adapt yourself. In the laborious twists and turns of figuration, characteristic for maximalist literature in general and hyperbolic realism in particular, we learn that Carnesalve is in one way quite like Carnevale, but in another "not quite" like it; the main difference being that the masquerade in Carnesalve is not "of the safe sort where the mask may be dropped at that critical moment it presumes itself as reality" (Gaddis [1955] 2012: 3). Fittingly, the passage clearly embodies the spirit of *sed tamen effabor*, made explicit by the efficient use of the word *yet*. In an apparent paradox, absolute transparency represents the peak of opacity and instead of being a condition of clear perception and knowledge turns out to be "mercilessly deceptive."

All of the above makes it unmistakably clear that Carnesalve is anything but an ordinary costume party. Instead, it is a potentially life-changing proto-drag event where the mask, close to its etymological origin, not only veils a person's face, but creates a new persona in the flesh. Consequently, Cyprian, Reef, and Yashmeen all undergo profound emotional and existential changes: Reef's hyper-masculinity is liquefied after he positively responds to Cyprian's erotic infringement; Cyprian learns to accept and enjoy his submission without bringing himself in life-threatening situations; and Yashmeen becomes pregnant in a creative and emancipated act of reproduction that interrupts the patriarchal structure of the triangular family:

> It was around this same time that Yashmeen discovered she was pregnant with Reef's child—and, as Cyprian would be pleased to imagine, in some auxiliary sense, in ambiguous lamplight and masked fantasy, his own (*ATD*: 891).

Despite the narrative *coitus interruptus* right after Reef starts to penetrate Cyprian, the narrative comes back to the scene later to reveal its results. This is characteristic for hyperbolic realism, which often fills in the gaps that orthodox postmodern literature would probably leave open or only revisit to further postpone their resolution in a dutiful literary embodiment of Derrida's philosophical concept of *différance*. However, hyperbolic realism often waits a long time before it provides a narrative solution. The syncopated character of these solutions therefore produces newly enigmatic and unresolved doubts and uncertainties. "You never sense the 'aftermath' because always, something else starts up along the way" (Kraus 1997: 75).

The Penultimate Self-Portrait of Edwin Johns

Benno von Archimboldi is not the only enigmatic artist of interest in *2666*. In a typically casual conversation in Part I, the English literary critic Liz Norton tells her Italian friend and colleague Piero Morini about a British painter who as a young man singlehandedly started an avant-garde movement "that would later be known as the *new decadence or English animalism*" (2666: 52). Not only because the movement remains largely unnoticed, Johns is presented as the exemplary anarchic anti-artist, bursting into the arts scene from the lower class as a threat to the establishment. According to a familiar cliché, his radicalism is in constant danger of falling into madness. Finally, in an outburst of inexplicable panic shortly before he is admitted to a psychiatric hospital, Johns cuts off his right hand, which happens to be "the hand he painted with" (2666: 87).

But Bolaño goes beyond the reproduction of the usual image that places Johns in a row with mad artists who ended up destroying themselves as they directly applied their radical aesthetic commitments to their bodies and lives.

The popular fantasy of the mad genius who cuts off his ear to demonstrate his detachment from a wrong society is paradoxically rejected or at least diverted in the very moment when Johns installs his mummified hand at the center of his final work of art. The painful irony is emphasized by the fact that his self-mutilation becomes one of the major factors of his successful exhibition, which takes place in a presumably alternative art gallery in a former working-class and now successfully gentrified neighborhood:

> The paintings weren't bad. Still, the show wouldn't have been so successful or had such an impact if not for the central painting, much smaller than the rest, the masterpiece that years later led so many British artists down the path of new decadence. This painting, viewed properly (although one could never be sure of viewing it properly), was an ellipsis of self-portraits, sometimes a spiral of self-portraits (depending on the angle from which it was seen), seven feet by three and a half feet, in the center of which hung the painter's mummified right hand (2666: 52–3).[6]

In Johns's hyperbolic self-portrait, which marks a certain endpoint of the long history of the genre, both as climax and *cul-de-sac*,[7] self-representation

---

[6]"Los cuadros no eran malos. Pese a todo, la exposición no hubiera tenido ni el éxito ni la repercusión que tuvo de no ser por el cuadro estrella, mucho más pequeño que los otros, la obra maestra que empujó a tantos artistas británicos, años después, por la senda del nuevo decadentismo. Éste, de dos metros por uno, era, bien mirado (aunque nadie podía estar seguro de mirarlo bien), una elipsis de autorretratos, en ocasiones una espiral de autorretratos (depende del lugar desde donde fuera contemplado), en cuyo centro, momificada, pendía la mano derecha del pintor" (Bolaño 2004a: 76).

[7]The strong material and aesthetic limitations of self-mutilation as a strategy of aesthetic expression are succinctly summarized in a famous statement by the German artist Martin Kippenberger: *I can't cut off an ear everyday* (see Haun 2008: 49).

culminates in a vertiginously incarnated *mise en abyme,* which immediately sparks Morini's attention, an attention that will soon turn into obsession. From the narrator's allusions, we suspect that for Morini, who is tied to a wheelchair, there must be more at stake than a merely personal fascination. We must read carefully to get there, as the narrator demonstrates a certain form of "ritual reluctance" (Pynchon [1965] 2000: 51) and strongly focalizes on the three other Archimboldians in the respective passages.

Toward the middle of the first part, accompanied by his friends and colleagues Pelletier and Espinoza Morini finally meets Johns face-to-face in a Swiss psychiatric hospital. Bolaño creates the chilling atmosphere of a duel that is about to take place between the melancholic intellectual and the manic artist. Morini asks a few questions, Johns gives effusive, incoherent, and multidimensional answers that oscillate between dilettante nonsense and profound originality. As the interview approaches its peak, the narrator plunges the scene in an eerie play of light and shadow—Bolaño's favored lighting conditions and one of his most efficient techniques to create sudden suspense: "Dusk had settled around Morini and Johns now" (2666: 91). And then Morini asks a question that seems to be the central impulse for his obsession for the wounded artist: "Why did you mutilate yourself?" (2666: 90–1).

As Johns prepares himself to answer, the darkness that already surrounds the two antagonists (*rodeados de penumbra*) rapidly intensifies. The nurse wants to switch on the light, Pelletier prevents it. Focalizing on Pelletier, the narrator's gaze, weirdly enough, turns to the color of the shoes of those present: the nurse's are white, Pelletier's and Espinoza's are black, Morini's are brown, "Johns's shoes were white and made for running long distance, on the paved streets of a city or cross-country" (2666: 91). The color of shoes, "their shape and stillness," is the last thing Pelletier sees "before night plunged them into the cold nothingness of the Alps" (91). And then, at the height of suspense, the mutilated artist tells the impaired paraplegic critic why he mutilated himself, "and for the first time his body relaxed, abandoning its stiff, martial stance, and he bent toward Morini, saying something into his ear" (2666: 91).

That is all—for now, at least. Johns stands up to shake hands with Espinoza and Pelletier, which increases the already grotesque character of the scene as we know that the artist must shake hands with his remaining left hand. He leaves the room in his white running shoes without shaking Morini's hands, and the three critics return to their hotel. The next day, Morini disappears, and we are left with an unanswered question: What did Johns tell Morini into the ear; what was the real reason to cut off his hand? Used to postmodern literature's celebration of ambiguity and unresolvable questions, we have every reason to believe that the answer will disappear in the same "cold nothingness of the Alps" (2666: 91) that had swallowed the five characters in the meeting room of a remote psychiatric hospital in Switzerland.

But once again (and for the first time in 2666), Bolaño demonstrates his dissatisfaction with a strategy familiar from narratives typically defined as modern or postmodern in which the narrator creates a central, enigmatic, and decisive moment for the sole purpose to keep it ambiguously unresolved. Incomplete as it may be, the novel provides an answer and thus to a certain extent a conclusion to Morini's pernicious inquiries. The *dénoumenent* takes place, once more, in an anti-climactic setting, a casual moment between the rather unusual romantic couple Morini and Norton when the Italian critic "adopting a casual tone of voice, said he thought he knew why Johns had cut off his right hand." For a moment, Liz doesn't even remember who that is, although she was the one who had told Morini about the radiating figure of the *nuevos decadentistas* in the first place. So why did he do it? For Money, says Morini. Money? Yes, money, Morini confirms: "'Because he believed in investments, the flow of capital, one has to play the game to win, that kind of thing'" (2666: 97).

Like many modern and postmodern writers, Bolaño loves to create suspense, bifurcations, and ambiguity, often instilled with a characteristic pathos of not-knowing. But just as often he is not quite satisfied with the simple celebration of openness, unresolvable tension, and symmetric ambiguity. Many times, always almost in fact, he revisits a riddle or open question laid out earlier to lead it to some kind of solution at least. However, these solutions are reliably undramatic and "mercilessly deceptive" (2666: 880) when compared to the initial amount of pathetic mystery. Suspense is not perpetuated into endless suspension; pathos falls into bathos.

The same intricate interplay of pathetic preparation and bathetic solution is felt when Archimboldi finally appears in Part V of 2666. Suspension in 2666 is often hyperbolically extended, but usually not infinitely maintained. Enigmas are solved, ambiguities disentangled, at least to some extent. The circumstances under which they are solved, however, remain contingent and casual. Within sometimes short, sometimes longer arcs of suspension, enigmas are led to partial solutions in which new enigmas, questions, and mysteries emerge. In the same vein, at the end of Part 1, the narrative episode of the British artist comes to its final conclusion. The narrated circumstances of his death, however, could hardly be less dramatic. Sitting at the edge of a rock, accompanied by a female nurse and a burly *muchacho*, looking out on a sublime landscape that includes the inevitable waterfall, Johns seems to be peacefully drawing, with his left hand, of course, "with which he had become quite proficient." Yet a brief moment later, "the accident happened. Johns stood up on the rock and slipped, and although the man tried to catch him, he fell into the abyss. That was all" (2666: 150–1).

The Melancholy of Totality

Eso era todo. Was that really all there was? What remains when *hyperbolic realism* decides that a particular motif or narrative episode has been exhausted, that some kind of totality, however temporary, fragile and incomplete it may be, has been achieved? Where to go after the last directions are given in Pynchon's "corrupted pilgrim's guide" (*ATD*: 566)? And what is left to see after Bolaño adds his last brushstrokes to his monumental "sketch of the industrial landscape in the third world" (*2666*: 294)?

Not much more, we might say, than resignation, a certain sense of powerlessness and a few dazzling descriptions of a spectacular landscape from which humans are soon to be eradicated.[8] Both novels have this pessimistic, deeply melancholic dimension, despite all the jocularity, the abundant accumulation of life-affirming minutiae, and despite the seemingly conciliatory conclusions of both novels.

It is a very specific kind of melancholy; a melancholy of or after totality more than a melancholy of lack—a melancholy of the absolute following the experience that some kind of representational completeness has been achieved which nevertheless leaves us with a feeling of collective defeat and political impotence.

A striking image for this less canonized type of melancholy is found in what is arguably one of the most fascinating accounts of the problem of totality, Jorge Luis Borges's *The Aleph*. When the first-person narrator ("it's me, it's Borges," Borges [1945] 1971: 11) goes down the basement of the Viterbos, he hardly thinks it possible that he will really meet his beloved and deceased Beatriz there. But after having glimpsed in a crystalline moment "*all* of Beatriz' images" (1971: 12), he faces the next problem: "How, then, can I translate into words the limitless Aleph, which my floundering mind can scarcely encompass" (1971: 13)? How to translate it into a language constructed with "a set of symbols whose use among its speakers assumes a shared past" (1971: 13)? Borges's writerly despair that

---

[8]More than in *ATD*, extinction as the imminent horizon of human existence is a strong motif in Part V of *2666*. It seems to be a constant concern of Archimboldi's poetic project, too, as we can see in the scene where the narrator tells us of Lotte's reactions to Archimboldi's novel *The King of the Forest* and of the moment when it dawns to her that the author of the book must be her brother: "The style was strange. The writing was clear and sometimes even transparent, but the way the stories followed one after another didn't lead anywhere: all that was left were the children, their parents, the animals, some neighbors, and in the end, all that was really left was nature, a nature that dissolved little by little in a boiling cauldron until it vanished completely" (*2666*: 887).

follows on the encounter with the totality of the Aleph, then, has at least two reasons: the fact that the simultaneous givenness of infinite images is untranslatable, and the related fact that its paradoxical experience or, to be more precise, its vision is singular and thus incommunicable.

As if in panic, Borges's discourse becomes hyperbolic, rushing into a paradoxical quest for "inconceivable analogies" (1971: 13) in the infinitely resonant region of poetry. Perhaps the Aleph can be compared to "a bird that somehow is all birds," to "a sphere whose center is everywhere and circumference is nowhere," or a "four-faced angel who at one and the same time moves east and west, north and south," (1971: 13) an angel outdoing both the mythological face of Janus and Benjamin's angel of history (Benjamin [1942] 1969). All these analogies must fail, of course, since "they bear some relation to the Aleph" (Borges [1945] 1971: 13), their very sense is not to make sense within the framework of worldly categories and the geometry of everyday experience. So again, two sources nourish the writer's despair, the too-much of vision and the too-little and too-late of language:

> Perhaps the gods might grant me a similar metaphor, but then this account would become contaminated by literature, by fiction. Really, what I want to do is impossible, for any listing of an endless series is doomed to be infinitesimal. In that single gigantic instant I saw millions of acts both delightful and awful; not one of them amazed me more than the fact that all of them occupied the same point in space, without overlapping or transparency. What my eyes beheld was simultaneous, but what I shall now write down will be successive, because language is successive (1971: 13).[9]

In Pynchon's hyperbolic carnival, Carnesalve, the mask's absolute transparency enables a complete symbiosis of mask and body, which produces a perfect illusion. In Borges's *Aleph*, on the contrary, the indiscriminate and simultaneous presence of each and every cosmic element produces absolute opaqueness, "sin superposición y sin transparencia" (Borges [1945] 2017: 340). The result is a deep state of melancholy facing an unbridgeable rift between the simultaneity of vision and the constitutive lateness of language (see Chapter 6).

---

[9]"Quizá los dioses no me negarían un hallazgo de una imagen equivalente, pero este informe quedaría contaminado de literatura, de falsedad. Por lo demás, el problema central es irresoluble: la enumeración, siquiera parcial, de un conjunto infinito. En ese instante gigantesco, he visto millones de actos deleitables o atroces; ninguno me asombró como el hecho de que todos ocuparan el mismo punto, sin superposición y sin trasparencia. Lo que vieron mis ojos fue simultáneo: lo que transcribiré, sucesivo, porque el lenguaje lo es" (Borges [1945] 2017: 340).

As so often with Borges, literature seems to be discredited as a weak medium, as an artificial and always belated disfiguration of experience.[10] It is a deeply ironic dismissal, of course, as we can hardly think of an author more committed to the derivative, the counterfeit, the secondary, or the apocryphal. It is this very irony that paves the way for an act of hyperbolic defiance that, *nonetheless,* recollects something of what is deemed to be inexpressible in a familiar linguistic register. So let us look a second time at the passage from above, this time with its significant additional sentence:

In that single gigantic instant I saw millions of acts both delightful and awful; not one of them amazed me more than the fact that all of them occupied the same point in space, without overlapping or transparency. What my eyes beheld was simultaneous, but what I shall now write down will be successive, because language is successive. Nonetheless, I'll try to recollect what I can (Borges [1945] 1971: 13).[11]

Algo, sin embargo, recogeré. Against all odds, something will remain, but it remains under the spell of the linguistic protagonist of this chapter, the little concessive expression *sin embargo, sed tamen, nevertheless*. The future tense of the verb adds another dimension of promise and suspense to the speech act. No *cogito,* no transcendental subjectivity, can abolish the persistence of doubt and uncertainty in Borges's *Aleph*. Even where skepticism in the face of the impossible is temporarily vanquished, it stubbornly continues to punctuate and impregnate the literary text. Borges's suspense is of a different kind than the suspense we encounter in more conventional narratives where it intensifies the drama and prepares the solution of plot-oriented intrigues. In Borges, on the contrary, suspense is an integral part of the metaphysics of the text, it embodies his literary vision,

---

[10]See, for instance, Borges's preface to his first volume of stories containing the following, rather serious self-critical words: "[Los cuentos] [s]on el irresponsable juego de un tímido que no se animó a escribir cuentos y que se distrajo en falsear y tergiversar (sin justificación estética alguna vez) ajenas historias" (Borges [1954] 2017: 11). Less obviously self-critical and already as part of the meta-fictional repertoire are the introductory remarks to what is perhaps the only text in Borges's corpus where explicit sexual actions are intimated: "Mi relato será fiel a la realidad o, en todo caso, a mi recuerdo personal de la realidad, lo cual es lo mismo. Los hechos ocurrieron hace muy poco, pero sé que el hábito literario es asimismo el hábito de intercalar rasgos circunstanciales y de acentuar los énfasis" (Borges [1975] 2017: 435).

[11]"En ese instante gigantesco, he visto millones de actos deleitables o atroces; ninguno me asombró como el hecho de que todos ocuparan el mismo punto, sin superposición y sin trasparencia. Lo que vieron mis ojos fue simultáneo: lo que transcribiré, sucesivo, porque el lenguaje lo es. Algo, sin embargo, recogeré" (Borges [1945] 2017: 340).

which we might extend, with all due caution, to his vision of language, experience, and perhaps even the world itself.

It is a cerebral, yet intimately sensual form of suspense, which lures us into the realm of sublime experience where the world as a whole becomes visible as an ontological simulacrum. Nonetheless, *sin embargo*, literature holds on to its vocation of daring to portray some kind of totality, even if it does this in a decisively subjunctive mode. But even the most exalted moment of literary triumph cannot repeal the melancholy encrypted in the mutual exclusiveness of vision and narrative. Hyperbolic language may bring comfort to a mourning narrator, but it can't bring back to life the object of his grief: Beatriz Viterbo. Similar to the séance-like encounter of Kit and his dead father (Chapter 6), Borges's encounter with totality remains ephemeral and non-redemptive, the fragile success of a literary séance where otherwise separate worlds briefly converge before drifting apart again, drifting into oblivion, into the abyss, "into the cold nothingness of the Alps" (2666: 91).

8

Ekphrasis beyond Imagination

Compact, closed like a closed door.
But onto the portal openings were flayed,
scratched out by fingernails.
CLARICE LISPECTOR

Ekphrasis between Rupture and Longue Durée

Verbal descriptions of images are among the oldest literary techniques. Long before Homer's shield of Achilles and until the present day, writers, orators, and poets have resorted to the visual arts to motivate and enhance their linguistic adventures. But despite its transhistorical significance, ekphrasis in the Western tradition has of course been subjected to a series of shifts, evolutions, ruptures, and expansions. Let me briefly sketch three of them:

1. According to a popular view, ekphrasis has slowly been isolated from its usual epic or dramatic context and turned into a genre of its own, mostly in the form of the lyric poem. Notorious examples like Keats's *Ode on a Grecian Urn* or Rilke's *Archaïscher Torso Apolls* immediately spring to mind. Paradigmatically, a lyrical voice contemplates a single and outstanding work of art, which is often exhibited in a museum-like space, combining meticulous description with affective self-experiment and metaphysical epiphany.

2. A second evolution concerns less a condensation of ekphrastic practice than its expansion in at least two directions. On the one hand, ekphrasis transcends its self-imposed constraints as a faithful mimetic representation of art, which in turn increasingly liberates itself from the imperative of representational mimesis. Ekphrastic

practice, then, becomes a tool for pictorial description as such, not only motivated by works of art but by virtually any object, image, or *gestalt*. On the other hand, the ekphrastic repertoire is more and more applied to art beyond the visual dominance, a tendency that nourishes and is nourished by an increasing intercourse between the different arts, genres, and media.[1]

3 A third line of evolution points at something more abstract. It carries the notoriously precarious relationship between image and word, showing and telling, and seeing and speaking into the heart of the ekphrastic text itself. Think of Wilde's exemplary *Picture of Dorian Gray*, where gothic elements are brought to the ekphrastic act to ironically and hyperbolically dismiss the mimetic confidence of Bourgeois realism. In orthodox postmodern literature, ekphrastic failure often serves as an ally to a theory of expression whose first and foremost aim it is to radically discorrelate signs from things and make every attempt to negotiate between the symbolic and the real look foolish and immature. Here, above all, it is skeptical art, art that is heavily invested in perceptual and epistemic doubt, that nourishes intricate cases of anti-mimetic mimesis. A popular example of such a twisted form of mimesis, where an effect of derealization is produced by a seemingly meticulous imitation of ostensibly non-imitative art, is John Ashbery's long poem *Self-Portrait in a Convex Mirror*.

These are some of the dominant historical and genealogical outlines associated with the journey of ekphrasis throughout the centuries. But ekphrasis can also be considered under the aspect of a remarkably constant

---

[1] Here are only a few examples from the modern Western tradition: 1) music: Cortázar's description of jazz in *El Perseguidor* and his reference to music in many other texts; Proust's little tune of the invented composer Vinteuil; Thomas Mann's twelve-tone composition that his equally fictional composer Adrian Leverkühn creates with the help of the devil; 2) theater: Pynchon's extensive account of the fictional revenge play *A Courier's Tragedy*; 3) poetry: Orlando's long-durational writing project (*The Oak Tree*) in Virginia Woolf's eponymous novel that is written and re-written, abandoned and resumed in syncopated correspondence with its author's adventurous journeys through the centuries; Balzac's description of poetic processes, the writing of poems (or rather the recycling of his own juvenile poetic outpourings), and the act of printing poems in *Illusions Perdues*; 4) art criticism: again Balzac's *Illusions Perdues*; Stanislaw Lem's imaginary literary criticism, which can be seen as an important inspiration of Bolaño's invented catalogue of a whole tradition of modern American Fascist writers in *La Literatura Nazi En América*; Chris Kraus's essays on feminist art in *I Love Dick*; 5) fake art: Gaddis's *Recognitions*; Gide's *Les Faux-Monnayeurs*; 6) performance and conceptual art: Chris Kraus again; Donald Barthelme's hyper-minimalist literary set-ups such as *The Balloon*; 7) practices treated as art that are usually not seen as such, for example, cooking in Karen Blixen's *Babette's Feast*; and 8) the art of (financial) speculation: Gaddis's *J R*.

longue durée, where a few major characteristics that have been present from its documented beginnings are as valid as ever before, even if they are sometimes mistakenly understood as genuinely modern inventions. Here are four of them, arguably the most important ones (I will use *Achilles's shield* as a point of reference and orientation):

1 *Energeia.* Ekphrasis not only produces and reproduces an image in linguistic terms, but puts equal emphasis on the expressive gesture that produces the image in the first place. In the classical idiom of Aristotle, *enargeia/evidentia,* which brings the image in front of our eyes, is inseparably bound up with *energeia,* the dynamic process that brings the image/object to life. Retracing Homer's description of Achilles's shield, it often seems as if *energeia* prevails over *enargeia* as the much more efficient technique to visualize the abundant minutiae engraved on the shield's surface.

2 *Notional Ekphrasis.* "Notional ekphrasis" (Hollander 1988) relies on the simple fact that ekphrasis does not need to rely on actually existing works of art for its act of poetic (re)production. In any ekphrastic act, the underlying object or art work can be produced simultaneously to its presumably secondary description. Homer's description of the shield gestures toward this logic as it defies any realistic reconstruction of scale and artistic craft and posits Hephaestus as the only thinkable craftsman of the shield. W. J. T. Mitchell goes so far to view notional ekphrasis as the normal situation from which ekphrastic descriptions of actually existing works of art (Rilke, Keats, Ashbery) are just the exception. This strongly resonates with the notion of flat fictionality that I developed in Chapter 6. In the realm of fiction, then, it does not really matter if the work of art subjected to ekphrastic description does have a referential counterpart or if it doesn't. According to Mitchell, all acts of literary ekphrasis refer to equally fictional works of art.

3 *Self-referentiality.* Ashbery's self-reflective poem is of course not the first instance of ekphrastic self-reflexivity in the history of Western literature. Achilles's shield understood as synecdoche, as a miniaturized representation of a whole (the Greeks, the cosmos, etc.), offers an early example of this tendency. The cosmos depicted on the shield is organized around binary but complementary oppositions. The space on the shield available for representational activity is very large, but not infinite. Time on the shield is organized in a nonlinear, circular way. The cosmos is projected onto the two-dimensional surface of the shield from where it is translated into the one-dimensional succession of the epic poem. At the same time, both shield and text seek to produce three-dimensional effects

to compensate for the dimensional losses that occur on the way from one medium to another. One could even suggest that the epic poem itself serves as a kind of shield, as an instrument of defense which at the same time embodies the spirit of war—a surface that simultaneously attacks and protects.

4 *Intertextuality and intermediality.* As a representation of a representation (Heffernan 1993: 3), since its beginning ekphrasis is an emphatically intertextual endeavor, fascinated by the possible interplay of different media. At its core, then, the structure of ekphrasis is citational and highly susceptible for any kinds of intertextual infiltration. Such an intertextual contamination can go both ways. The shield of Achilles is already a product that draws its pictorial energy from the idiosyncratic forging and shaping of Greek mythology and cosmology. At the same time, it marks the starting point for uncountable imitations, variations, and *outdoings*. This history of ekphrastic competition starts, at the latest, with Vergil's description of the shield of Aeneas.

Oscillating between transhistorical *long durée* and historical rupture, ekphrasis is particularly apt to wrap up our analytic exploration of Pynchon's and Bolaño's late maximalist novels. Since the inventions and innovations of *hyperbolic realism* are rather compositional than stylistic, to understand how 2666 and *ATD* reconfigure and recombine ekphrastic elements for their specific purposes promises to provide new insights that also recapitulate some of the findings of the previous chapters. I will start with the usual close readings of some characteristic passages in both novels; and then move on to a broader discussion of the iconopoetic mise-en-scène characteristic for *hyperbolic realism*. I will also pick up the phenomenological motif that came up in previous chapters and use some of Merleau-Ponty's and Richir's philosophical insights to reassess some of the notorious questions surrounding the problems of the image and imagination in the literary text.

Photography as Modern Alchemy

Seen from the perspective of rupture, the invention of photography marks a decisive moment in the history of ekphrasis. As technology and practice, photography not only introduces a new aesthetic ambition into the field of art, it also provokes a crisis of representation, which runs in two directions at least.

The first critical dimension concerns the relationship between image and reality. When it comes to the mimetic power of painting, even the most hard-boiled realist must concede that the imitation of the real in a painting can only be the effect of a considerable amount of aesthetic labor. Photography, in contrast, comes with the promise of providing immediate and undistorted copies of a chosen section of the world. A still popular view on photography disregards or even dismisses the aesthetic labor invested in the composition of the image. The photographer's skills are thus not seen as aesthetic accomplishments, but rather as technical achievements; to become a photographer capable of creating mimetic objects, then, all you need is the equipment and the skills to operate the technology.

The second crisis emerges with the predominance that the technological dimension gains over the aesthetic dimension. This has a lot to do with what Benjamin has famously called the technological reproducibility of the image. In the wake of pictorial serialization, which in our digital age is pushed further and further to the extreme, images are in danger of losing their uniqueness (Benjamin's *aura*) and of becoming a devalued commodity, which is constantly and generally available.

At the beginning of the twentieth century, at latest, photography started to pose a serious threat to the mimetic hegemony of painting (and literature) by redefining the material ontology of the image. This could not be without (highly ambiguous) consequences for the situation of literary ekphrasis. On the one hand, photography makes the mimetic powers of literature look ridiculous in comparison to its own. On the other hand, the literary mainstream of the time refused to accept photography as an autonomous art form. High-cultured literary practice, however, used its newly found anti-mimetic license to venture into more anti-realist, self-reflective, and experimental forms of writing. Naturally, since we are in the field of culture, both positions can appear in productive tension in one and the same place, as we can see in Baudelaire's ambivalent relation to photography (Compagnon 2014: 91–134).

The time frame of *ATD* is situated at a historical threshold, a period in which photography is developing into a forensic technology that is said to produce evidence (or even truth) *and* emancipates itself as an autonomous art form. Pynchon's novel consistently testifies to this crucial role of photography at the end of the long nineteenth century. In an early scene, an as yet uninitiated Merle Rideout learns from the "gainfully self-employed" photographer Roswell Bounce about the somewhat magical process behind the new medium, "the mysteriously guarded transition from plate to print" (*ATD*: 64). In an atmosphere reminiscent of the lab of an alchemist, Roswell lits "a ruby darkroom lamp," gathers his enchanting materials, and mumbles the rare and exquisite names—"Pyrogallic, mumblemumble citric, potassium bromide ... ammonia"—of the chemicals he summons for his photogenetic magic trick. And "[N]ow watch. And Merle saw the image appear. Come from nothing. Come in out of the pale Invisible, down into this otherwise explainable world, clearer than real" (64). Visibly less concerned with the content of the image, most attention is directed to the artificial and artful process of its coming into existence. Diverted from content, Merle gets fully imbricated into the mystical play of light and shadow in the darkroom and on the dry plate, and the moment the picture bursts into sight produces a corresponding epiphany with the potential to provide his way of being in the world with a new drift. So far, photography had seemed to him "like an idiot's game" (*ATD*: 64), a dull activity without aesthetic value, a cheap way of making money by entertaining the ignorant masses. In the moment of his conversion, however, it is elevated to a magical, mystical practice, a modern counterpart to witchcraft as already suggested by Roswell's sorcerous mumbling of technical terms as if he were brewing a magic potion.

Only after one more step, we get more information of the image as a product of this technologically enhanced incantation of matter. Its ontological status is precarious; on the one hand, it emerges as a hyperreal epiphany, "clearer than real"—a piece of emphatic reality that hides its context and manufactured origin; on the other hand, it comes with a disturbing effect of irrealization, as an alien substance that creeps into "this otherwise explainable world" to plant wonder and discomfort into the heart of the worldly observer.

At the end of the paragraph, we are told that Merle's uneasiness is not only due to the darkroom's mystical atmosphere but has also something to do with the fact that the primary item produced by photography is not the realistic image but only the negative. Pynchon's emphasis on the inversion of light bears an immediate resonance with the novel's title and its broad range of connotations: *ATD,* against light, against the obvious, superficial, and everyday. Before the image can produce its hyperreal effect, each photograph must pass through a transitional and dark phase as a counter-image from where light is "witched somehow into its opposite."

In drawing together some of the structuring features of the novel such as the pervasive ubiquity of *as if* (Chapter 6) and the intricate chiasm of light and shadow (Chapter 5), Merle's initiation into photography reminds us to pay attention not only to the "positive" images on the surface, but also and perhaps even more so to the less obvious, less canonized, "negative" images hidden from plain sight or buried in the archives. It is precisely such hidden material undercurrents of history that the novel promises to excavate by exploring the underrepresented history of militant anarchism and labor struggles, the diversity of irreverent belief systems, the neglected colonial and imperial power struggles, and conflict zones that paved the way to the First World War or the war of interpretations surrounding the many scientific revolutions of that historical period.

As we finally get to see what is on the picture whose development has been so dramatically staged, we become witness to such a sudden exposure of an undercurrent part of the real. What appears on the picture, then, looks like inmates from a mental asylum who are staring back at the photographer, the spectator, and the archivist alike, as if they were rejecting their assigned role as muted objects for the mortifying gaze of the camera. The scene and the site are clearly recognizable, but they frustrate Merle's realist expectations at first. Over the course of the novel, as our eyes become gradually accustomed to the altered conditions of light, it seems more and more as if the negative image was the appropriate mode to let the inmates-as-images enter the "daylit" world (*ATD*: 566); a world that does everything in its power to keep them locked in and at a safe distance from normality.

It is thus not the novel's intention to flip things "back to normal," but to dwell on the negative to expose the full extent of a multilayered relief of reality which to the untrained eye is only visible in its most superficial contours. As we have seen in Chapter 4, Pynchon resorts to the fantastic and speculative not only but also to revoke a historical (and material) unconscious that is partly hidden and partly lost. Even where the historical document stares back at the viewer as if in bold defiance of our routines of making sense of the world (and the archive), *ATD* holds on to some kind of evidence that demands from the reader to engage with a form of "productive reality." Such a general view of the world is different from the modernist consensus that considers the real as inert and resistant matter (Blumenberg [1964] 2015).

Bolaño's Negative Epiphanies

Perhaps even more than Pynchon, Bolaño's fiction displays a constant fascination with the dark side of photography. Early in *2666*, our four critics meet *el suavo*. *El suavo*, "the Swabian," is a rather unknown, rather unsuccessful writer who in the early years after the war worked as a cultural promoter in a small city in Southern Germany. When he invited Archimboldi to read from one of his books, he wrote a biographical sketch about him for the local newspaper, the *Diario de Mañana de Reutlingen*. Not only this early and rare piece on Archimboldi is of great interest for the critics, they are also interested in its author, *el suavo*. Whereas Pelletier and Espinoza think of him as a busybody whose greatest accomplishment was to have an affair with the publisher's widow, Morini offers a riskier interpretation. In *el suavo*, he sees "a grotesque double of Archimboldi, his twin, the negative image of a developed photograph that keeps looming larger, becoming more powerful, more oppressive, without ever losing its link to the negative (which undergoes the reverse process, gradually altered by time and fate)" (*2666*: 39).

Morini uses the negative photograph as a metaphor to create a speculative connection between two writers who are both marginal when they meet and share a problematic youth as (innocent?, complicit?, staunch?) cogs in the Nazis's machine of war and destruction. The thought itself seems rather underwhelming, but like many times in Bolaño's work something else, something larger or more unusual makes its presence felt in the most inconspicuous moments. Like everything in Bolaño's fictional universe, the image, and in our case the image of the double ("the two images somehow still the same," 39), will finally disappear. However, its vanishing will not be complete. Instead, it will slowly and irregularly wither away exposed to "time and fate," just like Amalfitano's geometry book. At the same time, the image "without ever losing its ties to the negative" carries with it a mysterious weight "that keeps looming larger." The scene makes use of the ambiguity of the word *revelada,* which is primarily used to refer to the developed photograph (as the unveiling of its negative template), while at the same time evoking a dramatic moment of sudden disclosure.

Inspired by Bolaño's own words,[2] Carlos Guerrero has fittingly described such moments in Bolaño's fiction as negative epiphanies:

> [A] mechanism of concealment can be felt in several sections of 2666. Bolaño eschews all possible satisfaction of linguistically apprehending the conclusion of an image, such that it would expose, as Joyce's epiphany does, the hidden and inner qualities of a thing. In Bolaño, the blow supplied by revelation is omitted and whatever clarity an image could suggest brings us further from any crystallization of hermeneutic immediacy (Guerrero 2006, my transl.).

While I agree that Bolaño's epiphanies significantly differ from the modernist stereotype, I think that Guerrero's reading overestimates the intensity with which Bolaño supposedly plays off occultation against revelation. As we've seen in Morini's impromptu speech, Bolaño presents a much more nuanced vision of the relationship between the negative proto-image and its developed product as he treats them as chiastically entangled counterparts rather than as mutually exclusive opposites. This view is supported by another scene where a character wakes up thinking he had dreamed about a movie he had recently seen. "But everything was different. The characters were black, so the movie in the dream was like a negative of the real movie" (2666: 234). The more he tries to bring the two imaginary events, movie and dream, together, the more they start to diverge. The plot takes "unexpected turn[s]," the ending is different, too,

---

[2] In his autobiographical essay *Literature and Exile,* Bolaño writes: "[A]nd that's where Mario died, the way poets die, unconscious and with no identification on him, which meant that when an ambulance came for his broken body no one knew who he was and the body lay in the morgue for several days, with no family to claim it, in a final stage of development or revelation, a kind of negative epiphany, I mean, like the photographic negative of an epiphany, which is also the story of our lives in Latin America" (Bolaño 2004b: 40–1).

and finally the dream becomes "something completely different" (234). Not at all exclusionary, the relationship between negative template and positive product is one of uncanny repetitiveness: always the same, yet different. Similar to what Merle in *ATD* experiences during his conversion to photography, the characters appear as spirits, at the same time eerily distant and weirdly real. Taken to a higher level, the scene embodies on a smaller scale a typical dynamic of longer sequences and narrative arcs in *2666*, the gradual escalation of an initially unremarkable situation.

Guerrero is right when he speaks of the highly ambiguous relationship between image and narrative in *2666*: "The diegetic situation is slowed down and gives birth to an interfering image [*imagen solapada*] which is decentered from the main action but nevertheless inserted into it" (Guerrero 2006). The same logic can be applied to Bolaño's use of ekphrasis, but not without adding two important modifications. First, deceleration, digression, and Baroque amplification lie at the core of Bolaño's poetic project. It is thus imprecise to tie such techniques exclusively to the question of the image. In Bolaño's fiction in general and in *2666* in particular, even the most ephemeral characters are led to their moment of grace, no matter how ephemeral these moments may be.[3]

The second modification turns our attention away from the way images are inserted into the narrative environment and toward the inner dynamics of the image itself. The hidden core of Bolaño's textual images, just like that of his metaphors, is never fully disclosed, although a lot of detail, aspect, perspective, and interpretational options are usually offered. Moreover, the image in its temporal and rhythmic unfolding stages its own precarious nature and demonstrates an entropic drift, as it is in constant danger to fall apart or collapse. To say it once again, to say that Bolaño images vanish does not mean that they fall into complete nothingness. Instead, we observe that their imaginative potential is liberated and transformed so that it can reappear in another shape.

A particular image can thus become strangely alive (in the mode of as-if-ness, of course) and act against its own creator "as if [they] might be an ex-lover or a living (and unfinished) painting that had just got news of the painter's [or author's] death" (*2666*: 149). Or the image can burst into

---

[3]It must be noted that *grace* in this case is deployed in an extra-moral sense, in the same way it is used by Flannery O'Connor, though without her Catholic side tones: "I suppose the reasons for the use of so much violence in modern fiction will differ with each writer who uses it, but in my own stories I have found that violence is strangely capable of returning my characters to reality and preparing them to accept their moment of grace. Their heads are so hard that almost nothing else will do the work. This idea, that reality is something to which we must be returned at considerable cost, is one which is seldom understood by the casual reader, but it is one which is implicit in the Christian view of the world" (O'Connor 1970: 112).

pieces, "images with no handhold, images freighted with all the orphanhood in the world, fragments, fragments" (2666: 206). Or it can merge with the mental sphere to trigger nervousness and obscurity: "Pensar sin pensar. O pensar con imágenes temblorosas" (Bolaño 2004a: 463)—*thinking with shaky images.*

Dehiscence and Phantasia at the Margins of Perception

Bolaño's images: not just shaky, but always already on their way to decomposition. A frequent subtype of this general template is a type of image whose "material" texture seems to be torn apart from within. In Part IV, the crime reporter Sergio González stumbles from one disturbing encounter to the next until he ends up in the house of a fortuneteller. In her hypersensitive inner vision, a substantial difference reigns between "ordinary murder" and a femicide, a difference that an "ordinary" mind may not as easily sense. As González pauses and asks her to explain herself, she claims that "an ordinary murder (although there was no such thing as an ordinary murder) almost always ended with a liquid image, a lake or a well that after being disturbed grew calm again, whereas serial killings, like the killings in the border city, projected a heavy image, metallic or mineral" (2666: 571). The difference lies thus in her highly esoteric perception of different states of image aggregation, light versus *pesada*, clear versus blurred, and liquid versus "smoldering"—*una imagen que quemaba* (Bolaño 2004a: 794). If the fortuneteller's use of figurative language already seemed odd, it tilts toward complete confusion when she mumbles of "burned curtains, dancing, say, that burned curtains, dancing, but the more curtains it burned the darker it grew ... where the killings took place" (2666: 571).

What seems to be the example of language in its *état clinique,* nevertheless contains a conception of the image that strongly resonates with many other passages in *2666*. It is a conception that emphasizes what we could call the material weight of the image and tracks its entropic drift until the moment it finally vanishes.

In the previous chapter, I quoted from a section that signals an essential rupture in the characters' (and the novel's?) ontological attitude ("After that moment, reality for Pelletier and Espinoza seemed to tear like paper scenery ... " [2666: 179]). In *Amuleto*, the catastrophic Tlatelolco massacre of 1968 calls for a much more dramatic and verbose interruption:

> When we reached the operating room, the vision misted over, cracked, fell and shattered, and then the fragments were pulverized by a bolt of

lightning, and a gust of wind blew the dust away to nowhere or spread it through Mexico City (Bolaño [1999] 2006a: 153).[4]

If Carlos Guerrero rightly identifies three important ingredients of Bolaño's hyperbolic images—their relative resistance against the narrative flux (1), their character as negative epiphany (2), and their delayed reintegration into the narrative (3)—I would like to add a fourth dimension: the sudden implosion of the pictorial frame, the ripping apart of its material texture, and the burning and withering away of the very fabric that holds the image physically together (a physicality that is, of course, also metaphorical).

To distinguish this particular logic of pictorial decomposition from the standard pattern of deconstruction, I propose to call it *dehiscence*. It is a term that Merleau-Ponty started to use in the last finished part of *The Visible and the Invisible*. Interestingly, the same word appears two times in Samuel Beckett's first and lesser known novel *Dream of Fair to Middling Women*, where it bears some resemblance to the way Bolaño deploys pictorial decomposition. So let's have a look at those passages in Beckett's first novel and one more in Merleau-Ponty's last philosophical work:

> I think of Beethoven's earlier compositions where into the body of the musical statement he incorporates a punctuation of dehiscence, flottements, the coherence gone to pieces, the continuity bitched to hell because the units of continuity have abdicated their unity, they have gone multiple, they fall apart, the notes fly about, a blizzard of electrons, and then vespertine compositions eaten away with terrible silences (Beckett [1932] 1993: 139).

> His face surged forward at you, coming unstuck, coming to pieces, invading the airs, a red dehiscence of flesh in action. You warded it off. Jesus, you thought, it wants to dissolve. Then the gestures, the horrid gestures, of the little fat hands and the splendid words and the seaweed smile, all coiling and uncoiling and unfolding and flowering into nothingness, his whole person a stew of disruption and flux. And that from the fresh miracle of coherence that he presented every time he turned up. How he kept himself together is one of those mysteries. By right he should have broken up into bits, he should have become a mist of dust in the airs. He was disintegrating bric-a-brac (1993: 116).

---

[4]"Cuando llegábamos al quirófano la visión se empañaba y luego se trizaba y luego caía y se fragmentaba y luego un rayo pulverizaba los fragmentos y luego el viento se llevaba el polvo en medio de la nada o de la Ciudad de México" (Bolaño 1999: 119).

> When I find again the actual world such as it is, under my hands, under my eyes, up against my body, I find much more than an object: a Being of which my vision is a part, a visibility older than my operations or my acts. But this does not mean that there was a fusion or coinciding of me with it: on the contrary, this occurs because a sort of dehiscence opens my body in two [*parce qu'une sorte de déhiscence ouvre en deux mon corps*], and because between my body looked at and my body looking, my body touched and my body touching, there is overlapping or encroachment, so that we must say that the things pass into us as well as we into the things (Merleau-Ponty [1968] 1964: 123).

Dehiscence befalls both the image and the observing body, which is also the body that writes. Contemplation, then, or attentive perception of any sort is not a one-way street as the object insists on being more than just a correlate of the subject's intentionality. "I find much more than an object," says Merleau-Ponty, "a Being of which my vision is a part, a visibility older than my operations or my acts" (1968: 123). A far cry from dead inanimate matter, these objects fix their viewer with a provocative stare of their own, not unlike Shelley's *Medusa* ("It lieth, gazing") and Rilke's *Archaic Torso of Apollo* ("for here there is no place/that does not see you"). Yet in contrast to their famous predecessors' use of the object-gaze, Pynchon and Bolaño do not turn "the gazer's spirit into stone" (Shelley 1968: 357), nor do they pathetically appeal to the viewer's spiritual renewal (Rilke: "you must change your life," Rilke 1957: 67). What happens between observer and object, between writing body and written image is not a full identification; it is, in Merleau-Ponty's words, an "overlapping or encroachment," an intimate contact which upholds a certain distance between the two poles that structure the "actual world" (Merleau-Ponty [1964] 1968: 123).

From both Beckett and Merleau-Ponty, we gain a powerful conception of dehiscence that is not exclusively destructive and disruptive. If, in the beginning, Beckett's passages focus on a formalist understanding of art, they come to a programmatic definition of a whole aesthetics of dehiscence in which the ripping apart of the surface of the "musical statement" turns into a sudden release of poetic energies, "a blizzard of electrons" (Beckett [1932] 1993: 139). Merleau-Ponty's phenomenological variant, albeit a bit less dramatically, follows in the same vein. Dehiscence as it appears late in the written chapters of *The Visible and the Invisible* is not a hindrance for or failure of perception but its necessary condition.

The dehiscence of image, surface, and inner material textures clears the space for a more granular and layered phenomenality. It is an act of destruction whose aim is not to reveal what has been mysteriously hidden, not to expose what is behind the image, but what lies *beneath* and *besides* it. If dehiscence is a term that describes the moment of the image's decomposition, what this decomposition makes visible can be described with a term that has been around since the early beginnings of phenomenology (Husserl 2006). It is Marc Richir, however, who placed the concept at the center of his phenomenological *refondation*. But let us first listen to a poet's voice, the voice of Anne Carson:

> Whenever any creature is moved to reach out for what it desires, Aristotle says, that movement begins in an act of the imagination, which he calls *phantasia*. Without such acts neither animals nor men would bestir themselves to reach out of the present condition or beyond what they already know. *Phantasia* stirs minds to movement by its power of representation (Carson 1986: 168–9).

Phantasia, then, is an act of imagination, but it is more than just the creation of an image; it reaches "out of the present condition or beyond what [we] already know." Unlike more conventional acts of imagination, in *phantasia*, especially according to Richir's radicalization, there is no clearly distinguishable *sujet*, no pictorial object on which the gaze can center and settle. The production of meaning and the materialization of an object are temporarily suspended to make way for the brute appearance of phenomenalization or what Richir calls the *rien-que-phénomène*: "the anecdotic coherence of *phantasia*'s apperceptions is suspended by the blinking of *phantasia*'s invisible apparitions" (Richir 2000: 365). Following Beckett's blizzard of electrons, what *phantasia* produces are not images in any conventional sense, images with content, frames, and signatures, but pure appearance, flickering, pulsating, and intermittent outpourings of brute phenomenality that only temporarily and precariously crystallizes into what Bolaño calls "shaky images" (2666: 370), *imágenes temblorosas*.

Phantasia is thus located at the lowest layer of phenomenalization; it represents the "most archaic phenomenological register" (Richir 2000: 486). It is an *imaginatum* without a *fictum* (2000: 72), that is, the intensity of movement that reaches beyond itself without aiming at an objective correlate, a pulsation, a trembling, and a floating of appearance. The rhythm of its very appearance is erratic and unstable (2000: 290), it comes in "Protean, fleeting, fluctuating and intermittent flashes [*clignotements*]" (2000: 148). In two ways, then, this brings *phantasia*'s products close to Morton's conception of the hyperobject. On the one hand, the products of *phantasia* "entails the character of unreality" (2000: 84). On the other, they are only visible in indirect and vicarious ways, from a "higher" but also less processual phenomenological register such as more object-oriented imagination or symbolic language.

Hence, the relation between what we usually call imagination, on the one hand, and *phantasia,* on the other, is highly problematic, as it is only from an already structured and object-like point of view that the fleeting and flickering phenomena or proto-phenomena of *phantasia* can be glimpsed.

But at the same time, this "higher" register threatens to neutralize the nervous pulsations at the heart of phantasia and to suffocate its energetic breath in the process of what Richir calls *architectonic transposition*.[5]

The *phantastic* phenomena are thus only tangible as *entre-aperceptions*, flickering presences in the interstices of perception, imagination, memory, and language as an "echo of what remains irreducibly ungraspable" (2000: 182) in the "complex play between apperception and language" (2000: 175). Unsurprisingly, music, art, and poetry are among the privileged sites where the play of *phantasia* can be felt in its most intense and nuanced way. Although a lot of writing about art tends to hypostasize both the aesthetic event and the aesthetic experience, as curious spectators we should not perceive art as a conveyor of fixed images and/or illustrations of thematic and conceptual concerns. It would be equally dangerous, however, to reduce the work of art to nothing more but a bundle of hallucinations without any symbolic or conceptual potential (2000: 135). We must not understand Richir's approach as an aim to exclude intellectual, conceptual, or thematic discussions of art, but as a framework that grounds such discussions in the experience and unfolding of the *wild process of figuration*—the temporalizing, autopoietic event of sense-making (the *sens se faisant* in Richir's words, the *sens en train de se faire* in Merleau-Ponty's).

To get into contact with those excessively fleeting phenomena, we must *bracket* our natural attitude in good old phenomenological fashion. But beyond Husserl's classical method of *epoché*, Richir does not only call for the bracketing of this or that condition of perception, but for the bracketing of the subject as a whole. This leads us straight into an "inhuman" register of perception (Trigg 2013), the register of *phantasia*. It is a register that is not only inhuman but also more-than-human and therefore hyperbolic, so there is no reason not to call it as Richir calls it: *hyperbolic epoché* (Richir 2000: 482).

---

[5] "Transposition architectonique" is one of many concepts with a considerable amount of jargon in Richir's philosophy. It describes the transposition from one phenomenological register to the next through *coherent deformation*, for example, the transposition from *phantasia* to imagination. In that process, the "lower" register is not merely sublated into the "higher" one. In a phenomenological framework, *phantasia* and imagination do not describe different levels of reality but are only abstractly separable layers with their possibilities and limitations. Those layers must be permeable, otherwise they would be "mortes." This is what Richir calls *transpossibilité*, a notion he adopts from Henry Maldiney. The particularity of *phantasia* stems from the fact that this register is much more "overshadowed" by those "higher" registers where shapes and forms are more developed. Richir's attempt is not an insurrection of *phantasia* against all other registers but to show what lies behind those forms, "ce qui les fait vivre" (Richir 2015: 151). See also Richir (2006: 377).

Back to Bolaño. A closer look at his pictorial and ekphrastic descriptions reveals a constant interplay of dehiscence and *phantasia*. We witness such an interplay in Edwin John's self-mutilating self-portrait (2666: 53); in the description of the cycle of wall paintings about the lives and hardships of construction workers in Detroit (2666: 241); in the close-ups on a Mexican boxer's back tattoo (2666: 274); in a monumental depiction of the Virgin of Guadalupe painted on the outer walls of a car park (2666: 320); and in an alleged fresco that tells scenes from the lives of German Wehrmacht soldiers in the South-Eastern European territories occupied by the Nazis (2666: 742).

The beginning of such a scene often falls together with the awakening of the observer's attention as we see here: "out of curiosity, he went into the building" (2666: 742) or here: "On the side of a neighboring building he saw a mural that struck him as odd" (2666: 241). Then the attention is shifted toward the medium, vehicle, or material behind and beneath the image. Frequently, these surfaces deviate from standard size and represent remarkable objects in themselves: the huge cement wall of a car park (2666: 320); the walls of an abandoned ruin in a war zone (2666: 742); and the naked back of a Mexican boxer (2666: 274). This is the type of medial background that serves as an environment for Bolaño's mannered and detailed descriptions in which an unusual and unsettling content is often normalized through comparison only to become then projected back into a more fantastic rhetorical register. In a typically cumbersome way, the narrator often struggles to name and categorize things such as *el fresco, por llamarlo de alguna manera* (the fresco, if it could be called that) (2666: 742) or "the bottle—let's just call it like that—on the left" (2666: 348, transl. adapted).

While Bolaño's ekphrastic descriptions are brimming with concreteness, the objects it evokes are often not or only vaguely recognizable as they permanently oscillate between the two phenomenological registers of imagination and *phantasia* such as the "stone statue whose shape couldn't yet be made out" (2666: 742). But not only the image itself, also its surroundings are steeped in an atmosphere of pervasive irreality: "Everything else was darkness and vague shapes" (2666: 274). Within an often drastically realistic yet at the same time retracted and blurred setting, such as the "paved square, an imaginary square that had never existed in Kostekino" (2666: 742)—or had it?—a constant interference of documental, imaginary, and *phantastic* elements takes place.

Images in *2666* never come to us as full-fledged, round, and sealed objects; they unfold as tentative and highly figurative processes of concretization, dramatically in front of the observer's eyes. Not only do they excite wonder and astonishment, they produce anxiety and discomfort. This dimension of an affective agitation provoked by the image is by far more important than its proximity to some ideal of aesthetic perfection; and it is often the very violation of such an ideal that advocates the image's true aesthetic appeal: "The tattoo, although it was technically accomplished, looked as if it had been done in prison by a tattoo artist who for all his skill lacked tools and inks, but the scene it depicted was unsettling" (*2666*: 274).

In Bolaño's pictorial scenes, hermetic opacity usually prevails over hermeneutic transparency (Guerrero 2006), and most of those scenes are constantly threatened by an internal tension to tear them apart. But what always remains, as is made tragically clear in Edwin Johns's tragic last self-portrait, is the wild gesture of the generative process—the "savage, gloomy strokes"[6]—and the stubborn confusion of shifting, diverging, and ultimately irreconcilable perspectives: "This painting, viewed properly (although one could never be sure of viewing it properly), was an ellipsis of self-portraits, sometimes a spiral of self-portraits (depending on the angle from which it was seen), seven feet by three and a half feet, in the center of which hung the painter's mummified right hand" (*2666*: 53).

Unlike the well-lit objects of the art market and the museum, guarded by experts and collectors, Bolaño's *phantastic* objects are practically impossible works of art, made out of scarce materials and under precarious circumstances by unknown artists.[7] Only relentless attention discovers the secret aesthetic qualities of these images, which appear as archaic cave paintings or pre-modern representations lacking in depth and perspective. It seems to be the aesthetic ideal of these images to stay away as far as possible from any ideal of aesthetic perfection: "The drawings were crude and childish and the perspective was pre-Renaissance, but the composition revealed glimpses of irony and thus of a secret mastery much greater than was at first apparent to the eye" (*2666*: 742).

Resonating with the evolution of the genre, Bolaño often uses ekphrasis beyond its role as poetic description of a suggested or actually existing aesthetic object. Liberated from its necessary relation to an object, ekphrasis can also appear as independently hallucinatory flashbacks like the one Oscar Fate has in the desert of Sonora. Fate's hallucination refers to a more orthodox ekphrastic scene in which he and several other characters actually see a spectacular fresco of the Virgin of Guadalupe, whose disturbing appeal has to do with the fact that one of her eyes is open while the other is closed. In Fate's hallucinatory reactualization, the image becomes an obscene *pars pro toto* for the damaged ecology of justice at the North Mexican border, as one eye witnesses the excessive wrongs and structural violence in Santa Teresa while the other deliberately refuses to assume responsibility (note

---

[6] Note that the Spanish original *trazos* is reminiscent of *la traza*, trace, which highlights the fleeting character of these acts of sign-making.
[7] Sometimes, they don't even know it themselves.

that the eye is closed, not blindfolded). A few pages later, as Fate is thinking about the *feminicidios*, the image of the Virgin is melted with an image of a scale, "similar to the scales that Blind Justice holds in her hands" (2666: 348, transl. adapted).

At that moment, *phantasia* turns into a hyperbolic strategy, which destabilizes a formerly concretized image and cracks it open again to provoke and facilitate new processes of phenomenalization and meaning. In Fate's fantasy, the Santa Teresa version of Lady Justice is only vaguely and vicariously present, as a "non-present indeterminacy" (Richir 2000: 230) that is still waiting for its materialization. Her essential insignia, the scale, is alienated beyond recognition; instead of two weighing pans she holds two enigmatic objects that look like plastic bottles. The left bottle is transparent, sand trickles out of numerous holes. "The bottle on the right was full of acid. There were no holes in it, but the acid was eating away at the bottle from the inside" (2666: 348). The right bottle thus offers an example of dehiscence in the flesh: the fabric of the bottle whose function it is to contain its content is eaten away from within while a similar corrosion takes place at the heart of the narrative image, at the inside of Fate's cognitive system, and eventually, as we may conclude, at the core of the image of justice: "On the way to Tucson, Fate didn't recognize any of the things he'd seen a few days before, when he'd traveled the same road in the opposite direction. What used to be my right is my left, and there are no points of reference. Everything is erased" (2666: 348).

Andrea Tancredi's Impossible Avant-Garde Art

ATD is less populated with such outspoken, improbable, or unconscious artists than *2666* and many of Bolaño's other texts. One of those artists in *ATD*, however, the Italian anarchist and avant-garde painter Andrea Tancredi is a particularly interesting case: "Tancredi's paintings were like explosions. He favored the palette of fire and explosion. He worked quickly. *Preliminary Studies Toward an Infernal Machine*" (*ATD*: 585). Pynchon introduces Tancredi as a patchwork figure cobbled together from fragments of several post-impressionist, high modernist, and avant-garde artists. One could perhaps speak of him as an *artiste composé*, comparable with Flaubert's *objets composés* like that hat of Charles Bovary—a thing that, strictly speaking, cannot exist or only exists in our imagination as long as we temporarily suspend our proportional sense of reality.

In good old avant-garde fashion, Tancredi uses art—painting—with the final purpose to abolish art. Just like his political convictions, his aesthetics is one of sabotage. His artworks are projectiles directed against the very concept of color, against the "inertia of paint" (*ATD*: 586), turning them into an ally of the way photography in Pynchon's novel attacks and challenges the untimeliness of painting and other classical art forms.

The Tancredi episode is one of the most brilliant examples in *ATD* of Pynchon's reanimation of the hyperbolic craft of outdoing (Johnson 2010: 18). Like a skeptical harbinger of the future, Tancredi anticipates and to some extent surpasses some of the formal gestures of modernism and the avant-gardes that would only later become canonized. His quick and furious painting style, for example, may remind us of Jackson Pollock's action paintings or even prefigure the futurist's aesthetics of velocity. And his battle cry—"To reveal the future, we must get around the inertia of paint" (*ATD*: 586)—sounds like an essential avant-garde credo that is furiously trying to abolish the past and the ruling system by way of a daring juxtaposition of radical art and political revolution.

Tancredi's project to build a revolutionary *Infernal Machine* is of course an allusion to Duchamp's famous *Machine Célibataire,* with the crucial difference that Tancredi's machine is one to be used in a revolutionary struggle against capitalist and Fascist oppression. Outbidding the tradition of the *poètes maudits* and their commitment to scandalize the Bourgeois society, Tancredi's infernal machine is programmed as a vector for productive alienation and emancipatory nihilism. At the same time, as Pynchon stresses by taking up a theme that is one of Bolaño's most enduring obsessions, the wager with anarchistic counter-violence is always in danger of perpetuating or even exacerbating the very violence it hopes to abolish once and for all.

Tancredi's hyperbolic will to liberate color from its auxiliary role as a provider of form and recognizable function, to transcend it from within its intrinsic limitations, reads like a radicalization of impressionist and post-impressionist attempts to turn color into an esoteric weapon. Like an action painter, he wildly and brutally jots color patches on the canvas to then quickly remodel and perforate them "with an impossibly narrow brush, no more than a bristle or two, stabbing tiny dots among larger ones" (*ATD*: 586–7). The aim of this intense aesthetic practice, adorably named *divisionismo*, is, as stated by Tancredi himself, to break apart the "grammatical tyrannies of becoming" into their components and elements, to define the "smallest picture element, a dot of color which becomes the basic unit of reality" (587). Now we may think that *divisionismo* is just a hot-headed, hyperbolic spin-off from *pointillism*, but Tancredi seems to be after something much more radical than Seurat, both aesthetically and politically, at least if we believe in the words of one of his fellow painters: "'It isn't Seurat ... none of that cool static calm, somehow you've got these dots behaving dynamically, violent ensembles of energy-states, Brownian movement ... '" (587).

A similar contrast exists to the work of "Marinetti and his circle" (587), which, as we know today, became the most prominent example of an avant-garde movement that uses the aesthetic to celebrate virility and heroic sacrifice, promote violence, idealize war, and collaborate with Mussolini's fascism. Tancredi's anarchist futurism declares itself as the opposite of Marinetti's futurism, even if both movements share the same hatred: against the Bourgeoisie, against middle-class morality, tourism, religion, God, and decorative art. The fact that Tancredi hates some of the most important material and social factors that shaped the nineteenth century and would eventually create the conditions for two devastating World Wars does not mean, however, that he is a pacifist. His rejection of Capital, religion, and the Bourgeoisie is based on the same (or at least a similar) glorification of violence and brutal destruction than the one of his opponents; it is directed against individuals, things, and—typically for an anarchist's temperament—infrastructures. The strong limitations of his belief in the cathartic potential of violence becomes more than clear in his plea for a complete destruction of Venice, which again reads as the hyperbolic radicalization of the urbanistic myopia represented by modernist architects like Le Corbusier, with social hygiene as the new dominant religion: "Someday we'll tear the place down, and use the rubble to fill in those canals" (587).

The brutality of this vision suggests that more is at stake than simply some sort of hydraulic complicity of Left-wing futurism with an atmosphere of violent virility and blind destruction; Tancredi's militancy against the oppressors is also prone to simple failure. This is proven by his amateurish assault on Scarsdale Vibe, the obnoxious capitalist supervillain of *ATD*, which is precisely a failed attempt to put his infernal machine, "his precious instrument of destruction" (*ATD*: 742) to subversive use. The fatal encounter between the capitalist and the anarchist is staged as a standoff between two parties of a devilish aesthetic contact: "If Vibe was an acquirer of art, then here was Tancredi's creation, his offering" (742). But as already mentioned, his attempt fails, the infernal machine tragically turns itself against its inventor and finally kills him although the narrator doesn't tell us exactly how and why. All we know for sure is the fact of Tancredi's failure and the fact that his rebellious spell against Scarsdale ("Here it is, here is a bounded and finite volume of God's absence, here is all you need to stand before and truly see, and you know Hell", 742) remains unspoken.

In the novel's prominent context of unionist failure, the weakness of anarchism is joined by what Bolaño elsewhere describes as art's constitutive fragility and its tendency toward pointless self-sacrifice. For the time being, at least, corporate capital, which has the capacity to integrate art (and even revolution) as a commodity in its death-bound cycle, retains the upper hand. When Tancredi dies, the mortifying tendency of painting has already turned art into a dead object, that is, a commodity, "to be traded, on and on, for whatever the market will bear" (*ATD*: 738). That most of the escape routes offered by both Pynchon and Bolaño result either in madness or sacrifice—Edwin Johns cutting off his own hand and ending up in a mental asylum; Andrea Tancredi failing to set his machine in motion and being killed by Scarsdale's thugs—is a deeply depressive assessment of the emancipatory limits of revolutionary art. Without a functioning civic society, we could conclude, the artist might produce radical aesthetic form, but is not able to make a difference in the world. In this light, the impossible avant-garde aesthetics of Tancredi, his *divisionismo*, divides more than what it unites and falls prey to the same *dehiscence* it tries to pour into the art work for revolutionary purposes. In the moment he dies, Tancredi himself has turned into a *phantastic*, impossible object, crushed between the dirty fingers of a ruthless capitalist disguising itself as the beautiful soul of an art collector.

Hyperbolic Realism's *Phantasia*

Ekphrasis in Pynchon's and Bolaño's late maximalist novels is a fertile playground for *hyperbolic realism*'s aesthetic eclecticism. As we have seen in other chapters, both novels create various illuminating moments, in which heretofore unconnected elements are suddenly merged and synthesized. Most of the time, however, the results of these "negative epiphanies" (Guerrero 2006) are vague, disappointing or simply non-existing. When the extremely talented female mathematician Yashmeen Halfcourt has an epiphanic moment of spiritual awakening in the moment of seeing "the spine of reality" (*ATD*: 604), reality itself remains largely unimpressed and demonstrates its central traits of "impenetrability" and "incorrigibility" (Ferraris 2002: 160–1, my transl.).

But if epiphanies remain without consequences and if characters disappear or simply continue to move through the novel as if nothing had happened, things in the maximalist novels are usually not completely wasted. According to the flickering mode of phenomenalization fundamental for *ATD* and *2666*, the content or form of these moments reappears elsewhere, modulated or transposed into trivial phrases, hallucinations, phantasies, or dreams. From time to time, it seems as if a general ekphrastic energy circulates in the text, in which characters and the narrator tap into and opt out as they move along. To name just one example: three times in *2666*, a visual impression appears like the last *painting of a lunatic* (Bolaño 2004a: 53, 241, and 742).

Such a metaphorization of madness, which is not without its problems, occurs several times in both novels. Its structure can be explained by the two main concepts I used in this chapter: *dehiscence* and *phantasia*. In the very fabric of the image, something is ripped apart in a way that any idea of a coherent object collapses. This implosion sets into motion the free play of *phantastic* elements that are no longer contained by any pictorial frame. Just like the way a mentally ill is imagined to relate with the world, the interval between spectator and object is no longer a stable one, but oscillates between unsupportable nearness and insuperable distance.

Peripheralization is another essential feature of Bolaño's and Pynchon's ekphrastic poetics, often in touch with their sensibility for settings of extreme social inequality. Their images reliably appear outside of the white walls of museums and institutions exposed to weather conditions, damage, and decay. Their stronger porosity toward their social, discursive, and material environments, however, does not mean that dehiscence is meant as a negative or even disruptive process. More importantly, it has a liberating force as it lays bare what Richir describes as the most archaic phenomenological register beneath or beyond imagination, language, cognition, and normativity.

While it is impossible for a discourse that privileges rigid transparency to reach such a phenomenal register, it is still difficult for literary language, especially for the novel with its strong narrative bias to deal with *phantastic* phenomena. Hyperbole is one way of dealing with what lies beyond the grasp of narrative and the image-as-object, but as it is seen and approached from the standpoint of narrative and imagination. Insofar as the novel, and the maximalist novel with the single exception perhaps of Joyce's complete evacuation of the genre, inevitably sticks to some form of figurative mimesis, it never fully abandons the realm of representation. Located more in those safer spaces of imagination, memory, representation, and so on, mimesis nevertheless provides a ground which allows glimpses into a more archaic phenomenological layer like that milieu of the dead where "salvation does not yet exist" (*ATD*: 566). *Hyperbolic realism*, then, is not an attempt to oppose phenomenology and language, to divide signs from things, to put *energeia* against *enargeia*. Quite on the contrary, it is the ongoing effort to provide *genetic* and *architectonic* solutions for the passage and transposition from one of these levels to the other.

Genetic phenomenology and architectonic transposition are indeed some of Marc Richir's favorite concepts. Richir's philosophy, as much as Bolaño's and Pynchon's novels, is not interested in finding a symmetrical relation between process and stasis or rhythm and form. According to their constitutive lateness, after realism, after the avant-gardes, and somehow even after the end of the world, both novels are determined by a sense of entropy produced by an aesthetic force that we could describe as "unemployed negativity" (Bataille [1937] 1988: 90). Most of the stuff *hyperbolic realism* is made of (Chapter 3) runs through the prism of the flickering interplay between the visible and the invisible (Chapter 5)—and all its little images are rounded with a sleep (Chapter 8).

Reality is neither a complete illusion nor does its incorrigibility mean that we should return to some kind of pre-critical positivism. To be in the real today and in Bolaño's and Pynchon's late maximalist novels means that we start out from mimetically relatable situations from where we gradually slide into their "weird geometries" (Fisher 2016: 25) to end up in a world seen and experienced from the inside or flipside of matter (Bolaño 2004a: 873). From established meanings and recognizable objects, the focus is not always directed toward the overwhelmingly big but often toward the hyperbolically small yet "massively distributed in time and space" (Morton 2013: 1). From the paradigm of subjective access to the world, we are drawn in an intimate and visceral contact with the real—which is why, with some caution, we could also speak of hyperbolic realism as a realization of Bolaño's own fictional *visceral realism* (Bolaño [1998] 2007).

Within the realm of *phantasia*, the naively presupposed distance of an observer to their object tends to be suspended and replaced by an intimate contact with the wild and highly contingent temporalizing process of phenomenalization. Adopting the perspective of *phantasia* means that no practice of distant observation or conceptualization (as necessary and inevitable as these processes are) can abolish the pre-linguistic, promiscuous[8] entanglements of our bodies with *both* things and signs.

Phantasia, as opposed to and in addition to imagination and conceptual language, is a register that reminds us that all phenomenological layers and conceptual scales in literature ultimately appear within the same zero-dimensionality of fiction—a dynamic I have described as *flat fictionality* in Chapter 6. *Phantasia* thus points to the non-spatial, non-temporal, and non-experiential (inhuman) ground of existence, to the pre-formative performance of matter before it crumbles and crystallizes toward more graspable forms of spatial, temporal, and figurative experience.

Rightly deployed, *phantasia* does not escape from the fields of basic human interest, from history, technology, ethics, politics, and symbolic institutions (Richir 2018). Pynchon and Bolaño do not of course dismiss those interests to defend a stale ideal of aesthetic autonomy. But in allowing considerable room for art and experience that is not entirely contained by conceptual or even imaginary methods, *hyperbolic realism* renegotiates the very conditions of (human) time, space, and human-scaled experience. *Phantasia*, we could say with Jodorowsky, cannot escape death, but immortality can be obtained, although it is a radically secularized and skeptical form of immortality, which acts not—again—as an escape from social coexistence, but as its re-evaluation.

As the images burst and crack open (*dehiscence*), nothing remains but words, words, words (*the stubbornness of language*)—confusing, distorted, alienated, and alienating words (*phantasia, hyperbole*), which nevertheless bring us into closer contact with the real we are already embedded in

---

[8]Merleau-Ponty prominently uses *promiscuité* six times in *Le visible et l'invisible* (Merleau-Ponty 1964: 115, 153, 282, 288, 302, and 318).

(*promiscuity*). One of the most courageous adventurers into the wilderness of *phantasia*, Jorge Luis Borges, knew that the only immortality we deserve lies beyond memory—in the acceptance of our finitude and the affirmative alienation that comes as a consequence:

> To my way of thinking, that conclusion is unacceptable. As *the end approaches,* wrote Cartaphilus, *there are no longer any images from memory—there are only words*. Words, words, words taken out of place and mutilated, words from other men—those were the alms left him by the hours and the centuries (Borges [1947] 1998: 194).[9]

---

[9]"A mi entender, la conclusión es inadmisible. 'Cuando se acerca el fin,' escribió Cartaphilus, 'ya no quedan imágenes del recuerdo; sólo quedan palabras.' Palabras, palabras desplazadas y mutiladas, palabras de otros, fue la pobre limosna que le dejaron las horas y los siglos" (Borges [1947] 2017: 238).

PART THREE

9

Slow Adventures

> *any cat, any dog*
> *is worth more than literature*
> CLARICE LISPECTOR

The Adventure Novel after the End of Adventures

In Ricardo Piglia's highly acclaimed novel *Artificial Respiration,* nine years before Francis Fukuyama's controversial essay from 1989, Renzi, an important character of the book and Piglia's long-time alter ego, applies the famous claim of the end of history to the problem of adventures and experience itself:

> We all want, I say, to have adventures. Renzi told me that he was convinced that neither experiences nor adventures existed any longer. There are no more adventures, he told me, only parodies. He thought, he said, that today adventures were nothing but parodies. Because, he said, parody had stopped being what the followers of Tynianov thought, namely the signal of literary change, and had turned into the very center of modern life. It's not that I am inventing a theory or anything like that, Renzi told me. It's simply that I believe that parody had been displaced and that it now invades all gestures and actions. Where there used to be events, experiences, passions, now there are nothing but parodies. This is what I tried to tell Marcelo so many times in my letters: that parody had completely replaced history. And isn't parody the very negation of

history? Ineluctable modality of the visible, as the Irishman disguised as Telemachus would say during the Trieste carnival, in the year 1921, said Renzi cryptically (Piglia [1980] 1994: 110).[1]

Piglia readers know that throughout his work Renzi serves as a stand-in hyperbolist who is allowed to make the boldest statements about literature, politics, and the state of the world that the author himself does not directly make.[2] With this in mind, we should not forget that the scene above primarily represents an intradiegetic dispute between the first-person narrator's youthful nostalgia for adventures and Renzi's snobbish dismissal of the possibility of authentic experience after the end of history. Nonetheless, in Renzi's farewell to adventures Piglia encodes a dominant aesthetic and historical sentiment of his era that transcends the limits of the book.

Apparently unimpressed by Renzi's diagnosis, Bolaño's and Pynchon's late maximalist novels can be seen as revivals of the adventure novel after the end of postmodernism. Their action spans centuries, countries, and continents; their characters are constantly on the move and on the run, they get involved in murder and revenge, intrigues and exceptions, they are chased and chosen, they must overcome obstacles, and they must pass tests. Rapid changes of direction remind us of the picaresque novel; the episodic juxtaposition of sections and chapters make it difficult to see any harmonious order at first glance, which turns the reading itself into an adventurous journey through the vast and bumpy landscapes of the maximalist novels.

The site of these novels is the world, the planet or even an intersecting sequence of several worlds; it is clearly not the abstract and indefinite universe of high modernism. What they aim at in their hyperbolic intention are "very large finitudes" (Morton 2013: 60), not infinite abstractions.

---

[1] "Todos queremos, le digo, tener aventuras. Renzi me dijo que estaba convencido de que ya no existían ni las experiencias, ni las aventuras. Ya no hay aventuras, me dijo, sólo parodias. Pensaba, dijo, que las aventuras, hoy, no eran más que parodias. Porque, dijo, la parodia había dejado de ser, como pensaron en su momento los tipos de la banda de Tinianov, la señal del cambio literario para convertirse en el centro mismo de la vida moderna. No es que esté inventando una teoría o algo parecido, me dijo Renzi. Sencillamente se me ocurre que la parodia se ha desplazado y hoy invade los gestos, las acciones. Donde antes había acontecimientos, experiencias, pasiones, hoy quedan sólo parodias. Eso trataba a veces de decirle a Marcelo en mis cartas: que la parodia ha sustituido por completo a la historia. ¿O no es la parodia la negación misma de la historia? Ineluctable modalidad de lo visible, como decía el Irlandés disfrazado de Telémaco, en el carnaval de Trieste, año 1921, dijo, críptico, Renzi" (Piglia 1980: 137–8).

[2] Renzi's hyperbolizing spirit materializes itself most clearly when he reduces the totality of a particular author's work to one single question, a phenomenon I'd like to call the *Renzi question* (Sellami 2017). Here is one among many examples: "'Pero hay otra cuestión,' dice Renzi. '¿Cuál es el problema mayor del arte de Macedonio? Las relaciones del pensamiento con la literatura.' El pensar, diría Macedonio, es algo que se puede narrar como se narra un viaje o una historia de amor, pero no del mismo modo. Le parece posible que en una novela pueden expresarse pensamientos tan difíciles y de forma tan abstracta como en una obra filosófica, pero a condición de que parezcan falsos. 'Esa ilusión de falsedad,' dijo Renzi, 'es la literatura misma'" (Piglia 2000b: 28).

Blaise Pascal wouldn't have to be terrified by the vast space of *hyperbolic realism* as it is neither infinite nor empty.[3] If we follow Levinas's claim that metaphysics is the adventurous desire for the invisible and the infinite (Levinas [1961] 1979: 33–5), *2666* and *ATD* are not metaphysical novels. If they contain multitudes, they do not lead into an infinite space of endless reflections and self-reflections. If they seem to have several beginnings, they have a quite remarkable "sense of an ending," even as they extensively employ "tactics of incompleteness" (Carson 1986: 69). They may flirt with spirituality, sorcery and the supernatural, but they refuse salvation and the heroic gesture that demand from us "to die for the invisible" (Levinas [1961] 1979: 35).

Bolaño's Poetic Fracasology

The adventure genre plays a significant role in virtually everything Bolaño has ever written. The adventures of his restless protagonists reliably share two characteristics, at least: on the one hand, the frantic search for an enigmatic character or object, often hidden from or ignored by the larger public; and on the other hand, the protagonists' tendency to disappear and reappear according to erratic and unforeseeable rhythmic patterns.

The adventure theme is perhaps even more dominant in Bolaño's *Savage Detectives,* which masterfully combines the genre with the two threads of the detective novel and the *Künstlerroman*. The *Savage Detectives* weaves a plethora of patchy *testimonios* around the whereabouts of Arturo Belano and Ulises Lima, best friends, poets, and founders of the Neo-avant-garde movement of *visceral realism* in Mexico City, who are obsessed with the quest for biographical traces and lost poems of the (fictional) Mexican surrealist poet Cesárea Tinajero.

Tinajero is a typical textual enigma of Bolaño's fiction, a *centro intermitente*, a flickering center around which most of the novel's characters and occurrences rotate. As a character who is marginalized in at least four ways, as a woman from the Global South, as an avant-gardist and a poet, Cesárea is also the typical embodiment of Bolaño's strong penchant for the outskirts of the material and symbolic order. It is not at least their own marginal status that creates an elective affinity between, on the one hand, the two poets Belano and Lima who struggle for recognition within the

---

[3]"When I consider the short span of my life absorbed into the preceding and subsequent eternity, *memoria hospitis unius diei praetereuntis* (like the memory of a one-day guest [Wisd. 5: 15]), the small space which I fill and even can see, swallowed up in the infinite immensity of spaces of which I know nothing and which knows nothing of me, I am terrified, and surprised to find myself here rather than there, for there is no reason why it should be here rather than there, why now rather than then. Who put me here? On whose orders and on whose decision have this place and this time been allotted to me?" (Pascal [1670] 1999: 26).

hilariously opportunistic Mexican literary establishment, and Tinajero, on the other, who has already been forgotten by the generations after her.[4]

On a trip of the association of Mexican writers to Nicaragua, Belano and Lima disappear without a trace. As the long middle part of the novel multiplies the search in all sorts of ways, the novel shifts from the confessional tone of the first part to a polyphonic arrangement of a huge number of unsatisfying witness accounts that contain useless traces, contradictory information, and sometimes simply pointless cruft (Chapter 3).

The constellation Lima–Belano–Tinajero outlines the preferred type of adventure in Bolaño's fiction. Bolaño readers are invited to follow his protagonists' flickering adventures at the brink of the invisible, seduced into extremely remote places at the periphery of the periphery (Chapter 8). Bolaño does not confront his protagonist with typically heroic tests of courage, but nudges them into quixotic predicaments, situations we could describe as minor adventures, located in Bolaño's preferred social sphere at the margins of social respectability, the "lumpen-bohemia" (Draper [1986] 2011: 186). This slowness of Bolaño's adventures is amplified by the pace of the narrative pace; despite constant moving, Bolaño's novels—2666 a lot more than the *Savage Detectives*, we must say—often convey a strong sense of standstill and uneventfulness.

The idea of literature itself, how could it be otherwise, is included in Bolaño's preference for slow and minor adventures. While it seems hard to find a contemporary writer with a stronger belief in the idea of literature than Bolaño, whom the Mexican novelist Jorge Volpi has thus called "the last Latin American writer" (Volpi 2008: 77), literature in Bolaño's writing is characteristically surrounded by an aura of constitutive weakness. Throughout his work, the idea of literature's weakness is bound up with a long series of minor and major failures, but there is one that stands out: the failure or, rather, defeat of the progressive Left in Latin America, Bolaño's *generación perdida,* which had to cede political ambitions first to violent Right-wing military dictatorships and later to corrupt anti-social neoliberal regimes.[5]

---

[4] We don't learn a lot about their poetry from the narrator, but the few things that leak through tell us that they are subaltern existences who live in poverty and write against the established art of Octavio Paz and Pablo Neruda. They seem to be a Latin American, lumpen-bohemian re-enactment of the surrealists, and we can roughly identify Lima with Breton and Belano with Aragon. The search for Tinajero, her legacy, and what is presumably her single poem and the aggressive performances against the literary establishment, especially against Octavio Paz, seem to be their main poetic occupation.

[5] If 2666 stresses the neoliberal present with references toward globalized labor exploitation and the industry of drug trafficking, three of his shorter novels are directly concerned with the recent past and the traumas of the Left in Latin America. *Nocturno de Chile* and *Estrella Distante* narrate events around the coup against Allende and Pinochet's seizure of power in Chile. *Amuleto* deals with the events and the aftermath of the Tlatelolco massacre in Mexico City in 1968 where several hundreds of peacefully protesting students were killed by a military milicia.

At the turning point of the century, literature becomes a privileged case study for Bolaño's historical pessimism, a historical pessimism encoded in his often-commented metaphor of "the world (perceived as an endless shipwreck)" (*2666*: 504). Like the world itself, millennial literature faces the constant danger of endless shipwreck. As a promoter of adventure novels after the end of adventures, Bolaño partly returns to the origins of the modern European novel, writing under the distant star of Cervantes, constantly squinting at the two volumes of his edition of the *Quijote* (Bolaño 2004b: 34). In the (post avant-garde) moment where failure becomes inseparable from the very ontology of literature, writing assumes the laborious task of "fracasar con éxito," of *failing successfully*.

We should, however, refrain from too hastily identifying Bolaño's *fracosología* with the rehearsed celebration of poetic non-referentiality and the impossibility of expressing the world, let alone changing it—a cultural protocol often accompanied by a bow to a certain Beckettian wall tattoo ("try again, fail better"), which has by now become one of postmodernism's least negotiable battle cries. If it is true that Bolaño's texts are perforated with doubt and uncertainty, what we encounter in his late maximalist novel is not language and expression in its terminal state. Radical (ontological) doubt and "unemployed negativity" (Bataille [1937] 1988: 90) are no obstacles for expression, but its integral part. Almost always they are accompanied (but not forever and ever amortized) by a defying rhetorical gesture (*sin embargo, sed tamen effabor*) in the wake of the materialist stubbornness introduced to the Western tradition in Lucretius's *De rerum natura* (Chapters 6 and 7). Instead of semiotic insufficiency, the last word of Bolaño's aesthetics of failure is reserved for the tragic contrast between the abundance of poetic expression (Chapter 3) and literature's relative political powerlessness (Chapter 7, *The Melancholy of Totality*).[6]

Among Bolaño's works, *The Savage Detectives* is the most graphic example of this particular type of failure. In the adventures of Arturo and Ulises, proper names that echo some of the most canonized adventures of the Western imaginary, literature is not embroiled in a spectacular contradiction between the absolute and pure nothingness, but oscillates, in typically hyperbolic fashion, between the almost-nothing and the more-than-everything. The central secret at the heart of *The Savage Detectives* is not a spectacular metaphysical invisible (Levinas), but a very tiny object: a

---

[6]From the perspective of the Left, added to this tragic tendency is the dark presentiment that those artists and intellectuals most likely to carry out significant acts are conservatives, opportunists, and fascists. To name just a few fitting models from Bolaño's corpus: Carlos Wieder in *Estrella Distante*, the whole cast of *La Literatura nazi en América*, and the first-person narrator of *Nocturno de Chile*, a literary critic and fervent Catholic who gives tutoring lessons in communism (not just anticommunism!) to the entourage of Chile's dictator-to-come, Augusto Pinochet.

little poem, three lines that seem to be less than poetic verses, plus an odd title that seems to be less than a word: a sound, a suffix, or a syllable.

Obeying a well-known process, namely that excessive textual obscurity stirs up the desire and ambition of hermeneutic furor and hyperbolic interpretation (Hörisch 1998), one option is to read the title as a corrupted abbreviation of *navegación*.[7] Seen that way, the three different shapes of the "same" geometric line represents an increasingly turbulent ocean whereas the little rectangular figure stands as a symbol for a boat (or a coffin) in a maritime agony. According to this interpretation, Cesárea's tiny poetic legacy incarnates Bolaño's "absolute metaphor" (Blumenberg 1997), a metaphor that perceives the world as a whole as an enormous shipwreck and literature as a weak adventure and smaller failure embedded in it.

It is certainly no coincidence here that it is nothing else but poetry, suitably represented by an example of genre-defying *antipoesía*, which promotes Bolaño's onto-poetic miserabilism. Reading together textual, contextual, and paratextual elements of his work, readers become soon acquainted with a fundamentally ambivalent view on poetry that oscillates between heroic exceptionality and tragic powerlessness.[8] In *Amulet,* to cite just one of many possible examples, Auxilio Lacouture, the eccentric protagonist and narrator of the novel, finds a vindictive way of expressing the essentially romantic idea that, in the end, its powerlessness is poetry's only chance to survive (Chapter 6): "Metempsychosis. Poetry shall not disappear. Its nonpower shall manifest itself in a different form" (Bolaño [1999] 2006: 159).

Pynchon's Slow Adventures

One of *ATD*'s major narrative arcs dramatizes the historical conflict between unions and anarchists, on the one hand, and corporate capitalism and colonial/imperial extractivism, on the other. Like Bolaño, Pynchon

---

[7]Jordi Balada Campo (2015) takes this as an occasion to compare Bolaño's anti-heroic adventurism and particularly *Los detectives salvajes* with one of the most spectacular *fracasos con éxito* in the history of poetry: the life and work of Arthur Rimbaud.

[8]Marco Antonio Guerra, the university president's son, reaffirms poetry's exceptionality by voicing the seemingly romantic idea that poetry is the only existing clean practice, the only phenomenon outside of the market and capitalism: "Sólo la poesía no está contaminada, sólo la poesía está fuera del negocio" (Bolaño 2004a: 288–9; the idea is not adequately conveyed in Andrews's English translation). Notice the crucial distinction between literature, which is a part of the market, and poetry, which is not. But with poetry's eccentric position outside the market comes its practically complete lack of influence, a powerlessness of metaphysical magnitude, via which the poet is charged with the dubious task of becoming the official ambassador of Bolaño's aesthetics of failure, his *fracasología*.

emphasizes the historical defeat of the Left, exemplified by the fate of the Traverse family. In the wake of the family father's death, the sons and daughters of the family are spread across the globe, losing connection to political and collective struggles as they settle down for calmer private existences.

However, the anarchism motif is not completely lost, but migrates into social spheres more difficult to access. One of the funniest and saddest episodes of the novel is its *séjour* at the anarchist spa of *Yz-les-Bains*—a seemingly quiet haven, sheltered from the impositions of history and a world preparing for war. *Yz-les-Bains* seems to confirm the defeatism of the Left as it can only offer a melancholic retreat for its comrades. Seen through the lens of one of the novel's diagnostic missions, namely to sketch a possible genealogy for the twentieth century, the anarchist spa of *Yz-les-Bains* appears as a sad omen for the extremely limited possibilities of any future democratic socialism. Crushed between the rise of Communist totalitarian regimes and the misleading consensus of the capitalist liberal society, the only chance for a progressive Left inspired by unionist solidarity and anarchist rebellion to survive seems to be under the guise of wellness facilities.

Relegated to melancholic retreats, nostalgia and a grim sense of humor become the dominant modes of worldmaking of people with socialist intentions who shall belong, from now on, to a scattered tribe. Dispersion and scattering was of course already the major fate of Pynchon's characters in earlier novels, with the outstanding example of Tyrone Slothrop in *Gravity's Rainbow*. But as much as Slothrop is in danger of forever losing his body and his self through dissemination, scattering also seems to be his only viable option to escape from *Them* (the novel's notorious name for the malicious system that has tried to knot Slothrop deeper and deeper into its machinery of control ever since his relegated father literally sold him to *Them*. Late in the novel, two functionaries of *The White Visitation*, an important subsystem of *Them*, meet again after the War and try to disentangle the complicated relations and stakes of the zone at the time of the war:

> Of course a well-developed They-system is necessary—but it's only half the story. For every They there ought to be a We. In our case there is. Creative paranoia means developing at least as thorough a We-system as a They-system (Pynchon 1973: 638).

For every They there ought to be a We. But unfortunately, there isn't. Even (or especially) the most intimate relationships in *Gravity's Rainbow* are affected by the system's pervasive power; or they carry out its will, unconsciously and unwillingly most of the time. If Slothrop's fateful gift for prophetic erections is the most glaring image of the ways in which occult institutions such as *The White Visitation* control affect, libido, and the body of its victims (or accomplices), it is nevertheless only the tip of the iceberg of a much more general structure in *GR*. Another character in the novel, Franz Pökler, who works as an engineer for the Nazis learns that his only daughter Ilse is a prisoner of the labor camp right next to his working place. Only allowed to see Ilse for a brief period during summer vacation, he wonders each year anew whether the girl *They* send to him is really his daughter:

> So it has gone for the six years since. A daughter a year, each one about a year older, each time taking up nearly from scratch. The only continuity has been her name, and Zwölfkinder, and Pökler's love—love something like the persistence of vision, for They have used it to create for him the moving image of a daughter, flashing him only these summertime frames of her, leaving it to him to build the illusion of a single child (1973: 422).

Affectivity and intimacy in *Gravity's Rainbow* do not create bonds and connections; they serve as a currency and anesthetics.[9] Pökler's reasoning easily meets the conditions of paranoid thinking, which has remained one of the hottest candidates when it's time again to name the cognitive, hermeneutic, and affective transcendental of postmodernism. As a state of awareness, paranoia can nudge us to see new things, to increase our alertness and speed of reaction to the world. But as a limited cognitive scheme, it seems to be a rather helpless and inefficient tool when it comes to implementing change to improve our situation in meaningful ways.

---

[9]In *Gravity's Rainbow*, there seems to be one single exception to an otherwise utterly antiromantic world: the love story between Roger Mexico and Jessica Swanlake. "There's never much talk but touches and looks, smiles together, curses for parting. It is marginal, hungry, chilly—most times they're too paranoid to risk a fire—but it's something they want to keep, so much that to keep it they will take on more than propaganda has ever asked them for. They are in love. Fuck the war" (Pynchon 1973: 41–2). And yet, it seems as if our British-American lovebirds were completely dependent on that war and its atmosphere of imminent danger for the preservation and enhancement of their lust or maybe even of this other thing we could simply call love. The moment the war is over, Jessica remembers her name and glides away like a swan on the lake with her ugly duckling, Jeremy Beaver (yes!), her flavorless future husband. Roger, in return, does what responsible men are supposed to do and simply goes back to work. Shortly thereafter, however, he vanishes from the novel's radar for several hundreds of pages to only briefly re-emerge at its end. Within himself, Roger carries the insight that he must finally make peace with the end of this war and start to prepare himself not only against the day, but against the entire next decade, the triumph and terror of domestic consumerism unbound. "But it's too late. We're at Peace. The paranoia, the danger, the tuneless whistling of busy Death next door, are all put to sleep, back in the War, back with the Roger Mexico Years. The day the rockets stopped falling, it began to end for Roger and Jessica" (1973: 628). But against Roger's fears, as we all know only too well, the 50s would certainly not abolish paranoia, but help to prepare its rise as a dominant part of the Cold War years' dominant structure of feeling.

Being aware of your own misery without being able to change it is a deeply depressive condition. Cognitive paranoia knows it all or at least believes that it does know it all. But it has hardly any viable strategies to improve its own condition, let alone that of its environment. In one of the most memorable and celebrated episodes of *GR*, the talking light bulb Byron makes this hyperbolically, but unmistakably, clear:

> Byron, as he burns on, sees more and more of this pattern. He learns how to make contact with other kinds of electric appliances, in homes, in factories and out in the streets. Each has something to tell him. The pattern gathers in his soul (*Seele*, as the core of the earlier carbon filament was known in Germany), and the grander and clearer it grows, the more desperate Byron gets. Someday he will know everything, and still be as impotent as before. His youthful dreams of organizing all the bulbs in the world seem impossible now—the Grid is wide open, all messages can be overheard, and there are more than enough traitors out on the line. Prophets traditionally don't last long—they are either killed outright, or given an accident serious enough to make them stop and think, and most often they do pull back. But on Byron has been visited an even better fate. He is condemned to go on forever, knowing the truth and powerless to change anything. No longer will he seek to get off the wheel. His anger and frustration will grow without limit, and he will find himself, poor perverse bulb, enjoying it (1973: 654–5).

Someday he will know everything, and still be as impotent as before. Byron's rebellious dream of uniting all the bulbs in revolt seems prone to failure from the beginning, a vision that hopes to, literally, tap into all the world's scattered sources of energy to build an electric movement of resistance, a horizontal counter-network to the centralist *Grid*. It is the very peculiar tragedy of Byron that not only does his Tesla-like dream (after Tesla, the Serbian physicist, not the ideological self-driving car) end as a failure, as a dimmable light bulb he is doomed to live forever to never forget about it. This is the tragedy of cognitive paranoia, an endless smartness caught in a bad and infinite loop of powerlessness and the inability to act. As Sedgwick points out, depressive paranoia is an enacted "theory of negative affect" (Sedgwick 1997: 24), whose only positive outcome may be a cynical distance in relation to one's own self—the enjoyment of one's own miserable condition as ultimate and vain attempt to gain power over it.

Most characters in *Gravity's Rainbow* fall under the same dimmed-down light of a severely limited agency. Bearing strong resonances with Bolaño's historical defeatism, in Pynchon's narrative universes, at least on the surface, it is often the evil characters or those who comply with ruling forces whose actions are most likely to gain traction. In *GR*, it is Captain Blicero/Weissmann who seems to know best how to make use of *the Grid* in order to turn depressive, reactive paranoia into its creative, constructive, and anticipatory counterpart: "Blicero is a master. He learned quite early to fall into a trance, to wait for the illumination, which always comes. It is nothing he's ever spoken of aloud" (Pynchon 1973: 758). If Blicero ultimately falls prey to the same fate of failure that seems to affect everything and everyone in Pynchon's entropic universe, he will not go down without dragging his entire environment into his circle of death and infection.

To view paranoia as a central or even dominant feature of Pynchon's whole corpus (Bersani 1989, Apter 2006) is now common sense. Yet if it is true that paranoia circulates in many ways in Pynchon's work and particularly in his most important novel *Gravity's Rainbow*, a more cautious look suggests the author's historical and poetic sensibility for a nuanced understanding of various types and modes of paranoia and a wariness in reducing the enemy to a clearly defined or totalizing They-system.

Set against the postmodern tendency to reduce paranoia to its cognitive subtype, Sedgwick proposes a series of queer and reparative counter-modes of reading. In her famous introduction, Sedgwick complains with great verve about

> the exclusiveness of paranoia's faith in demystifying exposure: only its cruel and contemptuous assumption that the one thing lacking for global revolution, explosion of gender roles, or whatever, is people's (that is *other* people's) having the painful effects of their oppression, poverty, or deludedness sufficiently exacerbated to make the pain conscious (as if otherwise it wouldn't have been) and intolerable (as if intolerable situations were famous for generating excellent solutions) (Sedgwick 1997: 22).

As I wanted to show above, in *ATD* Pynchon's preferred reading routes are not those of paranoia, and we must ask if paranoia was ever so dominant a mode as many believe. What I have called Pynchon's reparative genre-poaching (Chapter 4) creates a framework for his characters to at least temporarily steal themselves away from the impositions of history, an act that should not be confounded with relativizing violence and historical pain.

"They fly toward grace" (*ATD*: 1085)—much has been speculated about the meaning of this last, this "halfway hopeful" (DeLillo 1997: 11) sentence pointing at the future fate of the Chums of Chance beyond the ends of what at times seems to be in danger of turning into a never-ending novel. By making room for grace in the midst of gravity, Pynchon sows a spiritual (or even religious) seed, resuming the book's irreverent interest in animism and other subaltern spiritual practices (Coffmann 2011). In contrast to orthodox paranoia not only as a "theory of negative affect" (Sedgwick 1997: 24), but as a way to produce closed systems and especially the closure of the future, *ATD* keeps open a few niches and escape routes at least to grant its characters the option of serendipity and evasion.

As usual in Pynchon's fiction, humor, parody, and counterfactual *phantasia* play an important role here, but they seem to come at a slower pace, much calmer than the preferred hyperactive mood of high postmodernism (Chapter 3) and more similar to the self-ridiculing theatricality of camp that oscillates undramatically between the lower and higher keys of culture (Isherwood [1957] 2012: 10).[10] The slow adventures of *ATD* unfold in an ever-expanding environment, radiating as flickering light over the very large but eventually not infinite ranges of the prairie. In this environment, human history appears on a larger canvas on which the whole nonhuman cast of spiritual, fantastic, and anarchic beings have the opportunity to encounter their moments of grace—no matter how brief and insignificant those moments may be.

---

[10]Sedgwick's little catalogue of classic camp with its emphasis on mannerism and deliberate ridiculousness reads like an abstract inventory of the novel's manifold hilarious scenes and moments: "the startling, juicy displays of excess erudition, for example; the passionate, often hilarious antiquarianism, the prodigal production of alternate historiographies; the 'over'-attachment to fragmentary, marginal, waste, or leftover products; the rich, highly interruptive affective variety; the irrepressible fascination with ventriloquistic experimentation; the disorienting juxtapositions of present with past, and popular with high culture" (Sedgwick 1997: 28).

10

The Labor of Figuration

*We talked as we had never talked before,
an outpouring.*
MAGGIE NELSON

*un mundo de arquitecturas en continua metamorfosis,
rumores que se configuran en significaciones,
archipiélagos del sentido*
OCTAVIO PAZ

Hyperbolically Realist

Do you like his work? I ask. The work of Joyce? I don't think there's another writer in this century that can be named in the same breath, he tells me. Well, I say don't you think he is a little too—how should I put it?—realistic [*un poco exageradamente realista*]? Realistic? says Renzi. Realistic? Without a doubt. But what is realism? he said. A representation based on an interpretation of reality, that is realism, said Renzi. In essence, he said later, Joyce set himself a single problem: How to narrate real events. What events? I ask. Real events, Renzi tells me. Oh, I understood moral events (Piglia [1980] 1994: 146).[1]

---

[1] "¿A usted le gusta su obra?, le digo. ¿La obra de Joyce? No creo que se pueda nombrar a ningún escritor en este siglo, me dice. Bueno, le digo, no le parece que era un poco, ¿cómo lo diré?, ¿no le parece que era un poco exageradamente realista? ¿Realista?, dice Renzi. ¿Realista? Sin duda. Pero ¿qué es realismo?, dijo. Una representación interpretada de la realidad, eso es el realismo, dijo Renzi. En el fondo, dijo después, Joyce se planteó un solo problema: ¿Como narrar los hechos reales? ¿Los hechos qué?, le digo. Los hechos reales, me dice Renzi. Ah, le digo, había entendido los hechos morales" (Piglia 1980: 184, my emphasis).

As we have seen in the previous chapter, Ricardo Piglia's lifelong alter ego Renzi loves to ask what I have called the Renzi question, a methodical trick that allows Piglia to reduce the entire work of a certain author to a single characteristic feature. In the passage quoted above, Renzi defines the work of Joyce, who might be seen as the most anti-realist of all anti-realist writers, as nothing else but *hyperbolic realism*. To be more precise, Renzi does not speak of *hyperbolic realism*, but of a work that is *hyperbolically realist*. It might seem pedantic to insist on this little difference. But there are a few things to gain from it, as we can see by looking at Tristan Garcia's brief cartography of the field of contemporary "new" realism alongside three grammatical categories: nominal, adjectival, adverbial (Garcia 2018, my transl.).

It is the last characterization as adverbial that comes closest to the particular type of new realism at work in Bolaño's and Pynchon's late maximalist novels. I hereby hope not only to work out a more precise relationship between the two main elements of my book's title, *realism* and *hyperbole*, but also to distinguish my efforts from the wide-spread tendency of literary criticism to combine the genre-defining noun *realism* with a descriptive or merely ornamental adjective such as magical, dirty, pastoral, traumatic, depressive, hysterical, peripheral, allegorical, etc. (Deckard 2012; Adams 2009; Fisher 2009; Rothberg 2000; Wood 2000; Buford 2008).

What all these efforts have in common, of course, is the awareness that realism 1.0, the ambition to produce an adequate image of reality, is no longer a viable option. Those seeking to make a case for a realism corresponding to our age are facing two challenges, at least: first, that the real is never pre-critically given to us as a whole or as a set of immediately accessible data; and second, that any literary rendering of the world must somehow produce an inevitably exaggerated and exaggerating "representation based on an interpretation of reality" (Piglia [1980] 1994: 146).

Combining the dominant noun (realism) with a specifying adjective, all the above-mentioned critical efforts, perhaps even the eminently polemic *hysterical realism,* try to respond to such challenges by supplanting the empty evocation of "an exterior reality *en bloc*" with "the search for criteria that subordinate our knowledge to something else than its own whim" (Garcia 2018: 44). However, the mere process of enriching a noun (realism), which had been fallen from grace for so long, with a more or less original adjective risks to reproduce the pre-critical understanding of reality as *manifest image*. Instead of a "representation based on an interpretation of reality" (Piglia [1980] 1994: 146), we risk to get a literary reproduction of the "myth of the given" (Sellars [1956] 1997), tinted with supernatural kitsch or decorated with imitative experimentalism.

What is more, there is a considerable element of arbitrariness to the choice of the specific adjective, which is then burdened with the responsibility of embodying the dominant structure of either the present world or a historical reality seen from the perspective of the emphatic now. In a way then, the popular critical strategy of *hysterical realism* and its allies risks to fall even behind the state of the art of nineteenth-century realism, which in its more sophisticated manifestations has of course never really believed in the possibility or benefit of creating a faithful image of society, nature, and life as a whole. In this light, any will to revive realism as a fruitful category for the understanding of contemporary literary aesthetics is faced with two principal (not necessarily incompatible) options. On the one hand, one can engage in thorough historical readings, establishing a more or less troublesome, more or less fragile continuity between a vast literary tradition that emerged asynchronically along the eighteenth and nineteenth centuries and certain forms of relevant, non-imitative contemporary writing. On the other hand, one can engage in more philosophically attuned readings that focus on the ways in which the literary text dramatizes and (re-)produces a concept of reality implicit in its aesthetic program.

Both options come with their own merits and limitations, but I believe that the second one is more promising, at least for my purposes. Following Garcia, I consider the hyperbolic in *hyperbolic realism* as an adverb, not as an adjective. This allows us to read Bolaño's and Pynchon's late maximalist novels not only as proponents of a new literary genre (Ercolino 2014),[2] but also as particularly interesting examples of a specific mode of writing, a *literary dispositive* that is not reducible to the ultimately arbitrary focus on the long and complex mega-novel.

If it is not altogether impossible and useless to look at these (late) maximalist novels in terms of genre—and Stefano Ercolino's *The Maximalist Novel* represents a heroic attempt in employing strategies of both distant and close reading to discern generic similarities—their understanding in terms of a writing mode, a *manière de faire* that points to a *manière d'être* (Macé 2011 and 2016), is more cognizant of the problem that we are dealing with contemporary cultural artifacts embedded in dynamic environments. We may later conclude that these texts belong to the same genre, but first we have to recognize that they are part of an evolving "new cultural geology" (McGurl 2011), to which Anthropocenic thought, speculative realism, and a certain branch of postwar phenomenology also belong. For my purposes, the question whether my corpus consists of one, two or thirty novels is not that important, since I purse a strategy that is speculative by nature and necessity, following the texts' permeability and porosity toward kindred literary spirits, resonant theoretical practices, and resonant likeminded onto-phenomenological configurations.

---

[2]The ten formal features with which Ercolino defines the postwar maximalist novel are extreme length, encyclopedic mode, dissonant chorality, diegetic exuberance, completeness, narrational omniscience, paranoid imagination, intersemiocity, ethical commitment, and hybrid realism.

In contrast to outstanding examples of maximalism like *Ulysses, Paradiso, Grande Sertão, The Man without Qualities, Infinite Jest*, or even Pynchon's and Bolaño's own earlier maximalist attempts, namely *Gravity's Rainbow, Mason & Dixon*, and *The Savage Detectives*, our authors' recent works profuse a sense of mitigated radicalism. This makes them appear more readable than their famous predecessors, but also open to criticism as they seem to partake in a conservative relapse of literature to the complacency of mimetic realism. Comparing Pynchon's and Bolaño's newer books with our short list of radical maximalist novels, critics might conclude that 2666 and *ATD* are less consistently experimental than *Ulysses*, less exquisitely hermetic than *Paradiso*,[3] less linguistically innovative and radically skeptical than *Grande Sertão*, less pointedly essayistic than *The Man without Qualities*, less distinctly metafictional than *Infinite Jest*, and less stylistically extravagant than each and every one of them.

In a widely known conversation with Larry McCaffery, David Foster Wallace said:

> I'm not much interested in trying for classical, big-R Realism, not because the big R's form has now been absorbed and suborned by commercial entertainment. The classical Realist form is soothing, familiar and anesthetic; it drops right into spectation (McCaffery 1993: 138).

Instead of an encompassing cosmological vision and a renewal of our aesthetic sensibilities, the spectacle of big-R realism of *ATD* and 2666 may seem not only aesthetically disappointing, but a lot more entertaining when provided by TV and other better-equipped agents of the cultural industry.

One can indeed claim that *ATD* and 2666 often recall the cultural format that dominated the last two decades: the TV series (especially in the long and sprawling form that privileges uncontained episodes and season-spanning narrative arcs). Pynchon's Colorado plot line, for instance, is reminiscent of HBO's *Deadwood*; another serial narrative format is evoked by *ATD*'s abundant allusions to the comic genre (*in the meanwhile*). Bolaño's atmospheric mixture of sex, drugs, and violence as much as the sharp contrast between a bunch of morally disappointing characters on

---

[3] Cortázar tried to make sense of *Paradiso*'s exceptional status in defining the adequate mode of reception not as reading, but as a preparation for reading, as meta-reading, so to speak: "En sus instantes más altos *Paradiso* es una ceremonia, algo que preexiste a toda lectura con fines y modos literarios; tiene esa acuciosa presencia típica de lo que fue la visión primordial de los eléatas, amalgama de lo que más tarde se llamó poema y filosofía, desnuda confrontación del hombre con un cielo de zarpas de estrellas. Una obra así no se lee; se la consulta, se avanza por ella línea a línea, jugo a jugo, en una participación intelectual y sensible tan tensa y vehemente como la que desde esas líneas y esos jugos nos busca y nos revela" (Cortázar 1967: 137).

the one hand and a tiny fraction of heroic exceptions on the other (Lalo Cura, Sergio González Rodríguez, Rosa Amalfitano, Guadalupe Roncal) seems to feed on the melodramatic cynicism of the *narconovela*.

In a way, a major public and critical success like *The Wire* seems to prove that TV has taken the lead in terms of telling the long story and uncovering its complex contexts. Perhaps even a hard-boiled reader and advocate of traditional literary values like James Wood implicitly compares the linguistic confinement of the late maximalist novel to the newly successful TV series, when he names boredom as one of the major effects of *ATD*'s failed realism:

> One of the problems with hysterical realism, of which this novel is a kind of zany Baedeker, is that one suffers both the hysteria *and* the realism: the worst of both worlds. There is the weightless excess, the incredibilities, the boredom that always attends upon cartoonish, inauthentic novelistic activity. But there is also the boredom attendant upon the rather old-fashioned, straightforward realism used to create this very escape from realism. Thus one of the most peculiar elements of this clearly ambitious and daring novel is that its stylistic syntax is relatively undaring, and so conventional. Of course much of it is pastiche, so in a sense it slips out of the charge of conventionality. But the practical effect is a grammar of realism that challenges nobody and nothing (Wood 2007b).[4]

Although Wood's stubborn conservatism may not allow him to see the problem from the perspective of competing media, his otherwise often compelling critique of Pynchon's longest novel reinforces the decline of reputation of the contemporary maximalist mega-novel, which must compete with the infinitely higher personal, technical, and visual resources of HBO & Co.

But Wood's argument gains its seductive power not primarily from the claim that *ATD* is too complex, too demanding, and too *hysterically* formalistic. Instead, the main reason for his discontent is the fact that Pynchon mobilizes an "old-fashioned, straightforward realism" whose missing aesthetic novelty is covered by the author's renowned cosmopolitan zaniness and historical erudition and whose ultimately conventional grammar is excused with the practically ineffective pretext of pastiche. Such a dismissal pushes *ATD* and, in the same vain, Bolaño's *2666* further away from orthodox postmodern celebrations of experimentalism like *Infinite Jest*. It is not everybody that will read this move as a step in the right

---

[4]Notice Wood's tiresome tic to dismiss *hysterical realism* on the basis of the biased assumption that it is inauthentic. For the sake of fairness, however, I have to mention that his critical reaction to Bolaño is overall positive, if not euphoric (Wood 2007a).

direction. For instance, a reader that is more skeptical vis-à-vis a realistic turn and its presumed attenuation of experimental extremes could see here yet another concession to the cultural hegemony of "capitalist realism," as it was aptly coined by Mark Fisher (2009).[5]

Despite their limitations—Wood's neglect of the larger media ecology and Fisher's overemphasizing of postmodern simulationism—such objections against *2666* and *ATD* are not entirely unsubstantiated. Seen at large, however, they are not very convincing either. If many scenes in these novels refer to a recognizable or even historically established reality, the "sandgrain manyness of things" (DeLillo 1997: 60) fanned out in front of the readers' eyes produces a sort of uncanny valley of too much description. Copious accumulation (Chapter 3) is in fact a crucial manufacturer of uncertainty in *ATD* and *2666* and could thus be added as an eighth item to Namwali Serpell's elaborate list of "seven modes of uncertainty" (2014). In the wake of the novels' foregrounding of what I have called flat fictionality (Chapter 6), the referential ties to historical reality become loosened. As a result, it becomes more and more difficult to separate what is real from what is unreal or, perhaps more importantly, what is substantial or relevant from what is only accidental. In *hyperbolic realism*, the discorrelation between words and events is not as aggressively asserted as is often the case in literature now canonized as postmodern. But such a discorrelation remains a fundamental condition for the narrative as well as for the narrated experience and perception of the characters.

If it is true that a lot of the material in Pynchon's and Bolaño's late maximalist fiction looks like the product of straightforward, mundane realism, its framework is not realistic, but metabolic (Chapter 4). Other than in some of the most sophisticated examples in Luz Horne's canon of *literaturas reales* (2011), Bolaño and Pynchon do not reduce mimesis to mere indexicality, but accommodate it in a field of metabolic intertextuality in which the inherited genres and literary techniques are partly imitated, partly upgraded, and partly "repaired." In that sense, *ATD* and *2666* are not only late cultural phenomena, they make their lateness explicit in at least two ways: as a literature that comes after realism and as a literature that comes after the avant-gardes.

Speaking of *ATD*, saying that mimesis tinged by metabolic intertextuality "shifts into the fourth gear" (Rinck 2015: 13, my transl.) is not only meant in some "strictly metaphorical way" (*ATD*: 433), but rather quite literally. Ganesh Rao's hilarious theory of people as vectors hereby serves as a *pars pro*

---

[5] A realism acting as a symbolic ally of the status quo. Assuming that late capitalism is an adequate name for our age, capitalist realism should perhaps be renamed as *late capitalist realism*.

toto for the ambition of the novel to expand the three warranted dimensions of historical reality/realism by a fourth axis: that of fantastic literature.

Now, coming back to Garcia's mapping of the field of contemporary realism, *hyperbolic realism,* which combines attitudes and elements from all three grammatical types (the nominal, the adjectival, and, most importantly, the adverbial), ventures into what Garcia sees as a fourth type of realism, a realism of the possible or even the impossible. This fourth type, which Garcia associates with the new phenomenon of speculative realism and Lewisian modal realism, seeks to translate the eternal business of literature into the more rigid realms of philosophy, in its attempt to know what seems or is unknown, to speak out what seems or is unspeakable and to grasp the reality of what seems or is unreal. Such a preference for paradox intermittently pops up at the surface of *hyperbolic realism*, in Bolaño's neo-surrealist imagery or when Pynchon uses mathematics to highlight a specific narrative paradox.

On the level of style, then, what appears as a quietist fallback into "old-fashioned, straightforward realism" (Wood 2007b) or a calculated concession to the literary market, can be seen as part of a conscious aesthetic strategy. In Chapters 5–7, I tried to show how the semiotic skepticism associated with postmodernity, modernism's infatuation with darkness and invisibility, and the laborious adventurism of plot and language of the maximalist novel are not banned from Pynchon's and Bolaño's late works, but refashioned in a more nuanced, discreet, and idiosyncratic way.

Flat fictionality, the act of placing the whole novelistic discourse under the sign of *as-if-ness* (Chapter 6), creates a pervasive atmosphere of unreality, which some theorists of today see as the predominant feeling of living in the Anthropocene (Morton 2013: 146). What we could call the realistic effect of flat fictionality, then, is not only to communicate the uncanny feeling that we are already living on a post-apocalyptic planet (Danowski & Viveiros de Castro [2014] 2016), but to provide the enabling condition for an expansion of what can be said. The atmospheric persistence of radical doubt, indiscriminate fictionality, and unemployed negativity, vanquished over and over again by the stubbornness of hyperbolic expression (*sed tamen,* Chapter 7), is the signature of Pynchon's and Bolaño's late maximalist novels. If these novels narrate a lot of moments of failure, the failure is much more political, ethical, and existential than linguistic and rhetorical. In *Gravity's Rainbow,* any attempt to establish a sustainable connection between the living and dead is made impossible by constant entropic noise (Kittler [1987] 2008). In *ATD*, in contrast, Kit Traverse and his father manage to mobilize the limited semiotic resources of the afterworld ("the stripped and dismal metonymies of the dead," *ATD*: 673) in order to verbalize at least parts of the generational, political, and ontological fractures that divide them. However, the fact that this act of post-mortal communication is only of a very ephemeral nature demonstrates literature's rather limited reparative powers. Even if the novel ends with a seemingly hopeful promise, in Pynchon's world there is no ultimate salvation from gravity, only the option of a provisional and constantly fleeting state of grace.

The notorious abundancy of *hyperbolic realism* (Chapter 3) shapes a world in which the visible is greatly and permanently outperformed by the invisible (Chapter 5). With the help of Richir and Merleau-Ponty, we have seen that this invisibility creates as much of an autonomous or "unemployed" phenomenological field as it is the invisible environment that enables phenomenalization in the first place. Metaphorical speech that is also hyperbolic is inserted into this environment. Metaphor binds the energies of its environment and operates as both a limiting and enabling mode of creating a "contact" with the real "through distance" (Richir 2015: 151). In the realms of *hyperbolic realism*, metaphors are neither absolute signifiers nor entirely meaningless (Rorty 1989: 19), they are (semi-)autonomous acts of expression that are at the same time parts of mutually entangled, interdependent acts of constant paraphrasing.

Thus, the reason why only a metaphor can explain what a metaphor is (Davidson 1978: 31) is not that metaphors could not be paraphrased in a complete way, but rather that there can be no act of paraphrasing that does not produce its new figurative excess and remainder, a new "halo of dizzying mystery" (2666: 659). The same dynamic applies to central enigmas in narratives of hyperbolic realism. The quest for narrative secrets does not inevitably lead into the "terrible indifference" (2666: 659) we might remember from celebrations of aporia according to orthodox postmodernism, but they are frequently solved, albeit in often bathetic and disappointing ways and at the end of long-ish arcs of suspension. However, postmodern skepticism is *not* supplanted by a new positivist confidence in narrative dénouement. All the solutions offered by hyperbolic realism remain provisional; episodic closure creates new enigmas and new possibilities, which characterizes these novels as complex structures, open and closed at the same time (Morin 2008).

Accordingly, the fact that radical and hyperbolic doubt is widely disseminated through these abundant discourses—but often partially and provisionally overcome (Chapter 7)—does not abolish the novels' intimate relation to linguistic uncertainty and the sinuous unfolding of their semiotic adventures. The destructive and deconstructive processes that often occur in moments of change are not merely semiotic and immaterial, but often tied to a literal tearing apart of the fabric of both the text and its narrated/imagined universe (Chapter 8). In the interstices of these "flayed [openings], scratched out by fingernails" (Lispector [1973] 2012: 70), what we glimpse is not merely the opposite of the real as manifest image, but the processes of the most fragile and precarious phenomenal realm, that of *phantasia*, which is the force that brings the image into being and has thus the potential to disturb and realign the image's ontology at any time.

With all this in mind, it is difficult to reduce *ATD* and *2666* to inauthentic products of literary tricksters and inflated discourses on the basis of a largely conventional "grammar of realism" (Wood 2007b).[6] What they promote is mimesis and realism in the fourth gear, a new planetary literature that explores the paradoxical nature of objects, words, and phenomena behind a façade of mimetic reproduction. As inferior adventures of laborious figuration, they offer an account of the complex, difficult, and increasingly impossible existence at or even "after end of the world," by trying to "express the ineffable without abolishing its character of ineffability" (Horne 2011: 185).

Against Ineffability

Pynchon's and Bolaño's late maximalist novels *2666* and *ATD* debunk the wide-spread myth of the ineffability of the real, but they do so without banning linguistic and perceptual doubt, ontological uncertainty, and the centrality of *phantasia* from the heart of their literary projects. One of the most perspicuous articulations of the current situation of literary expressibility can be found in Maggie Nelson's queer auto-theory essay *The Argonauts* (2015). Nelson's theory-savvy account of her love relationship with the trans and gender-fluid trans video artist Harry Dodge starts with a deliberately obscene juxtaposition of Beckett and anal sex that pauses on a note of perplexity[7] before it turns its attention to the age-old problem of what words can express and what they can't:

---

[6]If it is true that there is a lot of hot air in Pynchon's *ATD*, the inflation of airborne events are a mode of the novel's fantastic realism. After all, the narrative spends considerable amounts of time in the airship of the Chums of Chance, a distant standpoint from the messiness of life on earth's surface, but from where things can also be seen with a "balloonheaded clarity" (*ATD*: 157). The continuity or contiguity between our world and theirs is suggested in Lindsay's warning at the very beginning of the novel that by boarding the *Inconvenience*, we do not escape "into any realm of the counterfactual. There may not be mangrove swamps or lynch law up here, but we must nonetheless live with the constraints of the given world, notable among them the decrease of temperature with altitude" (*ATD*: 9).
[7]"October, 2007. The Santa Ana winds are shredding the bark off the eucalyptus trees in long white stripes. A friend and I risk the widowmakers by having lunch outside, during which she suggests I tattoo the words HARD TO GET across my knuckles, as a reminder of this pose's possible fruits. Instead the words *I love you* come tumbling out of my mouth in an incantation the first time you fuck me in the ass, my face smashed against the cement floor of your dank and charming bachelor pad. You had *Molloy* by your bedside and a stack of cocks in a shadowy unused shower stall. Does it get any better? *What's your pleasure?* you asked, then stuck around for an answer" (Nelson 2015: 3).

Before we met, I had spent a lifetime devoted to Wittgenstein's idea that the inexpressible is contained—inexpressibly!—in the expressed. This idea gets less air time than his more reverential *Whereof one cannot speak thereof one must be silent*, but it is, I think, the deeper idea. Its paradox is, quite literally, why I write, or how I feel able to keep writing.

For it doesn't feed or exalt any angst one may feel about the incapacity to express, in words, that which eludes them. It doesn't punish what can be said for what, by definition, it cannot be. Nor does it ham it up by miming a constricted throat: *Lo, what I would say, were words good enough*. Words are good enough (Nelson 2015: 3).

In light of many of current literary practices still held in the firm grip of (post)modernity's long arm, Nelson's mantra *words are good enough* reads like a pragmatist heresy against the prevalence of différance, simulationism, and metafictionality in certain circles at least. It strongly resonates, however, with some of the voices we have heard in this book, such as Luz Horne's remarks on indexicality in what she calls *literatures reales* or Richir's description of the *infigurable*, which is not the outer limit of an inevitably figurative literary discourse, but that which enables it and vouches for its relevance, so to speak. What all these positions have in common is that they do not send literature on a heroic mission to celebrate inexpressibility as a higher form of aphasia nor do they reduce the literary text to a discourse that speaks boastfully, but in classical syntax about new realities.

In contrast to Nelson's neo-pragmatist irreverence, Nelson's partner Harry, a visual artist is much more cautious about the power of words claiming that they are

> corrosive to all that is good, all that is real, all that is flow. We argued and argued on this account, full of fever, not malice. Once we name something, you said, we can never see it the same way again. All that is unnameable falls away, gets lost, is murdered. You called this the cookie-cutter function of our minds (2015: 4).

But Harry's lack of linguistic confidence neither reveals a textualist dogma nor does it launch an attack on language from its absolute outside. Instead, it takes its energy from the entanglement of embodiment, desire, and expression that Nelson tries to reanimate in her text, from the abundant proliferation of signs that produces potentially troubling effects of discorrelation. For how else would they have "argued and argued on this account, full of fever, not malice" than with words?

This is the initial aporia or, as Nelson has it, the founding paradox of her writing: not only the old idea of the later Wittgenstein that "the inexpressible is contained—inexpressibly!—in the expressed" (Nelson 2015: 3), but the newer one that confronts a pragmatist plunge into exuberance with an inevitable discorrelation of language and reality: "I argued along the lines of Thomas Jefferson and the churches—for plethora, for kaleidoscopic shifting, for excess" versus "the cookie-cutter function of our minds" and our expressive abilities (2015: 4).

After that, Nelson's book unfolds in an outpouring that constantly questions its own bias for plethora, kaleidoscopic shifting, and excess; an adventurous endeavor in which the founding paradox or paradoxes are not dialectically reconciled, but stylistically navigated, "we argued and argued," with an inevitably open end. Language is neither adequate or inadequate, it is simply there. Words are good enough, but language is never fully identical with itself; like the famous ship of the *Argonauts,* as it moves along, as it strives to survive, it must undergo a constant process of repair and refurbishment, always slightly out of sync with itself, either too much or too little—in short, hyperbolic.

Much later in the book, Nelson finds a certain "solution" for the tensed relationship between pragmatism and discorrelation:

> Afraid of assertion. Always trying to get out of "totalizing" language, i.e., language that rides roughshod over specificity; realizing this is another form of paranoia. Barthes found the exit to this merry-go-round by reminding himself that "it is language which is assertive, not he." It is absurd, Barthes says, to try to flee from language's assertive nature by "add[ing] to each sentence some little phrase of uncertainty, as if anything that came out of language could make language tremble."
>
> My writing is riddled with such tics of uncertainty. I have no excuse or solution, save to allow myself the tremblings, then go back in later and slash them out. In this way I edit myself into a boldness that is neither native nor foreign to me (Nelson 2015: 98).

Nelson's—and hyperbolic realism's—solution to the problem of the myth of the ineffable, then, is not to return to *rigid realism*, to the myth of a transparent language. Nor is it to rehabilitate the romantic genius who creates a divine-like poetic language that celebrates the beauty of hermetic form. Instead, even if by very different means, they both provide a form in which and through which *language can speak itself*. It might come as a surprise that this *inhumanism of language* is a recurrent idea of those phenomenological authors whose works I have used in this book to shed light on a few aspects of hyperbolic realism. It is an undercurrent theme, even for the authors themselves, often ignored, especially by phenomenology's critics for it does not quite fit into the popular reduction of phenomenology to a philosophy of personal experience. Against the accusation of phenomenology's necessary connection to an old-fashioned humanism, in Levinas's *Totality and Infinity*, we find these compelling words:

> Thus language commences. That which speaks (to) me and across the words proposes himself to me retains the fundamental foreignness of the Other [*l'étrangeté foncière d'autrui*] who judges me; our relations are never reversible (Levinas [1961] 1979: 101, transl. slightly altered).

Merleau-Ponty, in his *note de travail* from November 1959, is quite a bit more elaborate:

> Philosophy has never spoken—I do not say of *passivity*: we are not effects—but I would say of the passivity of our activity, as Valery spoke of a *body of the spirit*: new as our initiatives may be, they come to birth at the heart of being, they are connected onto the time that streams forth in us, supported on the pivots or hinges of our life, their *sense* is a "direction"—The soul always thinks: this is in it a property of its state, it cannot not think because a field has been opened in which *something* or the *absence* of something is always inscribed. This is not an *activity* of the soul, nor a production of thoughts in the plural, and I am not even the author of that hollow that forms within me by the passage from the present to the retention, it is not I who makes myself think any more than it is I who makes my heart beat (Merleau-Ponty [1964] 1968: 221).

In the mode and mood of *hyperbolic realism*, the author is neither dead nor sovereign, but acts as a receptive medium of *language that speaks itself*. The narrators are (symbolically) embodied beings, situated within a "productive nature" (Grant 2006) that surpasses them, makes them speak and makes their (artificial) heartbeat. Similar to Merleau-Ponty's claim that the soul cannot *not* think, and to Spivak's declaration that you "cannot *not* decide if you are actually in the field of justice" (Spivak 2012: 12), language, according to Nelson's elaboration, cannot *not* signify. At the same time, both the author and the narrator are not reduced to a simple function of the text's program. *Nous ne sommes pas des effets*, writes Merleau-Ponty (1964: 270). But in order to survive in the realm of productive alienation, the author needs to embrace the inhumanism of language by jumping into the "the well of the great poets, where all that can be heard is his [or her] voice gradually mingling with other voices" not knowing "who those other voices belong to" (Bolaño 2004b: 73).

Productive and, to say it with Serpell, ethically relevant uncertainty is not produced "by adding to each sentence some little phrase of uncertainty," but by letting your "tics of uncertainty" creep into the text and put them to work right there (Nelson 2015: 98). The author's act of expression only "succeeds" if she does not erase her hesitations and idiosyncrasies and allows herself the tremblings—not to slash them out later, as I would correct here, but to exaggerate them even further.

Nelson's programmatic disclosure resonates with what is much more implicit or *intermittent* (Chapter 4) in Bolaño's and Pynchon's late maximalist poetics. Together, they help us to overcome and, in great hyperbolic tradition, to outdo the postmodern master tropes of simulation, *différance* and metafictionality. In hyperbolic realism, reality experienced as ontological simulacrum does not reproduce an image of reality as spectacle. While postmodern simulationism is (still) based on a "philosophy of access" (Harman 2002), *hyperbolic realism* feeds on a distanced contact with the real that is *imprésentable,* but grounds and enables all our efforts of knowing, perceiving, and acting. It rejects the absolute difference between culture and nature or productive humanity and dead matter, and foregrounds the inhuman forces that traverse the human from within, gesturing toward an "ancestral past" (Meillassoux [2006] 2008) and a future horizon of extinction (Colebrook 2014), toward the very real and even imminent possibility of a world without us.

The abundance produced by hyperbolic realism, then, is not a sign of the triumph of linguistic narcissism. It is the result of an ongoing editing process of both language and our ways of being in the world, an editing of ourselves "into a boldness that is neither native nor foreign to [us]" (Nelson 2015: 98), but comes from the productive nature of language, which is folded into the productive nature of reality. To say it one last time, abundance in Pynchon's and Bolaño's late maximalist novels is not a vehicle of triumphalism, but a mode of uncertainty. The exteriority to which *2666* and *ATD* gesture is not that of Meillassoux's *grand dehors*. It is not absolute, but hyperbolic—hyperbolic because it always refers to more (and less) than what meets the eye, to the infinitesimally small and the very large, but it remains grounded in the situatedness of this act of gesturing even where it points to a situation in which this situatedness no longer exists.

As I have tried to show in Chapter 8, the concept of dehiscence, the material ripping apart of the very fabric of perception, the image or reality itself, might be seen as a much more materially grounded version of deconstruction. It cracks open the fixities of our "symbolic institutions" (Richir 2015: 154), the habits of imagination, mythology, language, memory, logical transparency, rhetoric reliability, and so on. But more than merely celebrating indifference, absence, and aphasia, it invites *phantasia* to make space for the "least things whose essence is flicker, flow" (Nelson 2015: 4) and reminds us that, while words are good enough, they are neither the only nor the privileged means by which we make contact with the real and by which we articulate that contact.

The close affinity between the hyperbolic and the inhuman provides an explanation for the intermittent irreality of these novels, the flickering presence of the weird and the eerie, and a textual abundance that is nevertheless constantly haunted by doubts and uncertainty. In *2666* and *ATD*, in contrast to Pynchon's and Bolaño's earlier works like *Gravity's Rainbow* and *The Savage Detectives*, the interruptions are less brutal, the shifts of direction less frantic, and the multi-perspective orchestration more subtle and discreet. It often seems as if the steady voice and idiom of the narrator, as it oscillates between ghostly omniscience and anonymous detachment, points to a gradual blending of character and material world.[8] In any case, what we are dealing with is not the regression to the confidence of a triumphant realism in which an omniscient narrator hovers as a synthesizing force above subordinate and subjunctive perspectives. Instead, plunging into the seemingly less radical novelistic worlds of hyperbolic realism, we become witnesses of a hyperbolic reality largely unfolding on its own account. But since we are not merely effects, to say it with Merleau-Ponty, we experience this specific kind of worldmaking not as helpless victims, but as *esprits de corps*, exposed (and exposing ourselves) to the "passivity of our activity" (Merleau-Ponty [1964] 1968: 221), folded into the flat fictionality of hyperbolic realism. Karl Ove Knausgård, a remote accomplice to hyperbolic realism, has brought home much of this atmospheric effect, in an essay about *2666*, which is just as well one about *ATD:*

> Reading *2666*, it seems that this sense of a center, based on an idea or an experience that something is near and something else is far away, has been dissolved or suspended ... Setting, place and events are not described as foreign, and there is no cognitive gap ... between the characters and what they see ... On the other hand, there is also no familiarity. The distance is always the same, the people are neither close to anything nor far from anything, it seems as if the environment has no effect on them, similar to an ambient experience on TV ... The world is in a sense seen to the end, and the fact that the characters are in a certain place for the first time does not change anything. This preceding awareness, which impregnates their gaze, creates a distance to the foreign that no trip or journey can abolish. If Tolstoy, with his descriptions of reality, has managed to portray the foreign as if we were seeing it for the first time, as if it were true and untroubled by our perceptual habits, Bolaño has

---

[8]In a slightly different, but lucid way, Ercolino (2014: 100) speaks of an *omniscience through recomposition*.

done the opposite. His description produces the weakening of the image of reality. Strangely enough, however, the result is similar to Tolstoy's, for the world that Bolaño describes is also mysterious, precisely because of the lack of familiarity and the lack of any attempt to penetrate it. We see it, and what we see is described in a way that neither the one nor the other is seen. It is inexplicable (Knausgård [2013] 2016: 250–1, my transl.).[9]

---

[9] I owe this reference to Johanna Nuber.

ψ) Epilogue: A Fifth Concept of Reality

> *Now it is time to wake,*
> *into the breath of what was always real.*
> THOMAS PYNCHON

For pre-modern minds, Hans Blumenberg (2020: 108) writes, the real is that which is unsuspicious. Today, the opposite has become true. In the Anthropocene, reality as such is under suspicion, as an obscenely overwhelming part of it is now affected by man, this most suspicious of animals. And yet, somewhat paradoxically, but as I have tried to show for many good reasons, a hermeneutics of suspicion is not very well positioned to capture the stakes of our time. This adherence to a hermeneutics of suspicion, much more than epistemological relativism, limits the applicability of orthodox postmodernism to make sense of the cultural riddles of our century.

Here lies one of the strategic reasons for my sustained interest in the two novels I've been wild-reading over so many pages, *Against the Day* (*ATD*) and *2666*. Their authors, Roberto Bolaño and Thomas Pynchon, are often counted among the first ranks of postmodernist literature, but their late maximalist fiction seems to be at odds with what one must historically and analytically associate with postmodernism, at least in more than a few aspects. The claim alone that the name tag of postmodernism is boring or "problematic" doesn't do the job, considering that many earlier texts of Pynchon and Bolaño thrive on conspirational logics, suggesting that "everything is connected" at the same time as the most important bits of information are withheld from both characters and readers. The narrative mode associated with this conspirational universe is noisy and hectic, it relies on the constant foregrounding of a thick network of intratextual and intertextual relations. Some critics have denounced pace, rhythm, and style of such narratives as hysterical; others may see them as the perfect aesthetic response to an unhinged reality in danger of becoming nothing more but a huge, energy-consuming simulation machine. And yet others seem to go so far as to celebrate the postmodern novel as a realism of a higher order, a realism, so to speak, that embodies the inescapable illusiveness of a fully computerized world.

If we follow Hans Blumenberg's fascinating attempt to organize the practice of novel-writing in the West as a whole in relation to its implied concept of reality,[1] the postmodern novel of the early digital age (1973–96, roughly) still subscribes to the modernist phase of said concept (Concept 4), to a notion of reality in which the real is that which is left as unappropriated by human access and perception. In other words, for both an orthodox modernist *and* a committed postmodernist, the more something eludes us, the more real it is supposed to be.

It cannot be denied that a considerable part of the modernist conception of the real is at work in *2666* and *ATD*—think of the driving secrets and suspenseful enigmas, the emphasis on remote locations with difficult accesses, the disappearance of plot lines and characters, the limited vision of the narrator, the pervasive atmosphere of fictionality and irreality, and the general opacity which results from an overabundance of details and information. However, underneath this recognizably modern conception, a new one creeps in. For this new concept, the real in its most emphatic or, say, contemporary sense is not defined by the inertia and muteness of the black box. For this fifth concept of reality (Concept 5) introduced in this book mainly via Pynchon's and Bolaño's hyperbolic realism, to whom it is of course not limited, the real is a productive process: dynamic, autopoietic, self-structuring, and agential. Its dominant time frame is not that of the history of Western civilization or capitalism; it is that of deep geological time, a frame reaching far behind (Meillassoux's ancestrality) and far beyond (Colebrook's extinction) the world seen through dominantly human scales. At the core of this conception lies a paradox, too, but it is very different from the one that defines high modernism, pointing at a situation where the fact that humans have become the major geological force of the planet provokes their expulsion from the center of the world.

As I have suggested several times in this book, *ATD* and *2666* constantly gesture toward a reality beyond or beneath human scales. It is a reality,

---

[1] Let us briefly recall the four (occidental) concepts of reality according to Blumenberg. Concept 1 = reality as instantaneous evidence (Platonic idealism); Concept 2 = reality guaranteed by an absolute witness (Middle Ages, theology, absolutist state, colonial rule); Concept 3 = reality as synthetic production of coherent contexts (Early modernity, experimental science, formal logic); Concept 4 = reality as that which resist human, civilizational, and technological appropriation (modernism, avant-gardes).

one could say by adapting Fred Moten, that is always "more and less than one" (Moten 2018: 1), "more and less than itself" (2018: 71), more and less than nothing, but also more and less than everything. But this does not mean that it is completely inaccessible or entirely absent. Distinct from both transparency and not-givenness, reality in Anthropocenic times is still deeply enigmatic, but the type of secret it accommodates is much better defined by what Moten calls an "open secret" (2018: 155) than by the nuclear[2] metaphor of a faceless, impenetrable black box.

It has been one of my major intentions in this book to demonstrate how hyperbole—not as a clearly recognizable rhetorical trope, but as a spectral figure, "a figment of a continuous intention, manifesting itself more often implicitly than explicitly" (Haverkamp 2002: 82)—articulates and by way of articulation (co-)produces this new conception of the real. Absolute resistance and complete withdrawal is no longer the characteristic signature of this contemporary formation of the real. But by no means should we simply return to the pre-critical attitude of the third concept (Concept 3) and its celebratory understanding of a hyper-rational subject engaged in a constant process of smoothly sorting all kinds of data into coherent and truthful lists and contexts. When Marc Richir speaks of the *rien-que-phénomène*, of wild beings and pure phenomenalization, his aim is not to rehabilitate a naïve "myth of the given" (Sellars [1956] 1997), but to trace how both fact *and* fiction, perception *and* hallucination, and truth *and* illusion emerge from one and the same phenomenological field—the field of anarchic *phantasia*.

But Richir's phenomenology is not only anarchic, it is also architectonic. In a similar vein, hyperbolic realism not only tries to hark back to the anarchic origins of our contemporary world, it is also interested in what happens in the passage from one phenomenological level to the next (e.g., from *phantasia* to imagination, from imagination to metaphor), from the phenomenal to the ontological realm, and, finally, in the transition from one concept of reality to another one. This might also explain the remarkable fact that, to shape and co-create that new concept of reality, hyperbolic realism uses narrative forms that often remind us, more than of the notorious modernist aesthetics of difficulty,[3] of the (Bourgeois) liberal realism of the

---

[2]Nuclear in two senses—as the nucleus of a nuclear age.

[3]Remember these famous words by T. S. Eliot: "We can only say that it appears likely that poets in our civilization, as it exists at present, must be *difficult*. Our civilization comprehends great variety and complexity, and this variety and complexity, playing upon a refined sensibility, must produce various and complex results. The poet must become more and more comprehensive, more allusive, more indirect, in order to force, to dislocate if necessary, language into his meaning" (Eliot [1921] 1948: 289).

nineteenth century associated with Blumenberg's third concept of reality (Concept 3).

Much less openly—we could also say: pretentiously—experimental than orthodox postmodernism, *2666* and *ATD* sometimes appear as conservative, even nostalgic reanimations of Roman Jakobson's type C realism (Jakobson [1922] 1987: 20–1).[4] From the point of view of Anthropocene theory, however, it is only consequent that these late maximalist novels do not promote their new ontological paradigm as a spectacular innovation— resonating with the fact that criticizing accelerationist progress and innovation for innovation's sake should now be one of cultural criticism's more important tasks. Not only have we never really been modern (Latour [1991] 1993), modernity has been and continues to be an important part of the problem (Moten 2018: 20). As much as Anthropocene writing involves a step toward the realization of modernity, it also files a petition against it.

Consequently, in its embrace of a new, fifth concept of reality, hyperbolic realism accommodates fragments of all four previous concepts. Concept 4 is obviously present in the central enigmas that drive the plots without being reducible to their function of creating interest and suspense. They implement the famous structure of the postmodern quest, with the important difference that the quest in hyperbolic realism yields more concrete results than some of those modernist and postmodernist narratives that seem to indulge in a metaphysics of ambiguity and ambivalence.

Concept 3 is not only audible in the narrative tone and the revalorization of the adventure genre, but is also at work, in a more abstract sense, in the privileging of structural coherence against epiphanic singularity. Patterns and regularities are not immediately visible, but can be perceived and reconstructed as distributed phenomena. This calls for readers, however, who are not always obeying their habits, tradition, or *Bildung*, but who are willing to engage with the text as its adventurous, experimenting co-creator.[5]

Unsurprisingly, concept 2 is much harder to spot in Pynchon's and Bolaño's late maximalist novels, but one can find it at work in those less

---

[4] Here is how Ercolino (2014: 163–4) sums up the particular relation between realism and anti-realism in the maximalist novel: "This new realism, a critical realism, should aim paradoxically, at a *defamiliarization* of the real, at the same time exploring its hidden folds, in an ethical impetus without precedent. The movement, characteristic of traditional realism, toward the familiarization of reality is abruptly inverted into an operation which no longer has much to do with realism as commonly understood; an operation imbued with the antirealism permeating twentieth-century literature and which marked the birth of the great American narrative." My own understanding is less invested in a dialectical reconstruction of the problem and even less in the genealogy of the great American narrative.

[5] A habit of reception that is, strictly speaking, required by both Concept 3 and Concept 4.

dominant moments when the texts go back to ancient, lost, and forgotten belief systems; spiritual practices; or animist epistemologies. Finally, there are even traces of concept 1, the Platonic conception of reality as instantaneous evidence. One example is true of the scene, when, after tedious ruminations, the mathematical genius Yashmeen Halfcourt experiences one of the several, but comparatively rare epiphanic experiences ("she had *seen* it, for the moment, so clearly") that hyperbolic realism grants its characters and readers. It is in this crucial scene that Yashmeen discovers or, rather, experiences the discovery of what she and Pynchon call the "spine of reality," as it makes itself present in a highly complex mathematical function that combines "real" and "imaginary" variables (*ATD*: 604). The narrator's retelling of that function remains incomplete and inconclusive, and the readers have no means to really see what Yashmeen has "*seen.*" But if we listen carefully to her interior monologue, this, after all, is not so important because "[T]hough the members of a Hermitian [matrix] may be complex, the eigenvalues are real" (604).

Therefore, without losing ourselves in the labyrinth of Yashmeen's mathematical intricacies, we can amplify her discovery of the "*Rückgrat von Wirklichkeit*" as a *pars pro toto* for the novel's strategy to juxtapose the historical and the fantastic, the perceptual and the imaginary. This leads us to the following formula: *Though many fantastic components of the story may be complex, their historical eigenvalues are real.* Adding an additional, counter-factual axis to embodied experience promises to *traverse* the three—or even four-dimensional frame to create a post-Euclidean mimesis of reality in the fourth (or even fifth) gear (Rinck 2015: 13).

For a short moment only, but that one moment, at least, Yashmeen can feel and perhaps even touch the spine of reality through the more-than-human tool of analytic number theory. Her vision amounts to a disguised acknowledgment of flat fictionality (Chapter 6): the premises are counterfactual and hard to believe, the whole generic framework is fictional (and even derivative), yet, the eigenvalues—no matter if we take them as phenomenological, ontological, or ethical—are undeniably real. To emphasize the shortness of that glimpse into the infrastructure of reality points to the fact that it will not lead to its domination; the epiphany will not last, it is shaped by hesitation and interruption, as the anacoluthon at the end of the passage demonstrates.

As a part of a more critical branch of Anthropocenic theory, hyperbolic realism defies the "ecological hubris" (Wiesing 2009: 69) that seeks to build and maintain access routes to reality in order to appropriate, excavate, extract, and consume its resources without ever bothering to understand said reality on its own terms. In my opinion, this is one of the most important reasons—and even a justification—for the fact that the aesthetics of hyperbolic realism is much less aligned with the triumphalism of the avant-gardes, that its way of worldmaking is less relentless, less invasive, and less virile than the ways of worldmaking we inherited from both high modernism and orthodox postmodernism, shaped by once heroic cultural values such as brutal destruction for the sake of renewal, unrestricted and unlimited growth, and relentless extraction.

Pynchon's and Bolaño's late maximalist novels do have some powerful allies among thinkers and writers that are taking on the challenge of life in the Anthropocene. Besides, they also have a few dispersed allies among pre-Anthropocenic intellectuals, although those allies are not always to be found where you'd most expect them. One of the most versatile contemporary interlocutors of hyperbolic realism, who has not been in the spotlights of this book, is Karen Barad. Her quirky synthesis of poststructuralist materialism, post-classical philosophy of quantum physics, and third-wave feminism/queer theory stands out from many other comparably eclectic attempts through its thoughtfulness and creativity. Her so-called "agential realism" is a clever attempt to uncouple agency from *anthropos* without falling back into the childish animism that tends to confound the agential affordances of human subjects with that of surveillance cameras, mushrooms, and slime molds. The more "idiotic" versions of flat ontology, which comes close to claiming that everything that exists exists in one all-encompassing register and then says no more, have rightfully been subjected to severe criticism from all sides. As of today, no serious proponent of Anthropocene theory seems to be invested in this path of realistic counter-rhetorics.

According to Barad's basic way more refined script:

[T]he knower does not stand in a relation of absolute externality to the natural world—there is no such exterior observational point. The condition of possibility for objectivity is therefore not absolute exteriority but agential separability—exteriority within phenomena. We are not outside observers of the world. Neither are we simply located at particular places in the world; rather, we are part of the world in its ongoing intra-activity (Barad 2007: 184).

What may look like a conciliatory gesture (*neither fully exterior nor merely reduced to a concrete position*) is in my view an articulation of a much more complex ecosocial scenery than the ones brought forth by most thinkers of the object-oriented or actor-network branches of Anthropocene theory. Neither adhering to Meillassoux's rhetoric of the great outdoors nor remaining within the claustrophobia of the transcendental subject, Barad turns to the revolutionary findings of Einstein, Bohr, and many others to redefine our ontological and epistemological situation as "agential separability—exteriority within phenomena."[6] Her pointing to the "ongoing intra-activity" of the world adheres to the fifth concept of reality as it is introduced above. It views reality not as an inert and resistant *bloc*, not as "Easy Think Substance," a "bland lump of whatever decorated with accidents" (Morton 2016: 47), but as productive, autopoietic, self-structuring, dynamic, and agential. Phenomena, according to Barad and in astonishing concordance with Richir's quantum phenomenology, do not result here from an interaction between the subject and the black-box a.k.a. Kant's *Ding an sich*. They are "intra-actions" within a shared environment, a vast but highly differentiated ontological field. Objectivity, like fiction, does not originate from an absolute outside, but from an *exteriority within phenomena*, not once and for all, but as the—always temporary—result of an ongoing effort of experimentation (in the case of objectivity) or figuration (in the case of fiction). Both objectivity and fiction do not stand outside the world, they are part of it, even as they create effects of radical distance within that world of which they are a part.

Exteriority within phenomena—this is not Meillassoux's absolute exteriority but a hyperbolic outsideness that haunts our immanence and creeps into our intimacy as "extimacy" (Miller 1994). "The reality is that hyperobjects were already here, and slowly but surely we understood what they were already saying. They contacted us" (Morton 2013: 201). That is why for hyperbolic and agential realism alike, the task is not to invent the next big phase in the linear history of the real, but "to wake into the breath of what was always real" (Pynchon 1973: 754). After all, the real has been around for quite some time now. At the same time, it has never *really* been *here* as it is rather *here-ish*, not completely here nor completely not-here, but always more and less than here: "As we stretch the local across the seeping transits we need not scale up to the Human or the global, but we cannot remain in the local. We can only remain *hereish*" (Povinelli 2016: 13).

In relation to the hyperbolically real, to say it one last time, we humans are both not-yet-there (Colebrook's extinction) and always too-late-too-the-game (Meillassoux's ancestrality). In a way, the fifth concept of reality thus represents the exact opposite to the Platonic notion that is the founding act of Western culture—not an intuitive, immediate access *to* the world without separation and distance (Concept 1), but the (often traumatic) proximity

---

[6] Barad's type of exteriority maintains a complex relationship to that of Levinas. On the one hand, like Levinasian exteriority is not reducible to "the interiority of memory" (Levinas [1961] 1979: 51); on the other hand, Barad's exteriority from within phenomenality differs radically from Levinas' metaphysics of an impossible to reach "absolute exteriority of the exterior being" (1979: 50).

and promiscuity *with* the real across ultimately unbridgeable chasms (Concept 5). This new configuration of the real can only be glimpsed from within, as an ongoing practice of synchronization and self-reflection—not the distant, sterile self-reflection of transcendental philosophy, but Merleau-Ponty's tactile self-reflection in which one touching hand surprises itself by touching another touching hand (Merleau-Ponty [1946] 1976: 109).[7]

For both *hyperbolic* and *agential realism*, the practices of experimentation are themselves material and processual. They are interdependent agencies, embedded in a concrete and impersonal field of juxtaposed environments, entangled with all kinds of inhuman apparatuses. It is only by virtue of these machines of experimentation that the forms of contact between the human and the nonhuman can be grasped. This is materialism not as the reification of the status quo of nature, but as an invitation to pursue our agencies within the compositional architecture of material and "open-ended practices" (Barad 2007: 146).

Literature, of course, is nothing else but one among those open-ended material practices. It is an inhuman apparatus, a machine of desire and reflection, used by humans to feel, perceive, and understand what is at stake in their complex entanglements with the world. At the beginning of the twenty-first century, reality reveals itself in often unsettling, overwhelming, promiscuous, traumatic, and, even if less frequently in novel, enticing and strangely beautiful ways. This newness, however, seems less obvious and abrupt as it may have been for those who have lived most of their lives within the long arc of (high) modernity. Today, much of the uncanny experience of Anthropocenic existence is tied to the feeling that we already live in a world "after the end of the world" (Danowski & Viveiros de Castro [2014] 2016; Morton 2013). Hyperbolically speaking, seen from a place after the end of the world, reality reveals itself as how it had already been long before humanity even appeared. It reveals itself, although in varying shapes and intensities, as how it had been for Plato as much as for his maid and his servants, for Medieval kings as much as for colonized fishermen and ascetic nuns, for Baroque philosophers as much as for exhausted factory workers or long-forgotten modernist poets. It reveals itself as how it will be and remain once "we" have disappeared from this planet like that deplorable face drawn in sand.

Seen from after the end of the world, reality—nature—, reveals itself as no different, after all, than ever before. It reveals itself as hyperbolic.

---

[7]The full quote in French its full beauty being untranslatable: "Le corps se surprend lui-même de l'extérieur en train d'exercer une fonction de connaissance, il essaye de se toucher touchant, il ébauche 'une sorte de réflexion'" (Merleau-Ponty [1946] 1976: 109).

REFERENCES

Adams, Don (2009). *Alternative Paradigms of Literary Realism*. New York: Palgrave Macmillan.
Agamben, Giorgio (2009). *The Signature of All Things: On Method*. New York: Zone Books.
Aira, César (1998). *Alejandra Pizarnik*. Barcelona: Ediciones Omega.
Aira, César (2002). *La prueba*. Buenos Aires: Era Ediciones.
Alexis, André (2019). *Days by Moonlight*. Toronto: Coach House Books.
Andersen, Tore Rye (2016). "Mapping the World: Thomas Pynchon's Global Novels." *Orbit: Writing Around Pynchon* 4 (1). http://dx.doi.org/10.16995/orbit.178.
Andrade, Oswald de ([1928] 1991). "Cannibalist Manifesto." Translated by Leslie Bary. *Latin American Literary Review* 19 (38), 38–47.
Apter, Emily (2006). "On Oneworldedness. Or Paranoia as World-System." *American Literary History* 18 (2), 365–89.
Arac, Jonathan (1979). "Rhetoric and Realism in Nineteenth-Century Fiction: Hyperbole in the *Mill on the Floss*." *English Literary History* 46 (4), 673–92.
Arrighi, Giovanni ([1994] 2010). *The Long Twentieth Century: Money, Power, and the Origins of Our Time*. London and New York: Verso Books.
Arrighi, Giovanni (2007). *Adam Smith in Beijing: Lineages of the Twenty-First Century*. London and New York: Verso Books.
Auerbach, Erich (1939). "Figura." *Archivum Romanicum: Nuova Rivista di Filologia Romanza* 22, 436–89.
Auerbach, Erich ([1946] 2003). *Mimesis. The Representation of Reality in Western Literature*. Princeton, NY: Princeton University Press.
Bajohr, Hannes and Eva Geulen (eds.) (2022). Blumenbergs Verfahren. Neue Zugänge zum Werk. Göttingen: Wallstein.
Balada Campo, Jordi (2015). "Ulises y Rimbaud en Roberto Bolaño, *Los detectives salvajes*." *Romanische Studien* 1, 85–110. https://www.romanischestudien.de/index.php/rst/article/view/11.
Barad, Karen (2007). "Agential Realism: How Material-Discursive Practices Matter." In *Meeting the Universe Halfway: Quantum Physics and the Entanglement of Matter and Meaning*, 132–88. Durham, NC: Duke University Press.
Barad, Karen (2003). "Posthumanist Performativity: Toward an Understanding of How Matter Comes to Matter." *Signs: Journal of Women in Culture and Society* 28 (3), 801–31.
Barth, John ([1967] 1995a). "It's a Long Story. Maximalism Reconsidered." In *Further Fridays. Essays, Lectures, and Other Non-fiction*, 75–88. Boston, MA: Little, Brown and Company.

Barth, John ([1967] 1995b). "The Literature of Exhaustion." In *Metafiction*, edited by Mark Currie, 161–78. London: Longman.
Barth, John ([1960] 1995c). *The Sot-Weed Factor*. New York: Doubleday.
Barthes, Roland ([1984] 1989). *The Rustle of Language*. Translated by Richard Howard. Berkeley: University of California Press.
Bataille, Georges ([1937] 1988). "Letter to X., Lecturer on Hegel … " In *The College of Sociology*, edited by Denis Hollier, translated by Betsy Wing, 89–93. Minneapolis: University of Minnesota Press.
Bataille, Georges ([1929] 1985). "Formless." In *Georges Bataille: Vision of Excess, Selected Writings, 1927–1939*, edited and translated by Allan Stoekl, with Carl R. Lovitt and Donald M. Leslie Jr., 31. Minneapolis: University of Minnesota Press.
Baudelaire, Charles ([1855] 1976). Œuvres complètes, Vol. 2, edited by Claude Pichois. Paris: Gallimard.
Beckett, Samuel ([1932] 1993). *Dream of Fair to Middling Women*. New York: Arcade.
Bellamy, Matthew J. (2018). "Drone Masculinity. James Bond and the Cultural Discourse of Covert Action." *Studies in Popular Culture* 41 (1), 128–61.
Benjamin, Walter ([1942] 2019). "Theses on the Philosophy of History." In Walter Benjamin. *Illuminations: Essays and Reflections*, edited by Hannah Arendt, translated by Harry Zohn, 196–209. Boston, MA and New York: Mariner Books.
Benjamin, Walter ([1933] 1999). "Experience and Poverty." In *Selected Writings*, Vol. I, Part 2: 1931–4, edited by Michael W. Jennings, Howard Eiland, and Gary Smith, 731–6. Cambridge, MA and London: Belknap Press.
Benoist, Jocelyn (2011). *Éléments de philosophie réaliste*. Paris: Vrin.
Bersani, Leo (1989). "Pynchon, Paranoia, and Literature." *Representations* 25, 99–118.
Bertoni, Federico (2007). *Realismo e letteratura: Una storia possibile*. Torino: Einaudi.
Black, Max (1979). "How Metaphors Work: A Reply to Donald Davidson." *Critical Inquiry* 6 (1), 131–43.
Bloom, Harold (1997). *The Anxiety of Influence: A Theory of Poetry*. Oxford and New York: Oxford University Press.
Blumenberg, Hans (2020). *Realität und Realismus*. Edited by Nicola Zambon. Berlin: Suhrkamp.
Blumenberg, Hans ([1964] 2015). "The Concept of Reality and the Possibility of the Novel." In *New Perspectives in German Literary Criticism*, edited by Richard E. Amacher and Victor Lange, 29–48. Princeton: Princeton University Press.
Blumenberg, Hans (1997). *Paradigmen zu einer Metaphorologie*. Frankfurt am Main: Suhrkamp.
Blumenberg, Hans ([1979] 1996). "Prospect for a Theory of Nonconceptuality." In Hans Blumenberg. *Shipwreck with Spectator*, 81–102. Cambridge, MA: MIT Press.
Blumenberg, Hans (1964). "Wirklichkeitsbegriff und Möglichkeit des Romans." In *Nachahmung und Illusion*, Poetik und Hermeneutik, Vol. I, edited by Hans-Robert Jauß, 9–27. Munich: Fink.

Böhme, Hartmut (2009). "Hilft das Lesen in der Not? Warum unsere Wissenschaftskrise eine Krise der Moderne ist." *Die Zeit*, March 12.
Bohrer, Karl-Heinz ([1981] 1994). *Suddenness: On the Moment of Aesthetic Appearance*. Translated by Ruth Crowley. New York and Chichester: Columbia University Press.
Bois, Yve-Alain and Rosalind Krauss (1997). *Formless: A User's Guide*. New York, NY: Zone Books.
Bolaño, Roberto ([2011] 2013). *Woes of the True Policemen*. Translated by Natasha Wimmer. New York: Picador.
Bolaño, Roberto (2011). *Los sinsabores del verdadero policíaca*. Barcelona: Anagrama.
Bolaño, Roberto (2009). *The Last Interview*. Last interview by Mónica Maristain, with an introduction by Marcela Valdes. New York: Melville.
Bolaño, Roberto (2008). *2666*, 3 Vol. Translated by Natasha Wimmer. New York: Farrar, Strauss & Giroux.
Bolaño, Roberto ([1996] 2008). *Nazi Literature in the Americas*. Translated by Chris Andrews. New York: New Directions.
Bolaño, Roberto ([1998] 2007). *The Savage Detectives*. Translated by Natasha Wimmer. New York: Farrar, Strauss & Giroux.
Bolaño, Roberto ([1999] 2006). *Amulet*. Translated by Chris Andrews. New York: New Directions.
Bolaño, Roberto (2006). *Last Evenings on Earth*. Translated by Chris Andrews. New York: New Directions.
Bolaño, Roberto (2004a). *2666*. Barcelona: Anagrama.
Bolaño, Roberto (2004b). *Between Parentheses: Essays, Articles, and Speeches, 1998–2003*. Edited by Ignacio Echevarria, translated by Natasha Wimmer. New York: New Directions.
Bolaño, Roberto (2004c). *Entre Paréntesis: Ensayos, artículos y discursos (1998–2003)*. Barcelona: Anagrama.
Bolaño, Roberto ([1996] 2004d). *Distant Star*. Translated by Chris Andrews. London: Harvill.
Bolaño, Roberto ([2000] 2003). *By Night in Chile*. Translated by Chris Andrews. London: Harvill.
Bolaño, Roberto (2002). *Una novelita lumpen*. Barcelona: Mondadori.
Bolaño, Roberto (2000). *Nocturno de Chile*. Barcelona: Anagrama.
Bolaño, Roberto (1999). *Amuleto*. Barcelona: Anagrama.
Bolaño, Roberto (1998). *Los detectives salvajes*. Barcelona: Anagrama.
Bolaño, Roberto (1996). *Estrella Distante*. Barcelona: Anagrama.
Borges, Jorge Luis ([1975] 2017). "Ulrica." In *Cuentos completos*, 435–9. Barcelona: Debolsillo.
Borges, Jorge Luis ([1954] 2017). "Prologue to the 1954 edition of *Historia Universal de la Infamia*." In *Cuentos completos*, 11–12. Barcelona: Debolsillo.
Borges, Jorge Luis ([1947] 2017). "El Inmortal." In *Cuentos completos*, 223–38. Barcelona: Debolsillo.
Borges, Jorge Luis ([1945] 2017). "El Aleph." In *Cuentos completos*, 330–44. Barcelona: Debolsillo.
Borges, Jorge Luis (1998). *Collected Fictions*. Translated by Andrew Hurley. New York: Viking.

Borges, Jorge Luis ([1945] 1971). *Aleph and Other Stories*. New York: Bantam Books.
Borowski, Mateusz and Malgorzata Sugiera (2006). "Realismus 2.0. Eine Frage der Perspektive." In *Seien wir realistisch. Neue Realismen und Dokumentarismen in Philosophie und Kunst*, edited by Magdalena Marszalek and Dieter Mersch, 267–92. Zurich and Berlin: diaphanes.
Bourcier, Simon de (2013). *Pynchon and Relativity: Narrative Time in Thomas Pynchon's Late Novels*. New York and London: Bloomsbury.
Bryant, Levi (2013). "A Conversation with Lucretius." https://larvalsubjects.files. wordpress.com/2013/04/bryantfordham.
Buford, Bill (ed.) (2008). *Granta 8, Dirty Realism*. London: Granta Books.
Buell, Lawrence (2014). *The Dream of the Great American Novel*. Cambridge, MA: Harvard University Press.
Bunia, Remigius (2007). *Faltungen: Fiktion, Erzählen, Medien*. Berlin: Erich Schmidt Verlag.
Butler, Judith (1993). *Bodies That Matter: On the Discursive Limits of Sex*. New York and London: Routledge.
Campe, Rüdiger (1991). "Die Schreibszene, Schreiben." In *Paradoxien, Dissonanzen, Zusammenbrüche: Situationen offener Epistemologie*, edited by Hans Ulrich Gumbrecht and Karl Ludwig Pfeiffer, 759–72. Frankfurt am Main: Suhrkamp.
Carson, Anne (1986). *Eros the Bittersweet*. Princeton: Princeton University Press.
Chakrabarty, Dipesh (2009). "The Climate of History: Four Theses." *Critical Inquiry* 35 (2), 197–222.
Chávez, Ricardo, Alejandro Ricardo, Vicente Herrasti, Ignacio Padilla, Pedro Ángel Palou, Tomás Regalado, Eloy Urroz and Jorge Volpi (2004). *Crack: Instrucciones de uso*. Mexico City: Mondadori.
Clute, John (2007). "Aubade, Poor Dad." *New York Review of Science Fiction* 222.
Coffman, Christopher K. (2011). "Bogomilism, Orphism, Shamanism: The Spiritual and Spatial Grounds of Pynchon's Ecological Ethic." In *Pynchon's Against the Day. A Corrupted Pilgrim's Guide*, edited by Christopher Leise and Jeffrey Severs, 91–114. Newark: University of Delaware Press.
Colebrook, Claire (2014). *Death of the PostHuman*, Essays on Extinction, Vol. I. London: Open Humanities Press.
Compagnon, Antoine (2014). *Baudelaire: L'irréductible*. Paris: Flammarion.
Corral, Wilfrido H. (2001). "Novelistas sin timón: exceso y subjetividad en el concepto de la 'novela total.'" *Modern Language Notes* 116 (2), 315–49.
Cortázar, Julio (1967). "Para llegar a Lezama Lima." In *La vuelta al día en ochenta mundos*, 135–55. Mexico City: Siglo XXI.
Cortázar, Julio ([1963] 2003). *Rayuela*. Madrid: Catédra.
Cortázar, Julio ([1963] 1966). *Hopscotch*. Translated by Gregory Rabassa. New York: Pantheon Books.
Curtius, Ernst Robert ([1948] 2013). *European Literature and the Middle Ages*. Translated by Willard R. Trask, with a new introduction by Colin Burrow. Princeton and Oxford: Princeton University Press.
Curtis, Adam (2009). *Oh Dearism*. London: BBC. Film. https://www.youtube.com/watch?v=8moePxHpvok&ab_channel=UKNewsMediaBlog.

Daalsgard, Inger H. (2011). "Readers and Trespassers: Time Travel, Orthogonal Time, and Alternative Figurations of Time in *Against the Day*." In *Pynchon's Against the Day. A Corrupted Pilgrim's Guide*, edited by Christopher Leise and Jeffrey Severs, 115–38. Newark: University of Delaware Press.
Daniel Grausam (2011). *On Endings. American Postwar Fiction and the Cold War*. Charlottesvillie, VA: University of Virginia Press, Charlotesville/VA.
Danowski, Deborah and Eduardo Viveiros de Castro ([2014] 2016). *The Ends of the World*. Translated by Rodrigo Nunes. Cambridge: Polity.
Davidson, Donald (1978). "What Metaphors Mean." *Critical Inquiry* 5 (1), 31–47.
Davis, Mike (1990). *City of Quartz: Excavating the Future in Los Angeles*. London and New York: Verso Books.
Deckard, Sharae (2012). "Peripheral Realism, Millennial Capitalism, and Roberto Bolaño's 2666." *Modern Language Quarterly* 73 (3), 351–72.
Deleuze, Gilles ([1988] 1992). *The Fold*. Translated by Tom Conley. Minneapolis: University of Minnesota Press.
Deleuze, Gilles and Félix Guttari ([1980] 1987). *A Thousand Plateaus: Capitalism and Schizophrenia*. Translated by Brian Massumi. Minneapolis: University of Minnesota Press.
DeLillo, Don (1997). *Underworld*. New York: Scribner.
Denson, Shane (2016). "Crazy Cameras, Discorrelated Images, and the Post-Perceptual Mediation of Post-Cinematic Affect." In *Post-Cinema: Theorizing 21st-Century Film*, edited by Shane Denson and Julia Leyda, 193–233. Falmer: Reframe Books.
Denson, Shane (2014). "Of Steam Engines, Revolutions, and the (Un)natural History of Matter: A Techno-Scientific Interlude." In *Postnaturalism: Frankenstein, Film, and the Anthropotechnical Interface*, 205–78. Bielefeld: transcript.
Deresiewicz, William (2008). "How Wood Works: The Riches and Limits of James Wood." *The Nation*, November 19.
Derrida, Jacques ([1967] 1997). *Voice and Phenomenon. Introduction to the Problem of the Sign in Husserl's Phenomenology*. Translated by Leonard Lawler. Evanston, IL: Northwestern University Press.
Descola, Philippe ([2005] 2013). *Beyond Nature and Culture*. Translated by Janet Lloyd. Chicago: University of Chicago Press.
Dorfman, Ariel and Armand Mattelart ([1971] 1975). *Para leer al Pato Donald*. Buenos Aires: Siglo XXI.
Draper, Hal ([1986] 2011). *Karl Marx's Theory of Revolution*, Vol. III., The Dictatorship of the Proletariat. New Delhi: Aakar Books.
Duyfhuizen, Bernard (1991). "'A Suspension Forever at the Hinge of Doubt.' The Reader-Trap of Bianca in *Gravity's Rainbow*." *Postmodern Culture* 2 (1), 1–27. http://pmc.iath.virginia.edu/text-only/issue.991/duyfhu-1.991.
Elias, Amy J. (2011). "Plots, Pilgrimage, and the Politics of Genre in *Against the Day*." In *Pynchon's Against the Day. A Corrupted Pilgrim's Guide*, edited by Christopher Leise and Jeffrey Severs, 30–46. Newark: University of Delaware Press.
Eliot, George ([1859] 1999). "The Lifted Veil." In *The Lifted Veil/Brother Jacob*, edited by Helen Small, 1–45. Oxford: Oxford University Press.

Eliot, T. S. ([1921] 1948). "The Metaphysical Poets." In *Selected Essays*, 281–91. London: Faber and Faber.
Engelhardt, Nina (2018). *Modernism, Fiction and Mathematics*. Edinburgh: Edinburgh University Press.
Engelhardt, Nina (2013). "Mathematics, Reality and Fiction in Pynchon's *Against the Day*." In *Thomas Pynchon and the (De)vices of Global (Post)modernity*, edited by Zofia Kolbuszewska, 212–31. Lublin: Wydawnictwo KUL.
Ercolino, Stefano (2014). *The Maximalist Novel: From Thomas Pynchon's* Gravity's Rainbow *to Roberto Bolano's* 2666. New York and London: Bloomsbury.
Felski, Rita. *The Uses of Literature*. Malden, MA, and Oxford: Blackwell.
Ferraris, Maurizio (2002). "Inemendabilità, Ontologia, Realtà Sociale." *Rivista di estetica* 19 (1) 160–99.
Fifield, Peter (2013). *Late Modernist Style in Samuel Beckett and Emmanuel Levinas*. New York: Palgrave Macmillan.
Fisher, Marx (2016). *The Weird and the Eerie*. London: Repeater Books.
Fisher, Mark (2009). *Capitalist Realism: Is There No Alternative?* Winchester: Zero Books.
Fitzpatrick, Kathleen (2006). *The Anxiety of Obsolescence: The American Novel in the Age of Television*. Nashville: Vanderbilt University Press.
Forestier, Florian (2015). *La phénoménologie génétique de Marc Richir*. Cham and Heidelberg: Springer.
Foster, Hal (1996). *The Return of the Real*. Cambridge, MA: MIT Press.
Franke, Anselm (2016). "The Third House." *Glass Bead*, Site 0: Castalia, The Game of Ends and Meanings, 1–15. http://www.glass-bead.org/article/the-third-house/?lang=enview.
Franzen, Jonathan (2002). "Mr. Difficult: William Gaddis and the Problem of Hard-to-Read Books." *The New Yorker*, September 30.
Fuguet, Alberto (2001). "Magical Neoliberalism." *Foreign Policy*, 125, 66–73.
Fuguet, Alberto and Sergio Gómez (eds.) (1996). *McOndo: Antología de la nueva literatura hispanoaméricana*. Barcelona: Mondadori.
Fukuyama, Francis (1992). *The End of History and the Last Man*. New York: Free Press.
Fukuyama, Francis (1989). "The End of History?" *The National Interest* 16, 3–18.
Gaddis, William ([1955] 2012). *The Recognitions*. Victoria, TX: Dalkey Archive Press.
Galloway, Alexander R. (2013). "The Poverty of Philosophy: Realism and Post-Fordism." *Critical Inquiry* 39, 347–66.
Garcia, Tristan (2018). "Une boussole conceptuelle: Orientation épistémique et orientation épistémologique des réalismes contemporains." In *Choses en soi: Métaphysique du réalisme*, edited by Emmanuel Alloa and Elie During, 41–56. Paris: PUF.
Genette, Gérard ([1982] 1997). *Palimpsests: Literature in the Second Degree*. Translated by Channa Newman and Claude Doubinsky, foreword by Gerald Prince. Lincoln and London: University of Nebraska Press.
Genette, Gérard (1966). "Hyperboles." In *Figures*, Vol. I, 245–52. Paris: Seuil.
Gess, Nicola and Sandra Janßen (eds.) (2014). *Wissens-Ordnungen: Zu einer historischen Epistemologie der Literatur*. Berlin: De Gruyter.

Giroux, Susan Searls (2002). "The Age of Irony?" *Journal of Advanced Composition* 22 (4), 960–76.

Goldstein, Jürgen (2020). *Hans Blumenberg: Ein philosophisches Portrait*. Berlin: Matthes & Seitz.

Gondek, Hans-Dieter and László Tengelyi (2011). *Neue Phänomenologie in Frankreich*. Frankfurt am Main: Suhrkamp.

Grant, Iain Hamilton (2006). *Philosophies of Nature after Schelling*. London: Continuum.

Guerrero, Carlos (2006). "Escritura e hipérbole: Lectura de 2666 de Bolaño." *Espéculo. Revista de Estudios Literarios* 34, n. p. https://webs.ucm.es/info/especulo/numero34/hiperbol.html.

Haberkorn, Tobias (2021). *Das Problem des Zuviel in der Literatur: Welt in Sprache bei Rabelais und Montaigne*. Amsterdam: Lesemagazijn.

Harman, Graham (2012). *Weird Realism: Lovecraft and Philosophy*. Winchester: Zero Books.

Harman, Graham (2002). *Tool-Being: Heidegger and the Metaphysics of Objects*. New York: Open Court.

Haun, Anne (2008). "Martin Kippenberger: Götterdämmerung." In *Die Inszenierung des Künstlers*, edited by Anne Marie Freybourg, 48–53. Berlin: Jovis.

Haverkamp, Anselm (2004). "Unbegrifflichkeit: Die Aufgabe der Seinsgeschichte (Blumenberg und Heidegger)." In *Latenzzeit: Wissen im Nachkrieg*, 73–82. Berlin: Kadmos.

Haverkamp, Anselm (2002). "Metaphora dis/continua: Allegorie als Vorgeschichte der Ästhetik." In *Figura cryptica: Theorie der literarischen Latenz*, 73–88. Frankfurt am Main: Suhrkamp.

Heffernan, James (1993). *Museum of Words: The Poetics of Ekphrasis from Homer to Ashbery*. Chicago: University of Chicago Press.

Higgins, Brian and Hershel Parker (eds.) (1995). *Herman Melville: The Contemporary Critics*. Cambridge: Cambridge University Press.

Hoffmann, Todd (2017). "The New Realism: Seeking Alternatives to Postmodern Pessimism." *Theory & Event* 20 (2), 426–49.

Hollander, John (1988). "The Poetics of Ekphrasis." *Word & Image* 4 (1), 209–19.

Hörisch, Jochen (1998). *Die Wut des Verstehens: Zur Kritik der Hermeneutik*. Frankfurt am Main: Suhrkamp.

Horne, Luz (2011). *Literaturas reales: Transformaciones del realismo en la narrativa latinoamericana contemporánea*. Buenos Aires: Beatriz Viterbo.

Hoyos, Héctor (2019). *Things with a History: Transcultural Materialism and the Literatures of Extraction in Contemporary Latin America*. New York: Columbia University Press.

Hoyos, Héctor (2015). *Beyond Bolaño: The Global Latin American Novel*. New York: Columbia University Press.

Hume, Kathryn (2011). "The Religious and Political Vision of *Against the Day*." In *Pynchon's* Against the Day. *A Corrupted Pilgrim's Guide*, edited by Christopher Leise and Jeffrey Severs, 167–90. Newark: University of Delaware Press.

Husserl, Edmund (2006). *Phantasie und Bildbewußtsein*. Edited by Eduard Marbach. Hamburg: Meiner.

Husserl, Edmund ([1913] 1983). *Ideas Pertaining to a Pure Phenomenology and to a Phenomenological Philosophy*, Vol. I, General Introduction to a Pure Phenomenology. Translated by Fred Kersten. The Hague: Martinus Nijhoff.
Husserl, Edmund ([1939] 1975). *Experience and Judgement*. Translated by James Spencer Churchill and Karl Ameriks. Evanston, IL: Northwestern University Press.
Husserl, Edmund ([1911] 1956). "Philosophy as a Strict Science." Translated by Quentin Lauer. *CrossCurrents* 6 (3), 227–46.
Irr, Caren (2014). *Toward the Geopolitical Novel: U.S. Fiction in the Twenty-First Century*. New York: Columbia University Press.
Iser, Wolfgang (ed.) (1966). *Immanente Ästhetik, Ästhetische Reflexion: Lyrik als Paradigma der Moderne*, Poetik und Hermeneutik, Vol. II. Munich: Fink.
Isherwood, Christopher ([1954] 2012). *The World in the Evening*. Minneapolis: University of Minnesota Press.
Jager, Bernd (2004). "The Historical Background of van den Berg's Two Laws." In Jan Hendrik van den Berg. *The Two Principal Laws of Thermodynamics: A Cultural and Historical Exploration*, translated by Bernd Jager, David Jager, and Dreyer Kruger, 1–31. Pittsburgh: Duquesne University Press.
Jakobson, Roman ([1922] 1987). "On Realism in Art." In *Language in Literature*, edited by Kristyna Pomorska and Stephen Rudy, 19–27. Cambridge, MA: Harvard University Press.
Jameson, Fredric (2013). *The Antinomies of Realism*. London and New York: Verso Books.
Jameson, Fredric (1981). *The Political Unconscious: Narrative as a Socially Symbolic Act*. Ithaca, NY: Cornell University Press.
Janicaud, Dominique (1991). *Le tournant théologique de la phénoménologie française*. Paris: Gallimard.
Johnson, Christopher D. (2010). *Hyperboles: The Rhetoric of Excess in Baroque Literature and Thought*. Cambridge, MA: Harvard University Press.
Joyce, James ([1939] 2000). *Finnegans Wake*. London. Penguin Books.
Joyce, James ([1922] 1992). *Ulysses*. London: Penguin Books.
Käkelä-Puumala, Tiina (2007). *Other Side of This Life: Death, Value, and Social Being in Thomas Pynchon's Fiction*. Dissertation, University of Helsinki.
Karl, Frederick R. (2001). *American Fictions 1980–2000: Whose America Is It Anyway?* Bloomington, IN: Xlibris.
Karl, Frederick R. (1985). "American Fictions: The Mega-Novel." *Conjunctions* 7, 248–60.
Kittler, Friedrich ([1987] 2008). "Pynchon and Electro-Mysticism." Translated by Kathrin Günther and Martin Howse. *Pynchon Notes* 54–5, 108–21.
Klein, Richard (1973). "The Blindness of Hyperboles/The Ellipses of Insight." In *Diacritics* 3 (2), 33–44.
Knausgård, Karl Ove ([2013] 2016). *Das Amerika der Seele: Essays 1996–2013*. Translated into German by Paul Berf and Ulrich Sonnenberg. Munich: Luchterhand.
Kraus, Chris (1997). *I Love Dick*. Los Angeles: Semiotext(e).
Küpper, Joachim (1988). "Zum Romantischen Mythos der Subjektivität: Lamartines *Invocation* und Nervals *El Desdichado*." *Zeitschrift für französische Sprache und Literatur* 98 (2), 137–65.

Latour, Bruno (2004). "Why Has Critique Run out of Steam? From Matters of Fact to Matters of Concern." *Critical Inquiry* 30, 225–48.
Latour, Bruno ([1991] 1993). *We Have Never Been Modern*. Translated by Catherine Porter. Cambridge, MA: Harvard University Press.
LeClair, Tom (1989). *The Art of Excess: Mastery in Contemporary Fiction*. Chicago: University of Illinos Press.
Leise, Christopher (2011). "'Exceeding the Usual Three Dimensions': Collective Visions of the Unsuspected." In *Pynchon's* Against the Day. *A Corrupted Pilgrim's Guide*, edited by Christopher Leise and Jeffrey Severs, 2–11. Newark: University of Delaware Press.
Lethem, Jonathan (2007). "The Ecstasy of Influence: A Plagiarism." *Harper's Magazine*, February, 59–71.
Letzler, David (2017). *The Cruft of Fiction: Mega-Novels and the Science of Paying Attention*. Lincoln: University of Nebraska Press.
Letzler, David (2012). "Encyclopedic Novels and the Cruft of Fiction: 'Infinite Jest's Endnotes." *Studies in the Novel* 44 (3), 304–24.
Levinas, Emmanuel ([1974] 1991). *Otherwise than Being, Or beyond Essence*. Translated by Alphonso Lingis. The Hague: Martinus Nijhoff.
Levinas, Emmanuel ([1961] 1979). *Totality and Infinity: An Essay on Exteriority*. Translated by Alphonso Lingis. The Hague: Martinus Nijhoff.
Levine, Elizabeth (2003). *The Serious Pleasures of Suspense: Victorian Realism and Narrative Doubt*. Charlottesville: University of Virginia Press.
Lévi-Strauss, Claude (1962). *La pensée sauvage*. Paris: Plon.
Levrero, Mario (2005). *La novela luminosa*. Montevideo: Ed. Santillana.
Lezama Lima, José ([1966] 2011). *Paradiso*. Translated by Gregory Rabassa. Normal, IL: Dalkey Archive Press.
Lezama Lima, José ([1966] 2000). *Paradiso*. Madrid: Alianza Literaria.
Lispector, Clarice (2015). *The Complete Stories*. Edited by Benjamin Moser, translated by Katrina Dodson. New York: New Directions.
Lispector, Clarice ([1973] 2012). *Àgua viva*. Translated by Stefan Tobler. New York: New Directions.
Lowry, Malcolm ([1947] 1971). *Under the Volcano*. New York: New American Library.
Loy, Benjamin (2019). *Roberto Bolaños wilde Bibliothek: Eine Ästhetik und Politik der Lektüre*. Berlin: De Gruyter.
Loy, Benjamin (2015). "Chistes par(r)a reordenar el canon – Roberto Bolaño, Nicanor Parra y la poesía chilena." *Romanische Studien* 1, 45–60.
Lucretius (2011). *On the Nature of Things*. Edited and translated by Martin Ferguson Smith. Indianapolis: Hackett Publishing.
Macé, Marielle (2016). *Styles: Critique de nos formes de vie*. Paris: Gallimard.
Macé, Marielle (2011). *Façons de lire, manière d'être*. Paris: Gallimard.
Mackay, Robin (ed.) (2007). *Collapse III*, Unknown Deleuze [+ Speculative Realism]. Falmouth: Urbanomic.
Madariaga Caro, Montserrat (2010). *Bolaño infra 1975–1977: Los años que inspiraron* Los detectives salvajes. Santiago de Chile: RIL editores.
Marcus, Ben (2005). "Why Experimental Fiction Threatens to Destroy Publishing, Jonathan Franzen, and Life As We Know It." *Harper's Magazine*, October, 39–52.

Maurice, Thomas (2013). "Le complexe du grimoire. Récit d'un cheminement personnel vers l'hyperbole." *Eikasia* 47, 899–912. https://www.revistadefilosofia.org/47-52.pdf.
McCaffery, Larry (1993). "An Interview with Foster Wallace." *The Review of Contemporary Fiction* 13 (2), 127–50.
McGurl, Marc (2011). "The New Cultural Geology." *Twentieth-Century Literature* 57 (3–4), 380–90.
McGurl, Marc (2009). *The Program Era: Postwar Fiction and the Rise of Creative Writing*. Cambridge, MA: Harvard University Press.
McHale, Brian (2011). "History as Genre. Pynchon's Genre-Poaching." In *Pynchon's Against the Day. A Corrupted Pilgrim's Guide*, edited by Christopher Leise and Jeffrey Severs, 15–28. Newark: University of Delaware Press.
McLuhan, Marshall (1962). *The Gutenberg Galaxy: The Making of Typographic Man*. London: Routledge & Paul.
Meillassoux, Quentin ([2013] 2015). *Science Fiction and Extro-Science Fiction*. Translated by Alyosha Edlebi. Minnesota: University of Minneapolis Press.
Meillassoux, Quentin ([2006] 2008). *After Finitude: An Essay on the Necessity of Contingency*. Translated by Ray Brassier. London: Continuum.
Mendelson, Edward (1976). "Encyclopedic Narrative: From Dante to Pynchon." *Modern Language Notes* 91, 1267–75.
Merleau-Ponty, Maurice ([1946] 1976). *Phénoménologie de la perception*. Paris: Gallimard.
Merleau-Ponty, Maurice ([1964] 1968). *The Visible and the Invisible*. Translated by Alphonso Lingis. Evanston, IL: Northwestern University Press.
Merleau-Ponty, Maurice (1964). *Le visible et l'invisible, suivie de notes de travail*. Edited by Claude Lefort. Paris: Gallimard.
Mignolo, Walter (2005). *The Idea of Latin America*. Hoboken, NY: John Wiley & Sons.
Miller, Jacques-Alain (1994). "Extimité." In *Lacanian Theory of Discourse: Subject, Structure and Society*, edited by Mark Bracher, Marshall W. Alcorn, Françoise Massardier-Kenney, and Ronald Corthell, 74–87. New York: NYU Press.
Moix, Ana María (2004). "Un torrente llamado Bolaño." *El país*, October 23, 6–7.
Moore, Thomas (1987). *The Style of Connectedness: Gravity's Rainbow and Thomas Pynchon*. Columbia: University of Missouri Press.
Moretti, Franco ([1994] 1996). *The World-System from Goethe to García Márquez*. Translated by Quintin Hoare. London: Verso.
Morin, Edgar (2008). *On Complexity: Advances in Systems Theory, Complexity, and the Human Sciences*. Translated by Sean Kelley. New York: Hampton Press.
Morton, Timothy (2016). *Dark Ecology: For a Logic of Future Coexistence*. New York: Columbia University Press.
Morton, Timothy (2013). *Hyperobjects. Philosophy and Ecology after the End of the World*. Minneapolis: Minnesota University Press.
Moten, Fred (2018). *Stolen Life*. Durham, NC: Duke University Press.
Nagel, Thomas (1989). *The View from Nowhere*. Oxford: Oxford University Press.
Negarestani, Reza (2008). *Cyclonopedia: Complicity with Semi-Anonymous Materials*. Melbourne: re:press.
Nelson, Maggie (2015). *The Argonauts*. Minneapolis: Graywolf.

Noll, João Gilberto (2002). *Berkeley em Bellagio*. Rio de Janeiro: Objetiva.
O'Connor, Flannery ([1957] 1970). "On Her Own Work." In *Mystery and Manners: Occasional Prose*, edited by Sally and Robert Fitzgerald, 107–20. New York: Farrar, Straus & Giroux.
Ortega, Julio (1992). *El discurso de la abundancia*. Caracas: Monte Ávila.
Padilla, Ignacio (2004). "Septenario de bolsillo." In *Crack: Instrucciones de uso*, edited by Chávez Castañeda, Alejandro Estivill Ricardo, Vicente Herrasti, Ignacio Padilla, Pedro Ángel Palou, Tomás Regalado, Eloy Urroz, and Jorge Volpi Debolsillo, 214–8. Mexico City: Mondadori.
Palmeri, Frank (2017). "Plutocratic Dystopia and Workers' Utopias in Morris's *News from Nowhere* and Pynchon's *Against the Day*." *Orbit: A Journal of American Literature* 5 (2), 1–27, DOI: https://doi.org/10.16995/orbit.219.
Panh, Rithy and Christophe Bataille (2013). *The Elimination: A Survivor of the Khmer Rouge Confronts His Past and the Commandant of the Killing Fields*. Translated by John Cullen. New York: Other Press.
Parks, Tim (2010). "The Dull New Global Novel." *New York Review of Books*, February 9. http://www.nybooks.com/daily/2010/02/09/the-dull-new-global-novel/.
Parra, Nicanor ([1969] 1983). *Obra gruesa: Texto completo*. Santiago de Chile: Andres Bello.
Pascal, Blaise ([1670] 1999). *Pensées and Other Writings*. Edited by Anthony Levi, translated by Honor Levi. Oxford: Oxford University Press.
Pfaller, Robert (2017). *Interpassivity: The Aesthetics of Delegated Enjoyment*. Edinburgh: Edinburgh University Press.
Piglia, Ricardo (2000a). "Noticias sobre literatura en un Diario." In *Formas breves*, 81–101. Barcelona: Anagrama.
Piglia, Ricardo (2000b). "Noticias sobre Macedonio en un Diario." In *Formas breves*, 13–28. Barcelona: Anagrama.
Piglia, Ricardo ([1980] 1994). *Artificial Respiration*. Translated by Daniel Balderston. Durham, NC: Duke University Press.
Piglia, Ricardo (1980). *Respiración Artificial*. Buenos Aires: Pomaire.
Pignarre, Claude and Isabelle Stengers ([2005] 2011). *Capitalist Sorcery: Breaking the Spell*. Translated by Andrew Goffey. New York: Palgrave Macmillan.
Pollock, Jonathan (2010). *Déclinaisons: Le naturalisme poétique de Lucrèce à Lacan*. Paris: Hermann.
Povinelli, Elizabeth (2016). *Geontologies: A Requiem to Late Liberalism*. Durham, NC: Duke University Press.
Powe, Bruce (1987). *The Solitary Outlaw*. Toronto: Lester & Orpen Dennys.
Price, Leah (2019). *What We Talk About When We Talk About Books: The History and Future of Reading*. New York: Basic Books.
Price, Leah (2012). *How to do Things with Books in Victorian Britain*. Princeton: Princeton University Press.
Purdy, Jedediah (1998). "Age of Irony." *The American Prospect*, July–August. http://prospect.org/article/essay-age-irony.
Pynchon, Thomas ([1965] 2000). *Crying of Lot 49*. London: Vintage.
Pynchon, Thomas (1997). *Mason & Dixon*. New York: Henry Holt & Company.
Pynchon, Thomas (1973). *Gravity's Rainbow*. New York: Viking.

Quintilian (2001). *The Orator's Education*, Books 6–8. Edited and translated by Donald A. Russell. Cambridge, MA: Harvard University Press.
Rancière, Jacques (1992). *Les noms de l'Histoire: Essai de poétique du savoir*. Paris: Seuil.
Richir, Marc (2018). *Phénomènes, temps et êtres. Phénoménologie et institution symbolique*. Grénoble: Editions Million.
Richir, Marc (2015). *L'écart et le rien: Conversations avec Sacha Carlson*. Grenoble: Millon.
Richir, Marc (2014). *De la négativité en phénoménologie*. Grenoble: Millon.
Richir, Marc (2006). *Fragments phénoménologiques sur le temps et l'espace*. Grenoble: Millon.
Richir, Marc (2004). Phantasia, *affectivité, imagination*. Grenoble: Millon.
Richir, Marc (2003). "Du rôle de la *phantasia* au théâtre et dans le roman." *Littérature* 132, Littérature et phénoménologie, 24–33.
Richir, Marc (2000). *Phénoménologie en esquisses: Nouvelles fondations*. Grenoble: Millon.
Richir, Marc (1998). "Qu'est-ce qu'un phénomène?" *Les Etudes Philosophiques* 4, 435–49.
Richir, Marc ([1982] 1993). "The Meaning of Phenomenology in *The Visible and the Invisible*." *Thesis Eleven* 36, 60–81.
Richir, Marc (1991). "Sens et paroles: Pour une approche phénoménologique du langage." In *Figures de la Rationalité: Etudes d'Anthropologie philosophique* 4, edited by the Institut Supérieur de Philosophie, 228–46. Louvain-La Neuve: Édition Peeters.
Richir, Marc (1982). "Le sens de la phénoménologie dans 'Le Visible et L'Invisible.'" *Esprit* 66 (6), June, 124–45.
Ricœur, Paul ([1965] 1970). *Freud and Philosophy: An Essay on Interpretation*. Translated by Denis Savage. New Haven, CT: Yale University Press.
Riffaterre, Michel (1994). "Intertextuality vs. Hypertextuality." *New Literary History* 25 (4), 779–88.
Rilke, Rainer Maria (1957). *Selected Poems*. Translated by Carlyle Ferren MacIntyre. Princeton: Princeton University Press.
Rinck, Monika (2015). *Risiko und Idiotie: Streitschriften*. Berlin: kookbooks.
Rodríguez González, Sergio (2002). *Huesos en el desierto*. Barcelona: Anagrama.
Rodríguez Freire, Raúl (2013). "Bolaño, Chile y la desacralización de la literatura." *Guaraguao* 44, 63–74.
Rorty, Richard (1989). *Contingency, Irony, and Solidarity*. Cambridge: Cambridge University Press.
Rosa, José Guimarães ([1956] 2015). *Grande Sertão: Veredas*. Rio de Janeiro: Nova Fronteira.
Rosset, Clément (1977). *Le réel: Traité de l'idiotie*. Paris: Minuit.
Rothberg, Michael. *Traumatic Realism: The Demands of Holocaust Representation*. Minneapolis: University of Minnesota Press.
Rovelli, Carlo (2017). *The Order of Time*. London: Allen Lane.
Rüter, Christopher (2018). *Hans Blumenberg: Der unsichtbare Philosoph*. Cologne: Tag/Traum Filmproduktion.
Sánchez Prado, Ignacio (ed.) (2018). *Mexican Literature in Theory*. London and New York: Bloomsbury.

Schnell, Alexander (2011). "Au-delà de Husserl, Heidegger et Merleau-Ponty: La phénoménologie de Marc Richir." *Revue germanique internationale* 13, 95–108. http://rgi.revues.org/1124.

Searls Giroux, Susan (2002). "The Age of Irony?" *Journal of Advanced Composition* 22 (4), 960–76.

Sedgwick, Eve Kosofsky (1997). "Paranoid Reading and Reparative Reading; or You're So Paranoid, You Probably Think This Introduction Is About You." In *Novel Gazing: Queer Readings in Fiction*, edited by Eve Kosofsky Sedgwick, 1–40. Durham, NC: Duke University Press.

Sellami, Samir (2017). "Die Kunst der Selbstauslieferung: Zum Werk Ricardo Piglias (1941–2017)." *Merkur* 816, Mai, 82–91.

Sellami, Samir (2015). "Zur Politik der Intertextualität in Roberto Bolaños *Estrella Distante*." *Romanische Studien* 1, 111–34. https://www.romanischestudien.de/index.php/rst/article/view/17.

Sellars, Wilfrid ([1956] 1997). *Empiricism and the Philosophy of Mind*. Cambridge, MA: Harvard University Press.

Sellars, Wilfrid (1963). *Science, Perception, and Reality*. New York: Humanities Press.

Serpell, Namwali (2014). *Seven Modes of Uncertainty*. Cambridge, MA: Harvard University Press.

Severs, Jeffery, and Christopher Leise (eds.) (2011). *Pynchon's* Against the Day. *A Corrupted Pilgrim's Guide*. Newark: University of Delaware Press.

Shaviro, Steven (2009). *Without Criteria: Kant, Whitehead, Deleuze, and Aesthetics*. Cambridge, MA: MIT Press.

Shelley, Percy Bysshe (1968). *Selected Poetry*, edited by Neville Rogers. London: Oxford University Press.

Shellhorse, Adam Joseph (2017). *Anti-Literature: The Politics and Limits of Representation in Modern Brazil and Argentina*. Pittsburgh: University of Pittsburgh Press.

Smith, Zadie (2000). *White Teeth*. London: Penguin.

Sousa Santos, Boaventura de (2014). *Epistemologies of the South: Justice against Epistemicide*. London: Taylor & Francis.

Sparrow, Tom (2014). *End of Phenomenology: Metaphysics and the New Realism*. Edinburgh: Edinburgh University Press.

Speranza, Graciela (2005). "Por un realismo idiota." *Boletín del Centro de Estudios de Teoría y Crítica Literaria* 12, 1–11.

Spiller, Robert (2009). "Fracasar con éxito o *navigare necessum est*." In *Poéticas del fracaso*, edited by Yvette Sánchez and Robert Spiller, 143–73. Tübingen: Gunter Narr.

Spitzer, Leo ([1928] 1961). "Zum Stil Marcel Proust's." In *Stilstudien*, Vol. II, Stilsprachen, 365–497. Darmstadt: Wissenschaftliche Buchgesellschaft.

Spivak, Gayatri (2012). "Why Study the Past." *Modern Language Quarterly* 73 (1), 1–12.

Stengers, Isabelle (2012). "Reclaiming Animism." *e-flux* 36, July. https://www.e-flux.com/journal/36/61245/reclaiming-animism/.

Stengers, Isabelle ([2002] 2011). *Thinking with Whitehead: A Free and Wild Creation of Concepts*. Translated by Michael Chase. Cambridge, MA: Harvard University Press.

Strandberg, Victor (2000). "Dimming the Enlightenment: Thomas Pynchon's *Mason & Dixon*." In *Pynchon and* Mason & Dixon, edited by Brooke Horvath and Irving Malin. Newark: University of Delaware, 100–11.
Tanner, Tony (1998). "Afterthoughts on Don DeLillo's *Underworld*." *Raritan* 17 (4), 48–71.
Toscano, Alberto and Jeff Kinkle (2015). *Cartographies of the Absolute*. Winchester: Zero Books.
Trigg, Dylan (2013). "'The Horror of Darkness.' Toward an Unhuman Phenomenology." *Speculations: A Journal of Speculative Realism* IV, 113–21.
Uslar Pietri, Arturo (1986). "Realismo Mágico." In *Godos, insurgentes y visionarios*, 133–40. Barcelona: Seix Barral.
Varela, Pablo (2010). "Hipérbole y concretud en parpadeo: En torno al último libro de Marc Richir 'Variaciones sobre el sí mismo y lo sublime.'" *Eikasia: Revista de Filosofía* 34, 439–58.
Vargas Llosa, Mario (1991). *Carta de batalla por 'Tirant Lo Blanc.'* Barcelona: Seix Barral.
Viveiros de Castro, Eduardo (2002). *A inconstância da alma selvagem e outros ensaios de antropologia*. São Paulo: Cosac Naify.
Volpi, Jorge (2008): "Bolaño, epidemia." *Revista de la Universidad de México* 49, 77–84. https://www.revistadelauniversidad.mx/articles/5b764f19-803a-41f4-9dd4-1d71567bff01/bolano-epidemia.
Waldenfels, Bernhard (2012). *Hyperphänomene: Modi hyperbolischer Erfahrung*. Frankfurt am Main: Suhrkamp.
Wallace, David Foster (1996). *Infinite Jest: A Novel*. New York: Back Bay Book.
Wallace, David Foster (1993): "E Unibus Pluram: Television and U.S. Fiction." *Review of Contemporary Fiction* 13 (2), 151–94.
Wark, McKenzie (2017). *General Intellects: Twenty-Five Thinkers for the Twenty-First Century*. London: Verso.
Whitehead, Alfred North (1929). *Process and Reality: An Essay in Cosmology*. New York: Macmillan.
Wiesing, Lambert (2009). *Das Mich der Wahrnehmung: Eine Autopsie*. Frankfurt am Main: Suhrkamp.
Williams, Raymond (1977). *Marxism and Literature*. Oxford: Oxford University Press.
Wolfram von Eschenbach (2006). *Parzival and Titurel*. Translated with notes by Cyril Edwards, with an introduction by Richard Barber. Oxford: Oxford University Press.
Wood, James (2014). "How Flaubert Changed Literature Forever." *New Republic*, December 12. https://newrepublic.com/article/120543/james-wood-flaubert-and-chekhovs-influence-style-and-literature.
Wood, James (2007a). "The Visceral Realist." *New York Times*, April 15. http://www.nytimes.com/2007/04/15/books/review/Wood.t.html.
Wood, James (2007b). "All Rainbow, No Gravity." *The New Republic*, March 5. https://newrepublic.com/article/63049/all-rainbow-no-gravity.
Wood, James (2000). "Human, All Too Inhuman." *New Republic*, July 24. https://newrepublic.com/article/61361/human-inhuman.

Woods, Gregory (1993). "High Culture and High Camp: The Case of Marcel Proust." In *Camp Grounds: Style and Homosexuality*, edited by David Bergman, 121–33. Amherst: University of Massachusetts Press.

Zanetti, Sandro (2009). "Logiken und Praktiken der Schreibkultur: Zum analytischen Potential der Literatur." In *Logiken und Praktiken der Kulturforschung*, edited by Uwe Wirth, 75–88. Berlin: Kadmos.

Zill, Rüdiger (2020). *Der absolute Leser – Hans Blumenberg: Eine intellektuelle Biographie*. Berlin: Suhrkamp.

INDEX

absolute
  conceptual 2, 5, 28, 36, 41,
    61 n. 13, 141
  infinity 26 n. 6, 41, 61 n. 13, 100,
    198
  metaphoric 137, 180, 194
  ontological 13, 91–2, 104, 135,
    145–8, 196, 199, 205, 208–9
  perceptual 100, 145–8
  and/as perfection 18, 52–4, 57, 93,
    96, 100, 102, 146, 164
  totality 12, 58, 72, 74, 92, 100, 112,
    122, 137, 139, 145–8, 176 n. 2,
    198
abundance 1–3, 47–62, 85, 98–9, 194,
  196, 199–200
  as excess 55–9, 64, 69–70, 79, 97,
    118–22, 126, 134, 191, 194, 197
  description 112, 134, 145, 151,
    179, 204
  intertextual 63–4, 190
abyss 5, 38, 42, 53–5, 132, 148
agency 10, 81, 90, 103, 111, 115, 120,
  122, 125, 183, 209
Aira, César 6, 25, 26 n. 6, 110
alchemy 88–9, 116, 152–3
Alps 42, 87, 143, 148
anarchism 18, 68, 101–2, 105, 115,
  129, 130, 142, 154, 165, 167,
  180–1, 185
ancestrality 13–14, 19, 82, 204, 209
  (*see also* Meillassoux)
de Andrade, Oswald 63, 80–81
animism 103, 115–17, 184, 207–8
antipoesía, anti-literature 70–1, 180
Arrighi, Giovanni 10–11
as if 42, 94, 107–48, 154–5, 157,
  184, 193, 200–1 (*see also* flat
  fictionality)

Auerbach, Erich 22–3, 36
autonomy 18, 28, 34, 43, 59, 72, 88,
  111, 118, 153, 170, 194
avant-garde 24–5, 57, 69, 82, 103,
  110, 118, 142, 165–9, 177, 179,
  192, 204, 207
  futurism 167
  and post-avant-garde 25, 70–2
  surrealism 21, 54, 177–8, 193

Barad, Karen 5, 126, 208–10
Baroque 33, 35, 38, 72, 79, 134, 157,
  210
Barth, John 47–51
Barthes, Roland 22, 197
Bataille, Georges 54, 92, 111, 169, 179
Baudelaire, Charles 41, 61, 153
Benjamin, Walter 79–80, 146, 153
Benoist, Jocelyn 13, 15, 72
Bertoni, Federico, 22–3
blindness 5, 37, 54–5, 102, 165
Bloom, Harold 82
Blumenberg, Hans 35, 155, 180
  Reality and Possibility of the Novel
    27–9, 203–10
Bolaño, Roberto
  Amulet 95, 109–10, 158, 178 n.
    5, 180
  Between Parentheses 71–2, 78 n. 18,
    83, 110, 156 n. 2, 179, 198
  By Night in Chile 96 n. 4, 178 n. 5,
    179 n. 6
  Distant Star 57, 69–74, 96 n. 4,
    133, 178–9
  Nazi Literature in the Americas
    70–2, 96 n. 4, 150 n. 1
  Savage Detectives 2, 57, 60, 70, 73,
    80, 170, 177–9, 180 n. 7, 190,
    200

Woes of Policeman 69–70, 74–5, 82
Una novellita lumpen 72
boom in Latin American literature 20–1
borders 51, 59, 94, 120, 158, 164
Borges, Jorge Luis 20, 75, 145–8, 171

cannibalism, cultural 80–2
capitalism
  corporate
  critique of 11, 204
  extractivism 67–8, 101, 122, 180, 207–8
  global 100
  late 60, 192
  millennial 99, 139
  neoliberalism 21, 27, 60, 178
  old 100–3, 180
Carson, Anne 161, 177
Chakrabarty, Dipesh 5, 10–11
chance 5, 23, 57–8, 77, 79
Ciudad Juárez 54 n. 7, 94–5, 164
Clute, John, "Aubade, Poor Dad" 65–9
colonialism 20–1, 68, 71, 78, 82, 86, 95, 101, 120, 125, 154, 180
  postcolonialism 11
contact (as mode of relation) 13, 72, 80, 117, 125, 127, 130, 160, 162, 170, 194, 199, 209–10
  promiscuity 170–1, 210
correlationism 12–17, 115 (*see also* Meillassoux)
discorrelation 80–3, 115, 150, 192, 196–7 (*see also* Denson)
Cortázar, Julio 3, 36, 56, 61, 150 n. 1, 190 n. 3
craft 55–8, 61, 68, 81, 116, 138 n. 4, 151, 166
crime 54, 58, 74, 94–9, 102, 158
Curtius, Ernst Robert 32
cynicism 99, 124, 132, 183–4, 191

Davis, Mike 68
dehiscence 158–70, 199
  rupture 115, 149, 152, 158
Deleuze, Gilles 118
  and Félix Guattari, *Thousand Plateaus* 9

DeLillo, Don, *Underworld* 4, 48, 50, 57, 59, 80 n. 22, 184, 192
Denson, Shane 80–3
Derrida, Jacques 18 n. 2, 61, 141
desaparecidos 21, 42, 60, 86, 138
Descartes, René 34, 39–40, 103, 134
deus malignus 39, 134
diagrams 76–7
différance 141, 196, 199
difficulty
  aesthetic 1–3, 29, 48–55, 61, 79, 138 n. 4, 176, 205
  existential 39, 195, 204
  rhetoric 32, 136, 169
doubt
  as concession 54, 147
  and defiance 48, 61, 138, 147, 155
  as disbelief 131–4, 138
  extravagant 134–5
  hyperbolic 39–40, 134, 195
  narrative 133, 135
  and pragmatism 196–7
  as skepticism 132–4, 138, 147, 150, 166, 170, 190, 192–4
  as suspense 143–8
  as uncertainty 4–5, 39, 133, 135, 139, 141, 147, 179
duality 89, 112–13
Duchamp, Marcel 75, 166

ecology 11, 13, 81, 83, 86, 118, 122, 127, 137, 164, 192, 207
ekphrasis 149–71
energy
  electricity 89, 94, 101–2, 183
  energeia 110, 151, 169
  entropy 18, 157–8, 169, 184, 193
  expressive 33–4, 83, 110, 121, 152, 168
  physical 87, 166, 183, 196, 204
Eliot, George 22, 33–4
  The Lifted Veil 135–6
Eliot, T.S. 56, 205 n. 3
enigma 16, 28, 38, 52, 55, 65, 74 n. 14, 77, 90, 95, 109, 125, 135, 141, 144, 165, 177, 194, 204–6
  mystery 21, 78, 89, 144, 194
  occult 100–4, 114, 154, 156, 177

riddle 109–10, 124, 144, 203
secret 88–9, 94, 101, 114, 139–40, 164, 179, 194, 204–5
Enlightenment 34, 68–9, 101, 103, 116
Ercolino, Stefano, *The Maximalist Novel* 2, 112, 189, 200 n. 8, 206 n. 4
ethics 10, 14, 35–6, 38, 64, 81, 86, 100, 170, 189 n. 2, 193, 198, 206 n. 4
experimentation 6, 20–1, 24, 59–61, 118, 149, 153, 185 n. 10, 188–92, 206, 209–10
extinction 199, 204, 209, 13–14, 19, 134, 110, 136, 145 n. 8

failure, *fracaso* 5, 33, 48, 58, 64, 74, 96, 99, 130, 150, 160, 167, 177–80, 183–4, 193
fantastic 38, 66–9, 75, 118–20, 122, 126–9, 155, 163, 185, 193, 195, 207
fascism 24, 73, 86, 150 n. 1, 155, 163, 166–7, 178–9, 182
feminicidios 53–4, 58, 78 n. 20, 95–9, 123, 131, 138, 158, 165
feminism 103, 150 n. 1, 208
figuration 4, 23, 31–5, 38, 48, 91–2, 108–15, 126, 140, 157, 162–3, 169, 187–201
 as disfiguration and *infigurable* 147, 196, 199
 as *figura* 35–37, 134
 geometric 77
finitude 12–13, 96, 115, 171, 176–7 (*see also* Meillassoux)
Fisher, Mark 15, 24–6, 118, 122, 170, 188, 192
flat
 characters 26
 fictionality 107–30, 151, 170, 192–3, 200, 207
 ontology 119, 208
Flaubert, Gustave 26, 50, 56, 165
forensic 58, 98–9, 153
Franzen, Jonathan 2, 49–51, 55–6

Fuguet, Alberto and Sergio Gómez, *McOndo* 20–1

Garcia, Tristan 11, 188–9, 193
Genette, Gérard 34, 64
genealogy 5, 15, 68, 105, 150, 181, 206 n. 4
Grant, Iain Hamilton 15, 116, 126, 198
grace 69, 117, 157, 184–5 (*see* salvation)
Greece 27, 32, 53, 59 n. 11, 151–2, 161, 204, 207–10
grotesque 2, 58–9, 79, 143, 155
 as carnivalesque 82, 139–42, 146, 176
Guerrero, Carlos 156–7, 159, 164, 168

Harman, Graham 12, 15, 119, 122, 199
Haverkamp, Anselm 35, 37, 205
Hegel, G. F. W. 41, 111–12
Heidegger, Martin 15–16, 35, 38, 93
Horne, Luz, *Literaturas reales* 25–6, 192, 195–6
Hoyos, Héctor 2, 6
Husserl, Edmund 16–19, 22, 39, 93, 111, 117, 138, 161–2
hyperbole, hyperbolic (*see also* abundance; Johnson; mannerism; metaphor; doubt)
 amplification 31–2, 157
 exaggeration 3, 5, 22–3, 29, 38, 67, 72, 86, 119, 121, 126, 132, 138, 188, 199
 exuberance 1, 34, 56, 67, 111, 189, 197
 geometry 16, 33, 37, 83, 170, 207
 outdoing 32, 67, 80, 108, 152, 166, 199

idiocy, of the real 25, 29, 154, 208, 14
imaginary 21, 42, 52, 69, 108, 120–4, 156, 163, 170, 179, 207
immanence 22, 43, 61, 209
inhumanism (of language and thinking) 19, 197–8
humanism, aesthetic 49–50

intermittence (*see also* Richir) 18–19, 27, 37, 42, 66, 93–104, 112, 114, 122, 133–4, 161, 193, 199, 200
irony 32–5, 164

Jakobson, Roman, "On Realism in Art" 22, 206
Jameson, Fredric 14, 23
jazz 86, 88, 150 n. 1
Johnson, Christopher D., *Hyperboles* 5, 34–5, 109 n. 4, 134–5, 138, 166
Joyce, James
   Finnegans Wake 48, 59
   Ulysses 1, 48, 59, 190

Kant, Immanuel 209, 10, 12, 28, 39–40
Karl, Frederick R., *American Fictions*, 2, 48
Keats, John, *Ode on a Grecian Urn* 149
Kittler, Friedrich 193
Knausgård, Karl Ove 200–1
Kraus, Chris 123, 141, 150 n. 1

Latour, Bruno 11, 119, 206
Letzler, David, *Cruft of Fiction* 55–8, 64, 79
Levinas, Emmanuel 4, 15–19, 42, 177, 179, 209
   Totality and Infinity 100, 198
Levine, Elizabeth 135, 138
Lévi-Strauss, Claude, *Pensée sauvage* 3
Levrero, Mario, *Novela Luminosa* 26 n. 5
Lezama Lima, José 59, 107, 128–9
lifeworld, *Lebenswelt* 16, 43, 86, 90
Lispector, Clarice 47, 85, 129, 149, 175, 194
Loy, Benjamin 25 n. 4, 69 n. 6, 70, 72
Lucretius, *De rerum natura* 136–8, 179

madness 5, 24, 34, 38–40, 76, 78, 121, 142, 167–8
   psychiatry 42, 103–4, 142–4

mannerism 4, 109–12, 126, 163, 185 n. 10
maps 6, 22, 57, 92, 104–5, 145
marginality 26, 42, 52, 68–9, 72, 128, 131, 155, 177, 182, 185
   periphery 42, 69, 74, 95, 99, 169, 178, 188
   subaltern 69, 103, 178, 184
Marxism 10, 12, 14
   communism 68, 82, 86, 179, 181
   socialism 102, 181
materialism 6, 27, 67, 72, 136–7, 179, 208–10
mathematics 40, 56, 100, 112–13, 121, 168, 193, 207
   geometry 33, 37, 75–7, 83, 146, 156 (*see also* hyperbolic geometry)
   numbers 37, 47–8, 95, 110, 121, 207
   obscure, obsolete 75, 103, 127
McGurl, Mark 11, 20, 56, 79, 189
McHale, Brian 65–8
Meillassoux, Quentin
   After Finitude 115, 199, 204, 208–9
   arche-fossil 13
   Extro-Sciecne_Fiction 79 n. 21
melancholy 5, 58, 74, 130, 143, 145–8, 179, 181
Melville, Herman 2, 48, 50, 61, 86
memory 81–3, 162, 169, 171, 199, 209
Merleau-Ponty, Maurice 4, 15, 37, 152, 162, 194
   chiasm 16, 90, 118, 114, 120, 154, 156
   Phenomenology of Perception 210
   Visible and Invisible 15–17, 38, 53 n. 5, 58, 90–3, 114–15, 117–20, 170 n. 8, 198, 200
   wild beings [*êtres sauvages*] and wild meaning [*sens sauvage*] 16–18, 91, 162
metabolic
   images 80–3
   intertextuality 79–82, 192
   processes 4, 50, 68, 81–3

metafiction 4, 25, 52, 55, 57, 60–1, 119, 190, 196, 199
metaphor
    absolute 180
    as practice 35, 50, 60, 82–3, 104, 108, 110, 114, 118, 127, 159
    critical 33, 35, 83 n. 25, 155, 205
    filée 107–14, 126
    hyperbolic 109, 114, 126, 128, 130, 194
    of the real 13, 53, 94, 113, 121, 179–80
    visual 85, 90, 112
metonymy 29, 82, 118, 126–30, 193
    as synecdoche 31, 109, 151, 164, 192, 207
mirrors 100, 102, 104–5, 112, 150
modernism
    dark 193
    high 28, 165, 176, 205, 208, 210
    technomodernism 20, 79, 204 n. 1
    as concept of reality 204, 206
Morton, Timothy 43–4, 115, 122, 126–7, 137, 161, 170, 176, 193, 209–10
    hyperobjects 41, 43–4, 122, 126, 161, 209
Moten, Fred 41, 205–6
mourning 85, 99, 148
myth of the given 18, 188, 205

narratology 66, 72, 80–1, 98, 100, 117, 132–5
Negarestani, Reza 43, 101
negativity
    aesthetic 29, 156–9, 168
    affective 68, 183
    existential 138
    phenomenological 28, 85, 92, 111
    photographic 154–7
    unemployed 43–4, 111–12, 169, 179, 193
Nelson, Maggie 187, 195–9
noise 53, 60, 74, 82, 104–5, 112
    (*see also* entropy)

novel
    adventure 65, 78, 175–85
    avant-garde 24
    Bildungsroman 59
    encyclopedic 2, 48, 55, 60
    global 2
    historical 66
    Künstlerroman 177
    modern, modernist 28–9, 179
    narconovela 96, 191
    nineteenth-century 26, 33–4
    philosophy of the 4, 176 n. 2
    postmodern 204
    science fiction 66–7, 79 n. 21

O'Connor, Flannery 6, 16, 138, 157 n. 3
ornament 114, 140, 167, 188, 209

pathos 55, 124, 132, 134, 144, 160
    bathos 124, 132, 144, 194
phantasia 19, 93, 194–5, 158–65, 168–71, 185, 194–5, 199, 205
phenomenology
    anarchic 115, 117, 185, 205
    architectonic 205
    epoché, reduction 18, 40, 162
    genetic 18, 169
    phenomenalization 17–18, 91, 93, 109, 111, 161, 165, 168, 170, 194, 205
    quantum 17–19, 113, 208–9
    speculative 19, 35, 93
photography 37, 86, 88–9, 115–16, 152–7, 166
Piglia, Roberto 24–6, 175–6, 187–8
planetary 10–1, 100, 195
postmodernism 2, 4, 9–10, 14, 20, 23, 32, 35, 37, 40, 47, 61, 65–6, 112, 119, 129, 132–3, 138, 141–4, 150, 176, 179, 182, 184–5, 191–4, 199, 203–8 (*see also* modernism; novel; phenomenology)
postwar
    fiction 20, 56, 78–9
    maximalism 189 n. 2
    phenomenology 4, 14, 15, 37, 189

pragmatism 4, 103, 116, 196–7 (see also doubt)
Proust, Marcel 34, 48, 59, 150 n. 1
Pynchon, Thomas
  bilocation 67, 90, 112–13, 114
  Crying of Lot 49, 57, 65, 101, 133
  Gravity's Rainbow 42 n. 4, 48, 57, 60, 65, 80, 101, 124, 181–4, 190, 193, 200
  Mason & Dixon 59, 68 n. 4, 190
  V. 65

Quintilian 31–4, 126

reading
  barbaric 69–73
  broad 10, 189
  close 35, 189
  distant 77, 189
  emancipated 3, 55, 61, 80, 190
  fictionalized 69–75
  maximalist 57
  as misreading 56, 72, 74, 86
  metatextual 25 n. 4, 190
  paranoid 5, 11, 68–9, 124, 129, 133, 182, 203
  pleasure of 65
  reparative 65–9, 74, 184, 194
  scene 73–4
  wild 3–6, 73, 77, 87, 103, 162, 176, 203
realism
  capitalist 24
  critical 23, 205–6
  hyperreal
  hysterical 2, 48–50, 57, 99, 188, 191, 204
  indexical 25–6, 192, 196
  in the fourth gear 83, 192, 195
  magical 20–21, 89, 126, 188
  mimetic 61, 190, 195
  new 12–7, 24–5, 188, 206 n. 4
  nineteenth-century 22–3, 26–7, 135, 189, 206
  return of the real 19–20
  speculative 12, 120, 189, 193
  traditional 83, 193, 206 n. 4

representation
  epiphany 4, 29, 88, 98, 109–10, 114, 118, 126, 129, 149, 154–9, 168, 206–7
  exhaustion 1, 47, 54, 57, 66, 69, 96, 100, 111, 145
  form, *informe* 3, 33–5, 49, 54, 60, 74, 79, 82, 122, 130, 139 n. 5, 150, 162 n. 5, 168–9, 180, 190, 197 (see also Bataille)
  ineffability 4, 53–4, 127, 136–7, 195–7
  mimesis 20, 23, 83, 116–17, 120, 134–5, 149–53, 169–70, 190, 192, 195, 207
  repetition 25–6, 86, 97–100, 117, 126, 129, 157
  sublime 49, 87, 90, 99, 116 n. 8, 144, 148
rhythm 58, 80
  of appearance and disappearance 4, 66, 87, 93, 100, 112
Richir, Marc 17–19
  interfacticity 80, 115
  intermittence [*clignotement*] 18–9, 42, 93, 161
  L'écart et le rien 38–40, 117, 162 n. 5, 194, 199
  meaning in the making [*sens se faisant*] 162
  Phénoménologies en esquisses 18, 93, 111, 161–2, 165
  symbolic institution 40, 117, 170, 199
  transposition 18, 162, 169
  transpossibilité 162 n. 5
  wild beings 26, 40, 92–3, 96, 103, 115, 162, 205 (see also Merleau-Ponty)
Ricœur, Paul 5
Riffaterre, Michel 63–4
Rilke, Rainer Maria 149–51, 160
Rinck, Monika 83 n. 25, 192, 207
risk 5, 13, 23, 31–2, 38, 39, 51, 73, 96, 103, 124, 126, 136–9, 155
Rosa, José Guimarães 41, 131
Rosset, Clément, *Le réel* 14, 25, 89

salvation, redemption 6, 69, 138 n. 4, 148, 169, 177, 194
Sartre, Jean-Paul 92, 111, 41
Sedgwick, Eve Kosofsky, "Paranoid and Reparative" 68, 183–5
Sellami, Samir 74, 176 n. 2
Serpell, Namwali 109, 133n2, 192, 198
simulacrum 120, 138–9, 148, 199
Smith, Zadie 48
Speranza, Graciela 14, 25
spirituality 73, 82, 103, 135, 160, 168, 184–5, 188, 207
spying 65–7, 88–9, 104, 140
Stengers, Isabelle 3, 6, 15, 115–16
  and Claude Pignarre, *Capitalist Sorcery* 101–4
surveillance 120, 124, 208

Tesla, Nicolas 89, 101–2, 183
testimonio 60, 98–9, 177
  and witnessing 2, 28, 164, 178, 204 n. 1
texture 37, 77, 82, 90, 92, 126, 138–9, 158–60
Toscano, Alberto 2, 12, 112
triumphalism 4–5, 134, 148, 199–200, 209
transcendental 11, 12, 15, 17, 28, 39–40, 43, 110, 122, 147, 182, 208, 210

uncertainty (*see also* doubt) 4–5, 39, 86, 118–19, 127, 129, 133, 135, 139, 141, 147, 179, 192, 194–200

Verne, Jules 65, 79 n. 21
visibility and invisibility 53 n. 5, 88–97, 102, 125, 160, 193–4
  darkness 4, 18, 54, 85–105, 143, 163, 193
  twilight, *semipenumbra* 87–8, 90, 94–5
Viveiros de Castro, Eduardo 103
  and Deborah Danowski, *Ends of the World* 193, 210
Volpi, Jorge 178

Waldenfels, Bernhard, *Hyperphenomena* 41–4
Wallace, David Foster 25–6, 48, 80–3, 190
  Infinite Jest 2, 31, 50, 58, 60–61, 79, 190–1
weird 37, 44, 52, 118, 122–3, 143, 157, 170, 200
Whitehead, Alfred North 13, 15
Wilde, Oscar, *Dorian Gray* 150
Wolfram von Eschenbach, *Parzival* 77–8 (*see also* adventure novel)
Wood, James 2, 48–50, 56–7, 188, 191–5
World's Columbian Exposition 1893, Chicago 120
World War I 41, 154, 167
World War II 77, 167

www.ingramcontent.com/pod-product-compliance
Lightning Source LLC
Chambersburg PA
CBHW050326020526
44117CB00031B/1818